CANCELLED WORDS

CANCELLED WORDS

Rediscovering Thomas Hardy

Rosemarie Morgan

London and New York

First published in 1992
by Routledge
11 New Fetter Lane, London EC4P 4EE

Simultaneously published in the USA and Canada
by Routledge
a division of Routledge, Chapman and Hall Inc.
29 West 35th Street, New York, NY 10001

© 1992 Rosemarie Morgan

Filmset in 10/12pt Palatino, Monophoto by
Selwood Systems, Midsomer Norton, Avon
Printed and bound in Great Britain by
Butler & Tanner Ltd, Frome and London

British Library Cataloguing in Publication Data
Morgan, Rosemarie
Cancelled words: rediscovering Thomas Hardy.
I. Title
823.8

Library of Congress Cataloging in Publication Data
Morgan, Rosemarie
Cancelled words: rediscovering Thomas Hardy / Rosemarie Morgan.
p.   cm.
Includes bibliographical references and index.
1. Hardy, Thomas, 1840–1928. Far from the madding crowd—
—Criticism, Textual.   2. Hardy, Thomas, 1840–1928—Editors.
3. Stephen, Leslie, Sir, 1832–1904.   I. Title.
823'.8—dc20   91–38326

ISBN 0–415–06825–8

To my father:

Tell him a faithful one is doing
        All that love can do
Still that his path may be worth pursuing,
        And to bring peace thereto.
                                    'The Haunter', Thomas Hardy

Contents

Facsimile pages

Facsimile pages

Acknowledgements

My appreciation and warmest thanks go to the staff of the Beinecke Rare Book and Manuscript Library at Yale University who not only gave me unlimited access to Hardy's holograph manuscript of *Far from the Madding Crowd*, but also generously supplied me with photocopies, photographic prints and much more besides in the way of friendly assistance, prompt attention, and unfailing goodwill. I also owe a special debt of gratitude to Bob Schweik, as one scholarly 'overlander' to another who has already 'blazed the trail' with *Far from the Madding Crowd*, and whose advisory comments on my manuscript were generously matched by his welcoming of new or divergent points of view. I should add here that all transcriptions in this study of Hardy's holograph manuscript are my own, and that my copy-editor, Sandra Jones, has been of immeasurable help in preserving their accuracy. I owe her very many grateful thanks. And, finally, to my staunch supporters at St Andrews University I wish to express my deepest appreciation. I owe much to Peter Coxon's steady stream of letters filled with Hardyana and other literary delights – as always, enthusiastic, sensitive, and affectionate. And if I took the manuscript of this book to Phillip Mallett half expecting to be 'kept in my place' by his scholarly acuity and intellectual agility, I was amply rewarded – as also by finding that I seem to have 'kept him in his place' as my erstwhile Ph.D supervisor generously expanding my narrative borders with his erudite marginalia!

Foreword

The purpose of this book is to present a collation and critical interpretation of the revisions made to Hardy's holograph manuscript of *Far from the Madding Crowd* for its first publication in *The Cornhill Magazine* (Smith, Elder & Co., 1874). In order to highlight all interlinear and proof revisions of this manuscript I have included, with each and every citation, a corresponding citation from *The Cornhill Magazine* in so far as it differs from the original. Hardy's holograph manuscript provided the copy-text, albeit with variations, for the *Cornhill* which, in turn, provided the copy-text for all subsequent editions including those we read today.

Hardy's post-*Cornhill* revisions effected very few substantive changes; most were confined to enlarging and defining the topography of 'Wessex' (see Appendices). His most extensive revisions occur either within the manuscript itself or at the proof-revision stage for the *Cornhill*. This is discounting accidentals. In keeping with the prevailing practice at the time, Hardy left the final punctuation of his text to the *Cornhill* compositors, who were instructed in the house-style of Smith, Elder & Co. Within the holograph manuscript itself there is no consistency of punctuation; there are long stretches of unmarked dialogue, exclamation marks used where compositors placed question marks and, in general, a decidedly 'open' punctuation. In revising for the Wessex editions of his novels in the 1890s Hardy made widespread removals of the commas supplied by his publisher's house-style; this conforms to his original method of writing with minimum use of commas in the holograph version of *Far from the Madding Crowd*.

What follows here is for the consideration of readers who may like to know something about my own methodology and the two textual versions of Hardy's novel I shall be comparing and contrasting. My focus throughout this book is upon the creative mind at work; I have, therefore, taken the manuscript and the *Cornhill* versions side by side, reading the one alongside the other just as Hardy's editor, Leslie Stephen, would have examined the one before admitting it into publication in the other. Where Hardy, sometimes on Stephen's advice and sometimes under the pressure

1

of his censorship, submitted changes not only in manuscript but also in proof, we can only map those changes with a view to interpreting their meaning, not their intentionality. Accordingly, each of the chapters that follow in this book offers specific interpretations of, say, the relevance of revisions made to Hardy's characterisation of Troy (Chapter 2), Oak (Chapter 4), Boldwood (Chapter 6) and Bathsheba (Chapter 7). Because literary criticism is itself ideological, all such interpretations tend to construct meaning rather than reflect it. Each chapter presents a close look at Leslie Stephen's involvement in the production – as, say, his advice upon the use of dialect and Hardy's characterisation of the rustics (Chapter 4), or upon matters of decorum and propriety (Chapters 6 and 8). Chapter 3 looks closely at Hardy's structural alterations, and Chapter 5 examines issues of class and rural labour, as and when these become the focus of his revisionary concerns.

It is not always easy or possible to distinguish between the willing and the unwilling revising hand, and even, on some occasions, between that of editor and author – although as certain patterns and characteristics begin to emerge, this becomes less obscure. This does not, overall, impair our critical observation and understanding of the creative mind at work. To this end, and to overcome the time-consuming work and laborious attention that would be involved if I simply presented a list of cancellations and revisions to be collated, compared and interpreted by the reader, my approach is not only editorial, in so far as I am presenting hitherto unpublished portions of Hardy's text, but also exegetical, interpretative and analytical.

The holograph manuscript

The manuscript of *Far from the Madding Crowd*, commissioned in 1873 by Leslie Stephen, editor of *The Cornhill Magazine*, was tentatively begun by September the same year (some early drafts discarded) and was submitted to Stephen in small sections, anticipating each of the twelve monthly instalments running from January to December 1874. The manuscript was completed in August 1874, and Hardy never set eyes on it again.

Many years later, in 1918 he was surprised to hear from his former publishers, Smith, Elder & Co., that it had been found in their offices – would he agree to its sale to raise funds for the Red Cross? He replied, on 23 January to Mrs Reginald Smith:

> How surprising that you should have found the MS of *Far from the Madding Crowd*! I thought it 'pulped' ages ago. And what a good thought of yours, to send it to the Red Cross, if anybody will buy it.

He recommends fastening the loose sheets together which, he says, will full of information as to pace: being difficult to describe in words they are given in the following diagram:-

'Straight on!' Jan exclaimed. Tracks like that mean a stiff gallop. No wonder we don't hear him. And the horse is harnessed — look at the ruts. Ay, that's one mare sure enough!

'How do you know?'

'Old Jimmy Harris only shoed her last week, & I'd swear to this make among ten thousand.

The rest of the gipsies must have gone on earlier, & some other way, said Oak. You saw there were no other tracks? They rode along silently for a long weary time. Coggan's watch struck one. He lighted another match & examined the ground again:

'Tis a canter now, he said throwing away the light. A twisty rickety pace for a gig. The fact is, they overdrove her at starting; we shall catch them yet.'

Again they hastened on. Coggan's watch struck two.

Facsimile 1 'Horses tramping' (MS 2–107)

2—108

When they looked again the hoof marks were as follows:

'That's' a trot, I know, said Gabriel

Only a trot now, said Coggan cheerfully. We shall overtake him in time.

They pushed rapidly on for yet two or three miles. Ah — a moment, said Gan. Let's see how she was driven up this hill. 'Twill help us. A light was promptly struck upon his gaiters as before, & he examined made.

Hurrah! said Coggan. She walked up here — & well she might. We shall get them in two miles for a crown.

They rode three, & listened. No sound was to be heard save a ~~hoarse mice~~ mill-pond trickling hoarsely through a hatch, & suggesting gloomy possibilities of drowning by jumping in. Gabriel dismounted when they came to a turning. The tracks were absolutely the only guide as to direction that they now had, & great caution was necessary to avoid confusing them with some others which had made

Facsimile 2 'Horses tramping' (MS 2–108)

make people bid higher, and then (rather charmingly) deprecates the notion of 'puffing' himself up in such a way.

The manuscript sold at Christies on 22 April 1918. The new owner was A. Edward Newton of Pennsylvania.

The number of manuscript chapters submitted for each *Cornhill* instalment falls between three and five, most of unequal length. Some early chapter numerations are not marked by Hardy's pen. There are 597 leaves in the mansucript, with four endpapers at front and rear, measuring $6\frac{1}{2}$ by $8\frac{3}{8}$ inches. Some leaves are fragmentary, some cut and pasted, some bear signs of previous use. The foliation is haphazard. Part 1 (Chapters I–XXI) is numbered 1–208; Part 2 (Chapters XXII–XLVI) is numbered 2–1 to 2–263; and Part 3 (Chapters XLVI, concluded, to LVII) is numbered 3–1 to 3–126. Many leaves have been renumbered, still bearing the cancelled number, and many carry numbers marked in the inner margin and/or gutter, many of which are themselves renumberings. This profusion occurs mainly in the centre of the book where there are signs of rapid writing. For example, the section beginning 'Horses Tramping' (Chapter XXXII) and ending 'Coming Home – A Cry' (Chapter XXXIX), carries an inner margin numeration four digits above that of the outer margin. Hence, leaf 180 carries the inner margin number of 184. But with Chapter L, 'On Casterbridge Highway', the inner margin numeration starts at 1. Thus leaf 181 is numbered 1 in the inner margin and as the chapters proceed the inner margin numbers show signs of previous numerical cancellations. Hence leaf 207 is numbered 23 in the inner margin which itself stands in place of 18-cancelled. There is no detectable rhyme or reason to any of this, aside from the obvious reuse of previously numbered leaves. Hardy evidently made many false starts and many experimental rough drafts, but his unusual manuscript foliations are not, in the main, helpful in determining the closeness of the roughest drafts in the manuscript to the period of inception. Nor can the different phases of composition in the manuscript be distinguished with any accuracy. We can only be assured of one thing: the manuscript stands as the surviving draft of *Far from the Madding Crowd* and as the copy-text for publication in *The Cornhill Magazine*.

Rapid writing throughout the central and late sections of the manuscript can be discerned by the damp imprint of the outer margin number upon the preceding verso. The damp imprint is most clearly defined in Chapters XXXII to XLVI, serialised July to November – the sections including Fanny's demise and death. This seems to indicate that these sections were written without interruption and at a very fast pace. Hardy, by this stage, was making fewer interlinear revisions but at the same time suffering increasing cuts and bowdlerisations at Stephen's hand.

Overall, the manuscript shows numerous interlinear revisions and verso augmentations, as well as several pencil-marked indications of proposed cancellations (Stephen's – Hardy never marked his manuscript in pencil), ranging from individual words to large segments. There are, for instance, five drawings of hoofmarks in the horses tramping episode, which have been excised by Stephen, as well as a lengthy segment in 'Adventures by the Shore'. The most notorious cut, concerning Fanny in her coffin, is also marked in the manuscript. Several sizeable cuts are, however, not marked in the manuscript at all.

The two-page Chapter XVI entitled 'All Saints' and All Souls'' is not part of the manuscript. This was written later, in proof, possibly to even up the length of the April instalment following some sizeable cuts to Chapter XV, or maybe even to add dramatic action to what was a rather meandering instalment.

Appended documents

Two, what appear to be saleroom notes, are appended to the front endpage of the manuscript. The first is numbered 2069 and reads:

> Presented by the Author and Mrs Reginald J. Smith, HARDY (THOMAS, O.M.) FAR FROM THE MADDING CROWD, Original Holograph MS., 597 pp. 4to, *new blue polished Levant morocco.* [3659]
>
> Bound in is an A.L.S., by the Author, respecting this MS., which he says was lost sight of for 40 years, also stating that one page that was missing has been supplied by him, 1918.

The second reads:

> Page 107 of Volume 1 of the Manuscript which was missing, was re-written by Mr Hardy in January 1918.

The A.L.S is from Hardy to his ex-publisher at Smith, Elder & Co., and is dated 23 January 1918 (printed in vol. 5 of *The Collected Letters of Thomas Hardy, 1914–1919*, edited by Richard Little Purdy and Michael Millgate, pp. 243, 244). The manuscript also contains a letter from Florence Hardy, dated 4 August 1918, to the new owner of the manuscript, A. Edward Newton of Pennsylvania. She writes:

> Dear Mr Newton,
>
> I am writing for my husband to thank you for your interesting letter. He hopes to be able to write a few lines to you soon, but just at present he finds himself unable to cope with his correspondence. He is pleased to know that the MS of his novel 'Far from the Madding Crowd' has found a place in your library, and hopes it may long remain there. The afternoon it was sold he and I visited the old home where it was written. We sat in the garden and looked up at the little window under which he sat as he wrote, more than forty years ago.

2 — 109

their appearance lately

What does this mean? — though I guess, said Gabriel, looking up at Coggan as he moved the match over the ground about the turning. Coggan, who had no less than the panting horses, had lately shown signs of weary weariness, again scrutinized the mystic characters.

He screwed up his face & emitted a long whew-w-w!

Lameness, said Oak.

Yes. Dainty is lamed: the near-foot-afore, said Coggan slowly, staring still at the tracks footprints.

We'll push on, said Gabriel remounting his humid steed.

Although the road along its greater part had been as good as any turnpike-road in the country it was technically only a byway. The last turning had brought them into the high road leading to Bath. Coggan recollected himself—

We shall have him now! he exclaimed.

Where?

Petticon Turnpike. The keeper of that gate is the sleepiest man between here & London — Dan Randell, that's his name — knowed en for years when he was at Casterbridge Gate. Between the lameness & the gate 'tis a done job.

Facsimile 3 'Horses tramping' (MS 2–109)

He thanks you for the facsimile of the letter you send, and is glad to have it. He had retained a copy of that letter, and strangely enough we were looking at it a few days before the facsimile came, little dreaming where the original was.

He thinks you may be interested to know that the other day he had a visit from three delightful young American soldiers and he was much struck by their high ideals and the lofty view they took of their participation in the war.

My husband thanks you for your most generous appreciation of his work and sends his best regards.

Signed, 'Yours very sincerely, Florence Hardy'.

Fragments

Two fragments of redundant drafts also survive (held in the Dorset County Museum). One, Chapter XXIII, the shearing-supper episode, consists of seven leaves, measuring $6\frac{1}{8}$ by $8\frac{1}{8}$ inches and numbered 2–18 to 2–24. This bears the pencilled date '1873' and an inscription in red ink, 'Some pages of the first Draft – afterwards revised. T.H.' Stephen wanted the chapter cancelled altogether and suggested adding a few paragraphs 'just explaining that there had been a supper'. Hardy instead rewrote the chapter in briefer form, omitting a rather sexually explicit reference to Fanny Robin to which Stephen had raised objections.

The second fragment, consisting of eleven leaves of blue paper measuring $5\frac{7}{8}$ by 8 inches, and numbered 106–a–k, also bears a red-ink inscription, 'Some pages of 1st draft – (Details of Sheep-rot – omitted from MS. when revised) T.H.' This fragment carries no chapter number, but since it begins, 'Troy soon began to make himself busy about the farm', and since it features the 'trickster' – Troy of the book's mid-section, Hardy possibly conceived of it as part of the August instalment, Chapters XXXIV to XXXVIII, where Troy takes up married life and puts Bathsheba's fortunes in jeopardy. Hardy's characterisation of Troy often became difficult to govern (see Chapter 2 of present volume for details), so perhaps he rejected the contents of this fragment for related reasons.

We know, from his account in F. E. Hardy's *The Life of Thomas Hardy, 1840–1928* (see note 1 to Chapter 1), that while writing *Far from the Madding Crowd* he would use scraps of paper, large dead leaves, woodchips and so on, when caught without his pocket-book, so presumably there were once many fragments and first drafts that remained provisional – as these appear to be. Their different measurements alone indicate that they never belonged to the completed holograph manuscript.

The *Cornhill* text

Facsimile of *The Cornhill Magazine*, vol. xxix, no. 169 and vol. xxx, no. 180, Jan.–Dec. 1874, printed on 673 pages with non-consecutive page numbering, and hard-bound with ten illustrated plates (originally twelve), measuring $22\frac{1}{2}$ cm, and twelve insert vignettes; all illustrations are from woodcuts by Helen Paterson. Several extraneous verso texts are included as and where Hardy's monthly instalment concludes overleaf.

The illustrated plates and insert vignettes

JANUARY: Plate depicts Bathsheba reviving Oak from smoke-suffocation.
                Vignette depicts Bathsheba carrying a small milkchurn.

FEBRUARY: Plate missing (original depicts Oak presenting himself to Bathsheba as the new shepherd).
                Vignette depicts Bathsheba housekeeping with Liddy.

MARCH: Plate depicts Bathsheba and Liddy practising Bible-and-Key divination.
                Vignette depicts Fanny Robin outside Melchester barracks in the snow.

APRIL: Plate depicts Bathsheba in new riding habit talking to Boldwood.
                Vignette depicts the maltster.

MAY: Plate depicts the shearing supper.
                Vignette depicts Oak shearing a sheep.

JUNE: Plate depicts Troy's sword display.
                Vignette depicts Bathsheba haymaking.

JULY: Plate depicts Bathsheba in the fir plantation.
                Vignette depicts Coggan and Oak tracking hoof-marks.

AUGUST: Plate missing (original depicts Bathsheba and Troy in intimate conversation – Boldwood lurking in shadows).
                Vignette depicts Oak in contemplation.

SEPTEMBER: Plate depicts Fanny asleep beneath a haystack.
                Vignette depicts the Casterbridge Union.

OCTOBER: Plate depicts Bathsheba and Troy beside the coffin.

Vignette depicts Troy planting flowers on Fanny's grave.

NOVEMBER: Plate depicts Troy swept out at Lulwind Cove. Vignette depicts Bathsheba in contemplation.

DECEMBER: Plate depicts Troy's appearance at Boldwood's party. Vignette depicts two large umbrellas in the mist.

Other texts consulted

(a) First edition in two volumes, large print, issued by Smith, Elder & Co., 1874. Volume 1, 333 pp., Chapters I–XXX, six illustrated plates measuring 22cm by Helen Paterson (reprinted from the *Cornhill*).

Frontispiece: February plate.
Facing p. 32: January plate.
Facing p. 158: March plate.
Facing p. 211: April plate.
Facing p. 262: May plate.
Facing p. 308: June plate.

Volume 2, 342 pp., numbered Chapters I–XXVII (effectively XXXI–LVII), six illustrated plates measuring 22cm by Helen Paterson (reprinted from the *Cornhill*).

Frontispiece: July plate.
Facing p. 53: August plate.
Facing p. 106: September plate.
Facing p. 167: October plate.
Facing p. 216: November plate.
Facing p. 299: December plate.

(b) First complete collected edition, issued by Osgood, McIlvaine, 1895, comprising 475 pages with an etching by H. Macbeth-Raeburn and a map of Wessex measuring 21cm. This is the first Wessex edition. The front is accompanied by a guardsheet with descriptive letterpress. The author's autographed inscription appears on the front endpaper. Macbeth-Raeburn's etching is entitled 'The Weatherbury of the Story' and is accompanied by the words, 'Drawn on the spot'.

Hardy's autographed inscription reads as follows:

In point of form, this is the best edition of the story with an illustration, published of late years. But the text has been corrected in a smaller and later edition with an illustration. The title is a quotation from the 19th stanza of Gray's Elegy.

Hardy dates this autograph July 1904. This edition carries most of Hardy's post-*Cornhill* substantive revisions, notably his partial reinstatement of some of the bowdlerised portions of the coffin scene, and the introduction of place names delineating a more precise topography in 'Wessex'. This topographical interest developed more actively and became more concretely defined in Hardy's work following immediately upon publication of *Far from the Madding Crowd*.

(c) Harper & Bros, 1899 edition (London and New York), 476 pp., which likewise carries a map of Wessex. No further significant changes.

Hardy made some revisions of accidentals for the Wessex edition (London: Macmillan, 1912), and also provided more topographical details. This more precise delineation of Wessex, the partly real, partly dream-country had, by now, become extensively mapped in his novels and poems.

Modern editions

Of all the editions currently available in bookshops and libraries, I would recommend the 1986 Norton edition (T. Hardy, *Far from the Madding Crowd*, ed. Robert C. Schweik (New York and London: W. W. Norton & Co, 1986)). This comprehensive edition adopts the Wessex edition as copy-text but also includes emendations of that text and provides a section on 'Variant readings'.

In this comparative analysis of Hardy's holograph manuscript and the *Cornhill* versions of *Far from the Madding Crowd*, I have struggled to avoid the vexed question of intentionality, but have struggled in vain. If there is a way of exploring the creative mind at work without second-guessing first Hardy's and then Stephen's developing interests and concerns, I have not discovered it. As Hardy himself said, readers may find more in a text than the author consciously puts there, so my hope is that I have cast nothing in stone but have rather unearthed one or two fragments in order to pave the way for the 'more' to be found.

1

Preamble

In these days of word processors and laserwriters, we no longer expect to find that proprietorial sense of pleasure and pride that Victorian editors took in transforming the most disorderly and chaotic of manuscripts into an elegant, well-proportioned book. And there is no doubt that when Hardy placed himself in the hands of Leslie Stephen, who commissioned *Far from the Madding Crowd* for serial publication in *The Cornhill Magazine* in 1874, he submitted his work to a Victorian editor whose professional pride was inseparable from his self-avowed passion for 'Improvement' – literary and moral in equal measure. For Stephen did not stop at tidying up Hardy's chaotic script, his unpunctuated dialogues, his inconsistent punctuation, his irregular spellings and his copious alterations. In addition to providing invaluable advice about periodical writing, such as the importance of sustaining narrative pace and keeping the plot in line, Stephen also provided Hardy with a short sharp course in Grundian conventions – conventions of literary propriety and decorum that were deeply ingrained in Stephen's consciousness but not in Hardy's, who appeared, as far as Stephen was concerned, to have 'no more consciousness of these things than a child'.[1]

With hindsight, we have the advantage over Stephen in seeing the progression of Hardy's iconoclasm, which predisposes us to the notion that he was simply chancing his arm with Mrs Grundy from the outset. Nevertheless, it is evident from a close reading of his holograph manuscript of *Far from the Madding Crowd* that we are here witnessing not so much a lack of consciousness as an uneducated consciousness now shaping itself into becoming 'a good hand at a serial'.[2] However ambivalent Hardy felt about Stephen's advice and influence, he appears at this stage of his career to be prepared to lay down his arms against Mrs Grundy in order to learn a few tactical literary approaches and something of the lie of the land.

Many of these approaches will, I hope, emerge in the following comparative analysis of the manuscript and *Cornhill* versions of *Far from the Madding Crowd*, which places a close focus on what I would call Hardy's heuristics, the creative writing process itself, the manner in which the literary invention of a first bestseller, from the origination to the cancellation of words, becomes for Hardy both a creative and a learning process. For it is, broadly speaking, the cancelled words that shaped this novel for serial publication in the *Cornhill*, which, in turn, provided the copy-text for all later volume editions, including those we read today. One very good reason why we are not reading the original manuscript version today is that no sooner had it provided Stephen with the copy-text for serialisation in the *Cornhill*, than it disappeared. Hardy assumed it had been pulped.[3] Following its publication in 1874 he never set eyes on it again. He never revised from it for later editions and – even supposing he might have wished to do so – he never retrieved or fully reinstated those portions bowdlerised for the benefit of Leslie Stephen's *Cornhill* readers.

Far from the Madding Crowd was Hardy's first major commission.[4] This was his first attempt at writing for a leading Victorian periodical under the guidance of a highly respected editor who kept him constantly aware of the needs of his middle-class audience. The yardstick by which Stephen measured the codes of decorum of this audience lay at his own back door, at the parsonage. His rule was, 'Thou shalt not shock a young lady', or, more precisely, 'Thou shalt not offend a country parson's daughter!' This, Stephen said, was the first commandment he had to enforce.[5]

This contingency alone would illuminate any study of Hardy's manuscript, if, in reading over his shoulder and watching the creative mind at work, we are also aware of the shadow of another standing alongside, so to speak, as Hardy submits his chapters from week to week, from month to month, under the scrutiny of Leslie Stephen's judicious eye: his steady flow of advisory letters and his lengthy discussions with Hardy at his London home acting as a constant rein to the author's creative imagination. Assessed in this light, the extent and significance of Hardy's revisions exact a pluralistic interpretation as we move from his own first writing to the cancellations and interlinear revisions made in the manuscript, then to augmentations marked in verso[6] on the preceding leaf, and then to changes made in proof – a practice more common at that time than now.[7] Finally, we have Leslie Stephen's editorial cuts, some of which are signified by visible pencil marks on the page.

We are looking, then, at changes of several different kinds. Some of them seem to reflect, as I say, a new awareness on Hardy's part brought about by the education of his consciousness in certain Victorian codes and conventions; others suggest artistic refinements and newly crafted devices of plot; others indicate the outright bowdlerisation of his editor.

Although, on occasion, the true owner of the 'good hand' is not always self-evident, several changes are certainly more consistent with Stephen's

170

Chapter XVIII

Boldwood in meditation: a ~~m~~ visit.

Boldwood was tenant of what was called the Lower Farm,
& his person was the nearest approach to aristocracy that
this remoter quarter of Weatherbury could boast of. Genteel
strangers, whose god was their town, who might happen to be
compelled to linger about this nook for a day, heard the
sound of light wheels, & prayed to see ~~a person or a gentleman~~ *good society to the degree of a parson or squire*
at the very least; but it was only Mr Boldwood going out for
the day. They heard the sound of wheels yet ~~so~~ once more, &
were re-animated to expectancy: it was only Mr Boldwood
coming home again.
His house stood ~~withdrawn~~ *recessed* from the road, & the stables, which
are to a farm what the *a* fireplace is to a house, were behind,
their lower portions being lost amid bushes of laurel. Inside
the blue door, open half way down, were to be seen at this
time the buttocks & tails of half a dozen warm & contented
horses standing in their stalls; & thus viewed presenting alterations of roan & bay in shapes like ~~.............~~ a
Moorish arch, the tail being a ~~contrast~~ streak *down the midst of each*, other there,
& lost to the eye gazing in from the outer light, the mouths of
the same animals could be heard busily sustaining the

Facsimile 4 'buttocks and tails' (MS 1–170)

15

thinking than with Hardy's. For instance, we have in the manuscript, in Chapter XVIII, Hardy's description of Boldwood's horses, which reads:

> Inside the blue door, open half way down, were to be seen at this time the buttocks and tails of half a dozen warm and contented horses standing in their stalls.

In the *Cornhill* there are no buttocks! Instead, there are 'backs':

> Inside the blue door . . . were to be seen . . . the backs and tails of half-a-dozen warm and contented horses . . .

A similar change occurs in Chapter XXII. In the manuscript, Gabriel Oak flings the sheep he is shearing over on its 'buttocks'; in the *Cornhill* these unmentionables do not appear. Oak, instead, has to fling his sheep on to its back. Clearly, no 'buttocks' for the country parson's daughter.[8]

The most notorious of the unmentionables was, of course, the unwed mother and her baby: Hardy's treatment of Fanny Robin's seduction and a lengthy passage (cut by Stephen) treating with her stillborn baby in the coffin. This example of Stephen's censorship has not, so far, received full critical attention, therefore I will be returning to it later, in Chapter 8, by way of amplification of recent critical observations.

But before embarking on a manuscript analysis and some of the other numerous textual changes that have so far gone unrecorded, I would like to mention an additional point of interest concerning the serialisation process of *Far from the Madding Crowd*. Hardy, we know, wrote the serial parts month by month – submitting to Leslie Stephen three to four chapters at a time for each serial number. But if you go to the original *Cornhill* publication, you will discover that not only were the parts written month by month but they were more or less matched month with month. That is, the temporal setting of the book – up until the denouement – corresponds with the calendar month of publication and the seasons of the real world.[9] Thus the late lambing time in Weatherbury (discussed by the rustics in Chapter XV) reaches the Victorian drawing-room in the April issue; the sheep-shearing scene appears in the May number; and the summer storms that threaten Bathsheba's hayricks come into the reader's month of August – and so on in that vein. Actually, in the normal course of events, summer storms usually occur, in the south of England, in late July. But as Hardy makes plain, the world of nature this year in Weatherbury is a little out of joint: 'tis a very queer lambing this year', says Oak, 'and we shan't have done by Lady Day.' Lady Day falls, incidentally, on 25 March, about the date when this number (the April number), was due to appear on the bookstalls. Back in Weatherbury, it is also a very queer season for the swarming of bees. As we are told in Chapter XXVII, they are not only swarming late this year, but they are also unusually hard to control, or as Hardy says, 'unruly'. However, if

2—7

flock without re-stamping it with her initials, came
again to Gabriel, as he put down the luncheon to drag
a frightened ewe to his shearing-station — flinging it over
upon its buttocks with a dexterous twist of the arm.
He lopped off the tresses about its head, & opened up
the neck & collar, his mistress quietly looking on.
"She blushes at the insult," murmured Bathsheba,
watching the pink flush which arose & overspread
the neck & shoulders of the ewe [where they were left]
bare by the clipping shears — a flush which was enviable,
for its delicacy, by many queens of the coteries, & would
have been creditable, for its promptness, to any woman in
the world.

Poor Gabriel's soul was fed with a luxury of content
by having her over him, her eyes critically regarding his
skilful shears, which apparently were going to gather
up a piece of the flesh at every close & yet never did
so. Like Guildenstern, Oak was happy in that he was
not over happy. He had no wish to converse with her:
that his bright lady & himself formed one group, exclusively
their own, & containing no others in the world, was
enough.

So the chatter was all on her side. There is a
loquacity which tells nothing, which was Bathsheba's; and
there is a silence which says much: that was Gabriel's.

Facsimile 5 'flinging it over upon its buttocks' (MS 2–7)

17

late-swarming, unruly bees are to be hived at all in the gardens of England, the time would be right – as Bathsheba knows – around the month of June; although no doubt the honeymaking readers of the June number would be denied a certain added attraction, namely the unexpected arrival at their garden gate of a dashing young sergeant of cavalry.

I draw attention to this close temporal correspondence, maintained by Hardy between the fictional world and the real, because it presents an aspect of accessibility and immediacy which would have been palpably felt by Victorian readers of the monthly *Cornhill*. The implications of this are not unimportant. For this 'here and now' quality subtly subverts the dramatic device Hardy uses to set his 'world apart': the spatial distance he sets between his pastoral world and the world of the Victorian drawing-room, into which unconventional young women farmers of a sexually daring nature may not otherwise gain admittance.

To my mind, this temporal correspondence with its aspect of palpable immediacy, which brings the events in Weatherbury right into our country parsonage, helps us to understand Leslie Stephen's anxiety as *Far from the Madding Crowd* begins to depart from cows and sheep and veers, instead, towards issues that he considered rather French and rather nasty.

Hardy touches, briefly, on this – the censorship issue – in his auto-biography, the *Life*: the three respectable ladies who had written to upbraid Leslie Stephen for an improper passage, which led him to caution Hardy about the seduction of Fanny Robin, and which drew from Hardy the response that he was anxious to please – he merely wished to be considered a good hand at a serial, although he might have higher aims one day.[10] His increasingly close acquaintance with Leslie Stephen would have left him in no doubt that as the editor of a widely respected periodical (the most influential medium of the day), Stephen would have seen it as his moral duty to act the part of censor, although he was always quick to insist that he was anything but a prude. The following letter is revealing, in this context. Written by Stephen in 1867:

> You say you have been reading some French novels lately. I am much given to that amusement, though I never read De Musset. By the way, I don't quite agree with your praise of them. Of course it is true that English writers – Thackeray conspicuously so – are injured by being cramped as to love in its various manifestations. Still, I doubt whether the French gains much by the opposite system. To say the truth, much as I like reading them, and especially Balzac and Sand, and little as I am given to over-strictness in my tastes, I do believe that the commonplace critic is correct . . . they are prurient and indecent . . . I don't think them delicate either in the sense of art or morals. They are always hankering and sniffing after sensual motives, and . . . the effect is apt to border on the nasty . . . I consider the lovemaking of

English novelists to be purer and more life-like. This touches certain theories, or if you like, crotchets of mine, on which I could be voluminous.[11]

Hardy was to learn just how voluminous – although it doesn't seem to have deterred him, later in his career, from 'sniffing after sensual motives' himself.

Difficulties arose between Hardy and Stephen partly because Stephen thought he would be getting something like *Under the Greenwood Tree*. He writes to Hardy, in November 1872:

> I hear from Mr Moule that I may address you as the author of *Under the Greenwood Tree*.
>
> I have lately read that story with very great pleasure indeed. I think the descriptions of country life admirable and indeed it is long since I have received more pleasure from a new writer.
>
> It also occurred to me, and it is for this reason that I take the liberty of addressing you, that such writing would probably please the readers of the Cornhill Magazine as much as it pleased me. *Under the Greenwood Tree* is of course not a magazine story. There is too little incident for such purposes; for, though I do not want a murder in every number, it is necessary to catch the attention of readers by some distinct and well arranged plot.[12]

Stephen goes on to invite Hardy to offer him his next novel, but being busily engaged in the writing of *A Pair of Blue Eyes* at this point, some time elapses before Hardy can send Stephen a few chapters of *Far from the Madding Crowd* with some succeeding ones in outline – in brief, what Stephen understood to be Hardy's story of a woman farmer, a shepherd and a sergeant of cavalry. It is now 1873 and time is running short. Shorter than Hardy had anticipated: Stephen has rearranged his schedule and would now like *Far from the Madding Crowd* to start in the January 1874 number of the *Cornhill*. But he still has not had sight of the complete manuscript. Neither has Hardy. Aside from a few rough drafts and chapter outlines he has not written it yet. 'As a rule', Stephen writes to Hardy,

> it is desirable that I should see the whole of the manuscript of a novel before definitely accepting it. Under the circumstances however and as I should wish to begin the publication of your novel before long, it may be desirable to decide at once.[13]

He does decide at once, fully confident that the author of *Under the Greenwood Tree* will, in his words, 'suit us admirably'.

What Stephen did not know, and what Hardy himself could not yet know, was that with the incorporation into this *Greenwood-Tree*-type tale of 'some distinct and well arranged plot', of more complex elements of incident and character, unexpected shapes and colorations began to appear. These give rise to dramatic complications and psychological implications not altogether in keeping with either the pastoral genre (of Stephen's expectations) or the melodramatic mode into which Hardy allows himself to fall, particularly when the dictates of suspense-plot and periodical deadlines accelerate the narrative heartbeat and dilate atmospheric pressure.

To some extent, Hardy surrenders to these unexpected shapes and colorations – shifting back and forth between varying modes and structures, seemingly bound by none. Demonstrating a narrative fidelity to the pastoral and a distinct flair for the absurdities and incongruities of melodrama, he also incorporates elements of fairy-tale romance juxtaposed with the verisimilitude characteristic of Victorian genre painting. In his free play with these modes, together with his aptitude for injecting psychological realism into the most commonplace of dramatic actions (such as Oak's sheep-shearing),[14] Hardy's creative imagination remains subject to few constraints, and this occasionally presents him with problems.

Some of these problems, as the following chapters will demonstrate, arise from his giving too free a play to the imaginative development of his characters who then have to be trimmed down to size, or endowed with a language more appropriate to their new role and function. Other problems arise when, in the vigour and flow of his writing, he becomes forgetful of the needs of his audience. This, in turn, can demand of him less 'realism' and more representational art – as, for example, in his modification of oaths and blasphemies (see Chapter 6 of present volume) which subtly negotiates the distance between free expression and propriety.

One such problem of imaginative overdevelopment occurs in his characterisation of his 'wicked soldier-hero' (as he liked to speak of Troy), who does not readily conform to any particular type. No doubt it is part of Hardy's purpose to feature Troy as an 'outsider' in the Weatherbury world, where he exists as an alien figure, a subject for rumour and hearsay who, even as Bathsheba's husband, remains ill-conversant with rural life and the concerns of the community. But the 'outsider', for Hardy, immediately presents him with a conflict of interests; a conflict of over-identification and psychic differentiation. Perpetually at odds with the world himself, perpetually experiencing a strong sense of alienation from contemporary ideologies, perpetually at loggerheads with literary reviewers and no less frustrated with passionate relationships (in later years, in self-referential terms, a 'misfit'), that balance between identification and differentiation that weighs in the creative imagination in varying degrees of acceptable and rejectable projections becomes, for

Hardy, the more problematical, the more ambivalent with alienated, 'outcast' characters. We can only guess at the extent of his struggle towards objectification of, and psychic differentiation from his literary 'progeny', so to speak, but we can, I think, reach a fairly educated guess in Troy's case. This we can do by treading closely in Hardy's own narrative footsteps; by evaluating his stance with Troy as it becomes increasingly ambivalent at both the conceptual stage of characterisation and at subsequent stages of consolidation in manuscript and proof revisions.

Hardy's authorial ambivalence towards Troy presents no immediate difficulties in the thematic sense; it does, however, produce several warps within the textual fabric of the novel, particularly where he is working towards a broader focus, a more impartial tone, a less trammelled perspective and a more consistent mode of presentation – as I will go on to show in close detail in the next chapter. Thematically though, as I say, things go well enough. In accentuation of his restless sense of limited freedom (and the novel's theme of strife – both noble and ignoble)[15] Hardy has Troy perpetually poised for exits he never successfully negotiates. As a member of the Dragoon Guards, he is posted from Casterbridge to Melchester at the very outset of the novel, and Fanny Robin, who will herself become marginalised by association with him, journeys through winter ice and snow to find him incarcerated in barracks with no exit permit. Later, on furlough, he removes to Bath, and this time it is Bathsheba who searches him out, only to get herself caught in a matrimonial trap wholly inappropriate to both of their youthful needs to dare each other and the world. Later still, as a married man, he takes himself off to the Budmouth racemeetings where his gambling ruinously depletes Bathsheba's hard-earned monies and emotional endurance in equal measure, while providing no satisfactory outlet for his restlessness. And finally he departs for America where, again, he finds himself impecuniously edged off to the fringe – at odds with himself and the world. All exits are in one way or another closed to him. Yet, despite these touches of the vagabond, the restless wanderer and the *déraciné*, Troy is neither the unregenerate villain nor the elevated anti-hero. Nor does he readily conform to type as the kind of reckless libertine already safely familiar to Stephen's 'young ladies' in Victorian melodrama. I say 'safely' because melodrama is a genre in which the sheer extravagance of emotion, sensation and violence strips immorality and vice of its shock value.[16]

The main problem lies then, in definition and identity – a good starting point for a critical examination of Hardy's literary creation of a major character in *Far from the Madding Crowd*. For the purposes of plot, Hardy seems to want the balladist's soldier-with-a-winning-tongue but, as we will go on to discover, as a major character who proves to be essential to the plot in moving the action ahead for periodical purposes, Troy also leads Hardy astray – notably into conceiving more scenarios than is warranted by theme or plot. Simultaneously, Troy also proves to be more complicated to define, more awkward to control, and more demanding of his author's attention than any other male character in *Far from the Madding Crowd*.

2

'What sort of man is this?'

Hardy's first impulse with Troy, in his first conception of him at the manuscript stage of writing, is to colour him not in the flamboyant tones of the seducer-stereotype, but in those Arcadian tones of Greek sensuousness so dear to his own heart. Although Troy has already entered the scene on the periphery, so to speak, first as the soldier incarcerated in Melchester barracks – 'as good as in the county gaol till to-morrow morning', as he tells the lovesick Fanny Robin – and, second, as the bridegroom she accidentally jilts at the altar and who heartlessly spurns her thereafter, it is not until the scene of the fir plantation and his erotic encounter with Bathsheba that Troy takes on the fuller dimension of a rounded, complex character. And it is at this point, in the chapter that follows (Chapter XXV), entitled 'The New Acquaintance Described', that Hardy plunges into Troy's story. Here we learn something of his vices, such as lying like a Cretan[1] and dissembling to women, all of which Hardy renders in tones of light irony and with the kind of uncensorious, wry benevolence we find in Henry Fielding's *Tom Jones*. This mildly indulgent tone is, however, rather more apparent in the manuscript than in the *Cornhill*. For example, as we are told that 'He never passed the line which divides the spruce vices from the ugly', so we are also told that:

> In his sacrifices to Venus he retained the ancient doctrines of the groves, and introduced vice, not as a lapse, but as a necessary part of the ceremony.

This little touch of pagan licentiousness is silently excised for Stephen's readers in the *Cornhill*.

Although Stephen maintains, in his correspondence with Hardy, a low profile on his role of censor, this does not reflect the regularity and rigour of his editorial intervention in actual practice.[2] This particular unauthorised cut reveals something of the intrusiveness of his method and something of what Hardy was later to call his 'grim and severe criticisms' – a phrase that (despite the mellowing of years) reveals Hardy's sense of harsh treatment at Stephen's hands. How could Hardy *not* have it entailed. But limitation of the capacity is never recognised as a loss by the loser therefrom: in this attribute moral or esthetic poverty contrasts ~~advanta~~ plausibly with material, since those who suffer do not ~~~~ see it, whilst those who ~~~~ see it do not suffer. It is not a ~~~~ denial of anything to have been always without it, & what Troy had never enjoyed he did not miss; but being fully conscious that what sober people missed he enjoyed, his capacity, though ~~ really less, seemed ~~more~~ greater than theirs.

He was perfectly truthful towards men, but to women lied like a Cretan, a system of ethics, above all others, calculated to win popularity at the first flush of admission into lively society, & the possibility of the favour gained being but transient, had reference only to the future –

In his sacrifices to Venus he retained the ancient doctrines of the groves, & introduced vice, not as a lapse, but as a necessary part of the ceremony. But he never passed the line which divides the spruce vices from the ugly, & hence, though his morals had never been applauded, disapproval of them had frequently been tempered with a smile. This treatment had led to his becoming ~~on~~ a sort of forestaller & regrater of other men's experiences of the glorious class, to his own aggrandizement as a Corinthian rather than

Facsimile 6 'his sacrifices to Venus' (MS 2–39)

been upset at this cavalier cancellation of his text? Not only did he thoroughly relish his literary allusions (poetic infusions into the prose), but also, in this instance, he had chanced at 'slipping one by' Mrs Grundy, only to find that despite all his deft efforts at emulating the neo-Classicists by camouflaging flesh-and-blood sexuality in the guise of classical antiquity, all his efforts have been in vain.[3]

And then there is the loss of artistic unity such an excision effects within the text: ultimately this Venusian reference provides the artistic balance to Hardy's characterisation of Troy in this chapter which relies heavily upon allusions to Greek folklore – from lying Cretans to the refined dissipation of the citizens of Corinth. As an allusion to things youthful and sensual, the excised passage and its reference to the rites of Venus is clearly intended as a prefatory note to the phrase it later justifies, which now runs in the *Cornhill* without qualification:

> He never passed the line which divides the spruce vices from the ugly; and hence, though his morals had hardly been applauded, disapproval of them had frequently been tempered with a smile.

This phrase, standing as it now does without the prefatory, justifying reference to Venus and the 'ancient doctrines of the groves', no longer makes any sense. In its present state, sandwiched between Corinthian dissipation and Cretan lying, there is nothing now (aside from the light irony of the allusions) of that soft and sensuous Greek joyousness with which to temper disapproval 'with a smile'.[4]

A less disruptive cancellation also occurs here. Whereas in the manuscript Hardy has Troy (the dissembler to women) 'perfectly' truthful towards men, in proof for the *Cornhill* this becomes 'moderately' truthful to men. This appears to be a downgrading with a purpose. Hardy, in revision, mainly concerns himself with the accuracy, authenticity and artistic refinement of details. He also concentrates on the clarification and coherency of characterisation and, with single word changes, upon subtly enhancing meaning and connotative depth. In this instance, purely in the interests of accuracy, authenticity and coherency, his 'wicked soldier hero' should not be 'perfect' in any respect, although the irony inherent in the phrase ('perfectly truthful towards men') serves aptly to throw up Troy's double-standards – he lies only to women! However, 'moderately' serves almost as well. More importantly, for our purposes, it also serves to show a willingness in Hardy to modify his own smiling benevolence, where Troy is concerned. This modification of the benevolent narrator's own inclination to 'temper' disapproval 'with a smile' allows for greater authorial leverage in effecting the unimpeded growth of his 'wicked soldier hero'.

Hardy's proof revisions to the next chapter, 'Scene on the Verge of the Hay-Mead', consolidate this downward curve in authorial benevolence.

25

This is where Bathsheba is offered Troy's gold watch, and where Hardy's revisionary efforts for the *Cornhill* are now devoted to modifying Troy's roguish charm by gentrifying him. To begin with, in his first conception of things, Hardy has no shred of glamour attaching to Troy; and the watch he offers Bathsheba has only a well-worn and distinctly well-earned symbolic value (of the kind that appealed strongly to Hardy). Troy tells Bathsheba:

> It is an unusually good one for a man like me to possess, he quietly[5] said. It was my poor father's. He was a medical man and always used it among his patients. The tick of that watch has run races with a thousand illustrious pulses in its time. It was all the fortune he left me.

The tone and focus here speak for themselves: no social pretensions, no pomposity, no class consciousness. But this is not what Hardy offers the *Cornhill* reader. In proof revision this little speech of Troy's now becomes:

> 'It is an unusually good one for a man like me to possess,' he quietly said. 'That watch has a history. Press the spring and open the back.'
> She did so.
> 'What do you see?'
> 'A crest and a motto.'
> 'A coronet with five points, and beneath, *Cedit amor rebus* – "Love yields to circumstance." It's the motto of the Earls of Severn. That watch belonged to the last lord, and was given to my mother's husband, a medical man, for his use till I came of age, when it was to be given to me. It was all the fortune that I ever inherited. That watch has regulated imperial interests in its time – the stately ceremonial, the courtly assignation, pompous travels, and lordly sleeps. Now it is yours.'

Similar class or status modifications of Hardy's original conception of Troy occur elsewhere in his proof revisions of *Far from the Madding Crowd*. Were they designed, perhaps, to offer the reader the more familiar stereotype of the vagabond charmer possessing murky connections with the gentry? Possibly – for it is true that such connections in the Wessex novels rarely endear us, and this might be helpful, in Troy's case, in edging him towards disaffection. Might they also, though, have a disconcerting effect on Hardy too, given his conflicting feelings about genealogies in general and his own in particular? Perhaps, by introducing this element of class separation, he establishes a marginal distance between himself and his character, in this instance between himself and his lordly 'pretender' who must, to all intents and purposes, eventually fulfil the role of the heartless seducer turned disruptive intruder in the Weatherbury world? On the

2—53

such sudden feeling in people. I won't listen to you any
longer. Dear me I wish I knew what o'clock it is — I am
going — I have wasted too much time here already.
The sergeant looked at his watch & told her. What haven't
you a watch Miss? he enquired.
I have not just at present — I am about to get a new one.
No. You shall be given one. Yes — you shall! a gift Miss
Everdene — a gift.
And before she knew what the young man was intending
a heavy gold watch was in her hand.
It is an unusually good one for a man like me to possess
he quietly said. It was my poor father's. He was a medical
man & always used it among his patients. The tick of that
watch has run races with a thousand illustrious pulses
in its time. It was all the fortune he left me.
But Sergeant Troy — I cannot take this — I cannot!
she exclaimed with round-eyed wonder. A gold watch —
what are you doing! Don't be such a dissembler!
The sergeant retreated to avoid receiving back his gift,
which she held out persistently towards him. Bathsheba
followed as he retired.
Keep it — do, Miss Everdene — keep it! said the erratic
child of impulse. The fact of your possessing it makes it
worth ten times as much to me. A silver one will answer

Facsimile 7 'the tick of that watch' (MS 2–53)

other hand, in a more practical sense – on a class level – this 'gentrified' Troy presents far more plausible competition for Boldwood and a far more appropriate suitor for Bathsheba (he is, after all, but an enlisted soldier which, in Victorian eyes, rated very low indeed on the social scale). At any rate, the *Cornhill* has, as we have seen, a rather pompous Troy offering a rather uneasy Bathsheba a gold watch engraved with a crest and motto, handed down to him, through his 'mother's husband', from the last lord of the Earls of Severn who, if we wish to read between the lines, yielded to his motto to the very last word.

The textual change we have glanced at in the *Cornhill* constitutes an important part of Hardy's larger scheme (with hindsight) to accentuate Troy's aristocratic origins. This development can be fully mapped as follows. Earlier, in Chapter XV, in his very first conception of Troy's background and connection with Fanny Robin (in the manuscript), Hardy has Boldwood respond to Oak's question, 'What sort of man is this Sergeant Troy?', with these words:

> 'H'm – I am afraid not one to build much hope upon in such a case as this,' the farmer murmured, 'though he's a clever fellow, and up to everything. Strange to say his father was a medical man who settled here several years ago because he preferred country to town – a taste which if indulged in means ruin to any professional man. He failed to scrape a connection together, and went away in debt leaving this son – a bright taking lad at that time – in a situation as copying clerk at a lawyer's in Casterbridge. He stayed there for some time, and might have worked himself into a decent livelihood of some sort had he not indulged in the wild freak of enlisting.'

However, *Cornhill* readers had the beginnings of a more colourful version:

> 'H'm – . . . though he's a clever fellow, and up to everything. A slight romance attaches to him, too. His mother, a French governess, was married to a poor medical man, and while money was forthcoming all went on well. Unfortunately for the boy, his best friends died; and he got then a situation as second clerk at a lawyer's in Casterbridge. He stayed there for some time, and might have worked himself into a dignified position of some sort . . .'

Here, we have Hardy's first reference to Troy's mother, 'a French governess', but not, as yet, the full reference as Hardy possibly first offered it to Stephen in proof revision for the *Cornhill*, which seems to have looked a little more like this:

> 'H'm – . . . A slight romance attaches to him, too. His mother was a French governess, and it seems that a secret attachment existed between her and the late Lord Severn. Soon after she was married to a poor medical man, and while money was forthcoming . . .'

This appears in the first edition (Smith, Elder & Co., 1874). Hardy is gradually working his way towards full disclosure but it is not until he revises for the first complete collected edition of the Wessex Novels, issued by Osgood, McIlvaine in 1895, that we have the entire unexpurgated version:

> 'H'm – . . . A slight romance attaches to him, too. His mother was a French governess, and it seems that a secret attachment existed between her and the late Lord Severn. She was married to a poor medical man, and soon after an infant was born; and while money was forthcoming all went on well. Unfortunately for her boy, his best friends died; and he got then a situation as second clerk . . .'

So now it is spelled out. The 'soon after' in this account carries rather a larger burden of suggestiveness than hitherto, and the text finally yields up the 'infant'.

As I will later show in more detail, Stephen had a peculiar sensitivity toward any mention of babies, particularly illegitimate babies. Thus, if the shape of the revised passage for the Wessex edition looks suspiciously like the original version submitted at proof stage to Stephen, who would have promptly excised the passage containing the baby ('and it seems that a secret attachment existed between her and the late Lord Severn ... and soon after an infant was born'), we may have every good reason for thinking that this aspect of Troy's characterisation is no late afterthought of Hardy's but rather an earlier, frustrated wish.

If we recall the outrage expressed by critics over Hardy's daring, in *Desperate Remedies* (1871), to portray a woman of respectable birth as the mother of an illegitimate child, Leslie Stephen's caution here (if that is what it is) would seem to be prudent enough. 'Nice women didn't . . .'; just as 'nice women', one hundred years later, did not contract sexually transmitted diseases. But evidently Hardy, who abhorred hypocrisy, double-standards and sexual prudery, was sufficiently irritated, or sufficiently frustrated, or in some way sufficiently provoked by his censors into making a point of revising this section later to insist on the fact that Troy is the bastard offspring of an illicit union between two 'respectable' people.

Certainly, if the story of the watch is to signify at all as a thread in Troy's history, it needs to be woven into the broader fabric of the community story, or the gossip which customarily serves to strengthen the security of the group while making targets of those who threaten it. Rather interestingly, Boldwood is the 'gossip' here. As a rule, until roused, he is reticent to a fault; but he is also, the keeper of many secrets, as well as the closest to gentry to be found in Weatherbury. Thus he is aptly cast as the respondent to Oak's question: 'What sort of man is this?'[6] And aptly enough his answer is, or would be if he were blunt about it, 'This man is a bastard.' But Boldwood is not given to forthright speech. Nor is he inclined to expose Troy as a threat to innocent young women. Nor does he regard the male, in this instance, as the object of blame. Instead, he rounds on the absent Fanny and reproaches her, albeit with commiseration, with being 'A silly girl – silly girl!' Thereafter, the scandalous seducer, suffering no checks upon his behaviour (checks of the kind Boldwood later tries to make when his *own* happiness is threatened), is free to act upon the old patriarchal motto, 'Love yields to circumstance': although this time around the seduction story becomes a second-generation repeat of the first with a tragic coda: the innocent mother and her newborn babe both die.

One ironic aspect of Stephen's cuts here is that the 'silly girl' herself must have sounded to the *Cornhill* reader, at this early point in the story, not quite as wantonly silly as Boldwood's original words intend. It is quite clear why Boldwood sees her as 'silly', for as he observes (in the manuscript), alluding to her liaison with Troy:

> she has now lost her character – he will never marry her – and what will she do?

But there is no reference to her lost character in the *Cornhill*. Evidently, this was too sexually explicit for Stephen, who had written to Hardy a few weeks before this instalment appeared in print to say that he had,

> ventured to leave out a line or two in the last batch of proofs from an excessive prudery of wh. I am ashamed: but one is forced to be absurdly particular.[7]

The *Cornhill* reader was therefore left to puzzle out the full implications of Fanny's silliness without Boldwood's elaboration, which by sheer dint of speculation might well have raised more eyebrows at the country parsonage than Stephen would have liked or intended.

Alternatively, the more unsuspecting reader, or even the less prurient reader, might have felt that Fanny's silliness lay solely in her blind faith in Troy; particularly her blind faith in his 'respectability'. Despite the fact that she is destitute and grateful to take money from a total stranger (Oak) on her way out of Weatherbury, and despite the fact that Troy, as an enlisted soldier, owns no higher social status than a servant, Fanny still speaks of him (in a letter returning the money to Oak) in the most elevated of terms:

> He would, I know, object to my having received anything except as a loan, being a man of great respectability and high honour

This takes me back to the point, earlier indicated in the 'the rites of Venus' section, which is that as far as Stephen was concerned, the less said about Troy's sexuality the better. If Boldwood was disinclined to spell out the facts, so too was Hardy's editor. Liddy's comment, in Chapter XXIV of the manuscript, that Troy is a 'gay man' and 'a walking ruin to honest girls, so some people say', did not meet with Stephen's approval. Out it went! Only the 'gay man' was retained for those never-to-be-shocked daughters of country parsons.

If the truth be told, the 'line or two' Stephen says he has 'ventured to leave out' has a remarkable propensity to multiply. Even forgetting his silent excisions, his visible markings in the manuscript tell us enough! Take, for example, 'honest girls' and their doings: they have a most unlucky way of catching his eye, and, instantly, the censoring pencil strikes. And he is particularly watchful over the intimate conversations between the women. In Chapter XXX, entitled 'Blame – Fury', Bathsheba, laughing with Liddy at the picture of herself as an 'Amazonian' woman, goes on to say:

I hope I am not a bold sort of maid – mannish?

'O no, not mannish', says Liddy,

but so almightly womanish that 'tis getting on that way sometimes. Ah! miss . . . I wish I had half your failing that way. 'Tis a great protection to a poor maid's virtue in these days of handsome deceivers.

Poised over 'a poor maid's virtue', Stephen's pencil draws the line, and the *Cornhill* has simply 'a protection to a poor maid in these days'. Later, evidently wanting to retrieve something of the mischievous tone of the women's talk, Hardy emends this line in a rather weak revision for the Wessex edition, so we now have:

'Tis a great protection to a poor maid in these illegit'mate days!

Apparently, Hardy anticipates his reader's skill in filling in the gap (pointed at in 'illegit'mate') that Stephen found too explicit in 'virtue'.[8]

Returning to Troy, whose sexuality becomes increasingly (in Hardy's revisions) associated with both illegitimacy and aristocracy, I should emphasise that in his gentrification scheme Hardy takes each and every opportunity to revise and upgrade Troy's background and class status. To this end, he seizes the moment of yet another conversation between the women, following Bathsheba's first encounter with Troy in the fir plantation, and revises their conversation accordingly. In his first conception of things, Bathsheba had crept, panting, into Liddy's room, and had asked:

Liddy, is any soldier staying in the village – sergeant somebody – rather young for a sergeant . . .?

However, 'young' is cancelled in the manuscript and Hardy replaces it

31

with 'gentlemanly': 'somebody – rather gentlemanly for a sergeant'. Not content with this little adjustment, Hardy shortly afterwards makes another. In the manuscript, Liddy exclaims:

> Such a clever young dand as he is! A doctor's son, brought up so well, and sent to Casterbridge Grammar School for years and years. Learnt all languages while he was there

But for the *Cornhill*, Hardy adds in proof:

> Such a clever young dand as he is! A doctor's son by name, which is a great deal; and he's an earl's son by nature!
> Which is a great deal more. Fancy! Is it true?
> Yes. And he was brought up so well, and sent to Casterbridge Grammar School for years and years. Learnt . . .

And if Liddy provides Hardy with a chance to upgrade Troy's status, so too does Fanny. Where, in the manuscript, she had simply written in her letter to Oak that Troy is a 'man of great respectability and high honour', Hardy now augments her words in proof for the *Cornhill* to read: ' – indeed, a nobleman by blood'.

A conceptual ambiguity arises here. Fanny is gullible to a fault – she reveres Troy's noble blood almost as if it exonerates him from conventional codes of behaviour and places him, by right, above all criticism – reminiscent of the tradition of the *droit de seigneur*. And this simple-minded faith of hers, this unquestioning trust in this particular class credo, renders her so poignantly a victim of gender and class domination that we can only grieve for her. In this respect, Hardy's augmentation – 'a nobleman by blood' – becomes, simultaneously, an aspect which endears poor Fanny while it renders the situation more stereotypical (and to that extent a degree less engaged, perhaps, on Hardy's part). To complicate matters still further, it also alerts the reader to Troy's snobbish name-dropping, or exploitation of his noble birth, and we now wince at what we see and fear for what we might see.

There may, however, be a contrary indication here: Hardy's gentrification of Troy may not be entirely alien to his own sympathies. Attraction and repulsion being two sides of the same coin, Hardy wavers over genealogies, sometimes despising sometimes admiring the thing that fascinates him – even the idea of his own 'blue-blood'. Perhaps then, all we can infer in Troy's case is Hardy's continuing ambivalence towards him. Salient to this point is that aspect of Troy's characterisation which is Hardy's own love of literary allusions. Troy's mother, described by Boldwood as a French governess but by Troy himself as a 'Parisienne', is that mother of all mothers in Hardy's book: she is a literary mother! From her, Troy has learned French proverbs, biblical tracts, Shakespearean speeches, and he even has a line from Thomas Campbell's song 'How

Delicious is the Winning'.[9] No other character in *Far from the Madding Crowd* can match Troy in this, and certainly no other performs as Hardy's mouthpiece in quite this stylish, literary way.[10]

Consequently, how and where to place Troy verges on the problematic for Hardy. It seems to me, from a close reading of his manuscript, that his 'wicked soldier hero' presents him with the difficult task of derogating a character who, in fact, makes constant appeals to his sympathy and imagination. Even in prefiguring Troy's downfall with the simplest of dramatic actions, such as his casual tossing away of his only fortune (his gold watch), which demands of Hardy a conscious act of class separation, there persists by virtue of the hindsight attention to it a narrative continuity of engagement.

Perhaps this engagement was largely due to the fact that Troy, who lived so vividly in Hardy's imagination, had to be continually wrested from that complex part of the artist's psyche that resists finality.[11] There is even a small segment late into the manuscript just at that ambivalent point when Hardy is struggling to effect Troy's departure where (leading up to the grave-planting scene), the narrative wanders off in Troy's direction and is visibly halted by Hardy's excising pen. This occurs at the point where Bathsheba returns home from the swamp. Entering the disused attic:

> Bathsheba went to the window and opened it. Whilst she stood there a faint distant rattle of mild musketry was audible.
>   'What's that

But she goes no further. Hardy stops here, puts his pen through the whole passage and substitutes Bathsheba's question: 'What shall I do to pass the heavy time away?'

Was Hardy thinking, at this point, of having Troy posted off with the Dragoon Guards? This is perhaps too much of a coincidence – their posting from local barracks at exactly the moment when Troy must escape Weatherbury. But if this was a possible scenario which faltered in Hardy's imagination and left him frustrated and restless, it could well explain the unbridled pace (in the manuscript) of the Lulwind Cove episode which, by contrast, not only carries Troy away but also Hardy himself – imaginatively speaking. He simply cannot stop himself, where Troy is concerned.

As to the original length of the Lulwind episode, we know that Leslie Stephen recommended one or two major cuts, notably in the paying scene and the shearing-supper, which he claimed delayed the action of the story. Did he, though, apply the same rationale of delayed action to the Lulwind episode in Chapter XLVII, entitled 'Adventures by the Shore', where Troy is swept out to sea? The extensive cuts to this chapter are of particular interest in the context of Hardy's characterisation of Troy because they are the only substantial cuts (aside from the coffin scene) that forcibly diminish the focus on a single central character in *Far from the Madding Crowd*. What is now a two-page chapter extends to twice that length in the manuscript version. The following is an extract:

> Troy had sunk down exhausted, and it was some time before he could speak connectedly, his deliverers meanwhile lending him what little clothing they could spare among them as a slight protection against the rapidly cooling air. He soon told them his tale, and begged to be put ashore at his bathing place, which he pointed out to them as being about a mile distant. Their boat was somewhat laden, but after a little demurring they agreed to row in the direction signified, and set him down. Troy however had considerably understated the distance, and what with this and keeping wide of the current they rowed more than two miles before the narrow mouth of the cove appeared. By the time that their keel crunched among the stones of the beach within the opening the sun was down, a crescent moon had risen, and solitude reigned around, rendering distinct the gentle slide of the wavelets up the sloping shore and the rustle of the pebbles against each other under the caress of each swell – the brisker ebb and flow outside the bay being audible above the mild repetition of the same motion here within.
>
> Troy anxiously scanned the margin of the cove for the white heap of clothes he had left there. No sign of them apparently remained. He leapt out, searched up and down – behind boulders and under weeds. Beyond all doubt the clothes were gone.
>
> By jingo, he said to them with a blank offhandedness; all I possess is gone; and I haven't a friend or penny in the world!
>
> The seamen took counsel, and one of them said. If you come aboard with us, perhaps we can find you a kit. We've been waiting in Budmouth for hands, and are short still. Can't get 'em to join. Captain's glad of anything he can pick up, and might take you.

Skipping over the next few manuscript paragraphs, we find Troy longing to escape

> all unpleasant reminders of his late wretchedness, and all responsibilities. The sad accessories of Fanny's end haunted him as vivid pictures which threatened to be indelible, making Weatherbury intolerable under any circumstances just now.

Hardy cancels much of this section himself, in the manuscript. Portions of it, however, he later retrieves and copies for use three chapters on – notably a section on Bathsheba where Troy's thoughts turn sourly upon the idea that:

> it seemed not at all unlikely that his wife might fail at her farming, and he would then become liable for her maintenance

3–9

of the Unknown a moving object broke the outline of the extremity, elongating the whole like a pencil propelled from its case, & immediately a ship's boat appeared, manned with several sailor lads, her prows towards the sea.

All Troy's vigour spasmodically revived to prolong the struggle yet a little further. Swimming with his right arm he held up his left to hail them, splashing upon the waves, & shouting with all his might. From the position of the setting sun his white form was distinctly visible upon the now dark hued bosom of the sea to the east of the boat, & the men saw him at once. Backing their oars & putting the boat about they pulled towards him with a will, & in five or six minutes from the time of his first halloo, two of the sailors hauled him in over the stern.

They formed part of a brig's crew, and had come ashore for sand. Troy had sunk down exhausted, & it was some time before he could speak connectedly, his deliverers meanwhile lending him what little clothing they could spare among them as a slight protection against the rapidly cooling air. He soon told them his tale, & begged to be put ashore at his bathing place, which he pointed out to them as being about a mile distant. Their boat was somewhat laden, but after a little demurring they agreed

Facsimile 8 'Troy had sunk down exhausted' (MS 3–9)

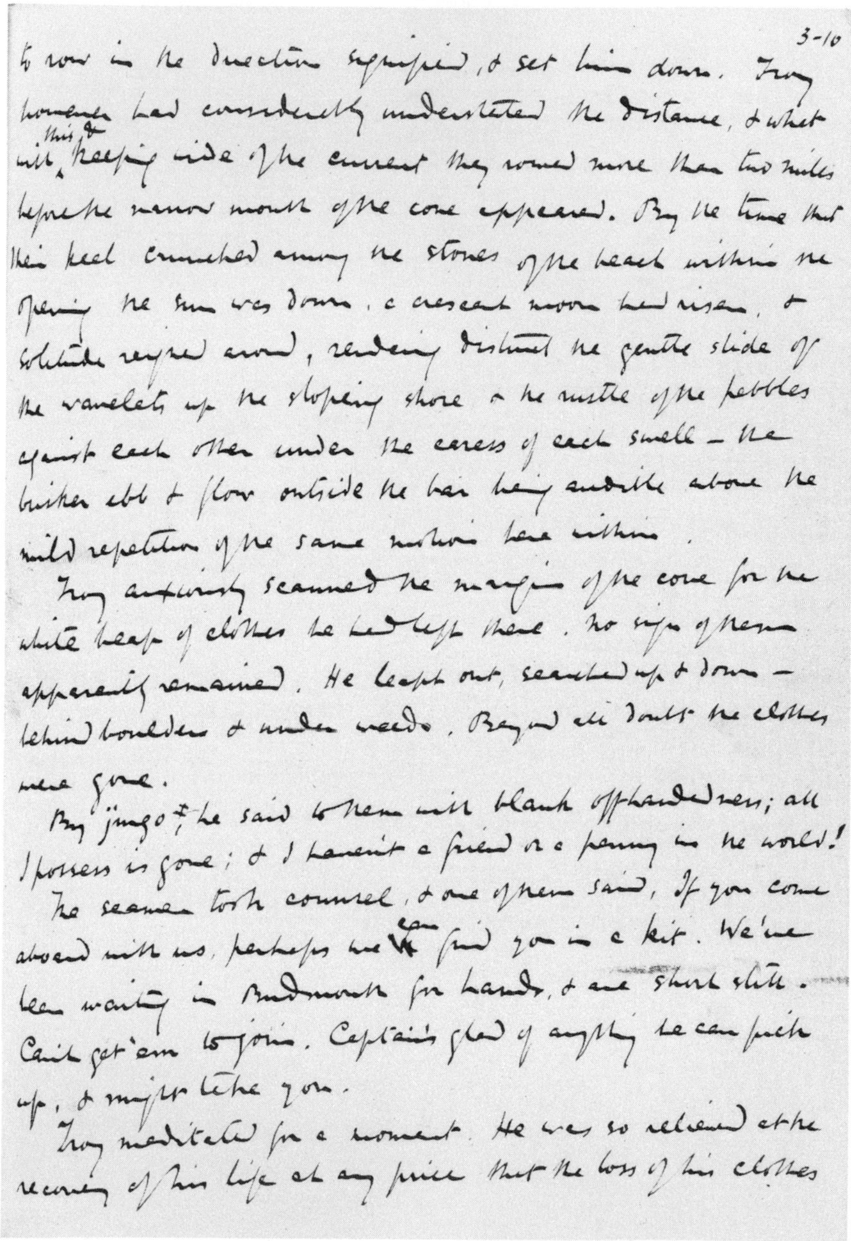

3-10

[Handwritten manuscript text, facsimile]

to row in the direction [...], & set him down. [...] however had [...] understated the distance, & what with [...] keeping [...] of the current they rowed more than two miles before the narrow mouth of the cove appeared. By the time that their keel crunched among the stones of the beach within the opening the sun was down, a crescent moon had risen, & solitude reigned around, rendering distinct the gentle slide of the wavelets up the sloping shore & the rustle of the pebbles against each other under the caress of each swell — the brisker ebb & flow outside the bar being audible above the mild repetition of the same motion here within.

[...] anxiously scanned the margin of the cove for the white heap of clothes he had left there. No sign of them apparently remained. He leapt out, searched up & down — behind boulders & under weeds. Beyond all doubt the clothes were gone.

"By jingo!" he said to them with blank offhandedness; "all I possess is gone; & I haven't a friend or a penny in the world!"

The seamen took counsel, & one of them said, "If you come aboard with us, perhaps we can find you a kit. We've been waiting in [...] for hands, & are short still. Can't get 'em to join. Captain's glad of anything he can pick up, & might take you."

[...] meditated for a moment. He was so relieved at the recovery of his life at any price that the loss of his clothes

Facsimile 9 'I haven't a friend or penny in the world' (MS 3–10)

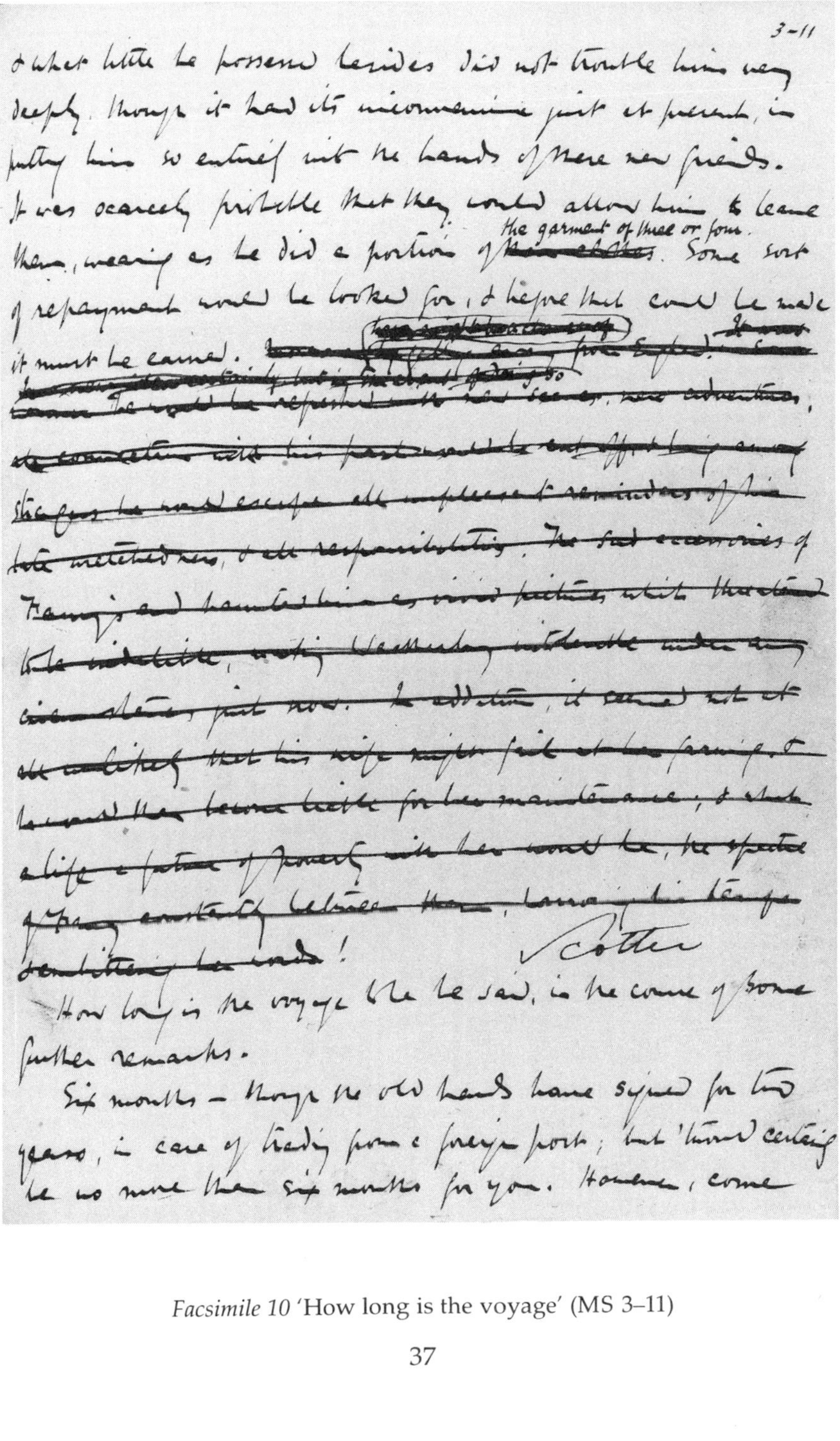

Facsimile 10 'How long is the voyage' (MS 3–11)

And what kind of life would it be with the 'spectre of Fanny constantly between them, harrowing his temper and embittering her words!'

Moving ahead through the manuscript another paragraph or so, we find Troy now accepting the invitation to leave:

> It would be doing Bathsheba a generous turn to leave the country, he thought grimly. His absence would be to her benefit as his presence might be to her ruin – though as she would never give him credit for his considerateness, he was hardly called upon to show it unless the gain was mutual.

And thus events flow on in the manuscript, moving from the external scene of lost belongings to the inner workings of Troy's mind as he mourns the loss of Fanny who haunts him as 'vivid pictures which threatened to be indelible'.

Hardy seems unable to abandon Troy even at this advanced stage of the plot, despite the fact that this is a logical point of departure. The question we have to ask then is: was it Hardy's or Stephen's excising pen that curtailed Troy's exploits by the shore? As we have seen, there are obvious signs in the manuscript that Hardy has tried to make some cuts in this episode, as if aware, himself, of having been carried away. And as we have also noticed, there are clear signs of his wishing to retain certain passages, some of which are inserted into a later chapter. This, then, suggests to me that whether the restructuring came about at Stephen's instigation or Hardy's, the very process of revision itself as Hardy worked his way line by line through this lengthy passage, could well have alerted him to the fact that by giving away the secret of Troy's disappearance at this point he was wasting precious dramatic potential. So, why not end this chapter, 'Adventures by the Shore', with Troy's rescue by the brig's crew without telling the reader about his emigration to America? This would serve two dramatic functions (and does!). The first function lies in the situational irony of the plot's conflicting truths. To all intents and purposes Troy has been drowned, as far as Hardy's Wessex characters are concerned. They do not know what we know; we know he was rescued. But we do not know what Hardy knows; Hardy knows he is not only rescued but also no longer in Wessex – as the reader still believes he is, in line with the revised version in which the brig-crew agrees to land him at Budmouth. It seems highly probable that these situational ironies would have appealed strongly to Hardy, once he discovered their potential in his text.

The second dramatic function, served by truncating this episode, develops out of the tension of the first. And the revised situation is now this: because we believe, but Bathsheba does not, that Troy is alive and presumably living in Wessex, we are doubly fearful for her now that

3–12

to the ship & read down the articles: we can put ye into Budmouth afterwards right enough.

They accepted the invitation, & away they went towards the roadstead. It would be doing Bathsheba a generous turn to leave the country, he thought grimly. His absence would be to her benefit as his presence might be to her ruin — though as she would never give him credit for his considerateness he was hardly called upon to show it unless the gain was mutual. And while he thought thus night drooped slowly upon the wide watery levels in front; & at no great distance from them, where the shore line curved round & formed a low riband of shade upon the horizon, a series of points of yellow light began to start into existence, denoting the spot to be the site of Budmouth, where the lamps were being lighted along the parade. The cluck of their oars was the only sound of any magnitude upon the sea, & as they laboured amid the thickening shades the lamplights grew larger, each appearing to send a flaming sword deep down into the waves before it, until there arose among other dim shapes of the kind the form of the vessel for which they were bound.

[End of October part]

Facsimile 11 'It would be doing Bathsheba a generous turn' (MS 3–12)

Boldwood, feverishly nourishing renewed dreams of possessing her, is about to resume his claims on her.[12]

Whatever the explanation for this extensive revision, the text (now copiously emended) withholds the full information about Troy's where-abouts until he returns and performs in the circus at Greenhill Fair.[13] Now, we are told, in Chapter L, that,

> After embarking on board the brig in Budmouth Roads as a new man with a new name he had worked his passage to the United States, where he made a precarious living in various towns as Professor of Gymnastics, Sword Exercise, Fencing, and Pugilism. A few months were sufficient to give him a distaste for this kind of life. There was a certain animal form of refinement in his nature, and however pleasant a strange condition might be whilst privations were easily warded off, it was disadvantageously coarse when money was short. There was ever present too the idea that he could claim a home and its comforts did he but choose to return to England and Weatherbury Farm. Whether Bathsheba thought him dead was a frequent subject of curious conjecture.

Actually, this is the emended manuscript version. The *Cornhill* absorbs a little more of the cancelled section in 'Adventures by the Shore', and excludes the 'new man with a new name'. Thus, (after proof revisions) the Greenhill Fair episode in Chapter L contains most of the above (about Troy's 'precarious living' in the United States) but also includes infor-mation from the cancelled 'shore' section, and instead of beginning 'After embarking on board the brig' it begins:

> The brig aboard which he was taken in Budmouth Roads was about to start on a voyage, though somewhat short of hands. Troy read the articles and joined, but before they sailed, a boat was despatched across the bay to Carrow Cove; but as he had half expected, his clothes were gone. He ultimately worked his passage to the United States, where he made a precarious living . . .

This is the version we have today. The only changes being first, the accidentals – Hardy himself preferred fewer commas, and this preference has been observed by later editors – and second, the alteration of Carrow Cove to Lulwind Cove.

This last revision was made some time after the *Cornhill* publication, when Hardy was revising for the Osgood, McIlvaine complete collected edition in 1895, as he began to develop the imaginative world of Wessex as a fictional region. 'Wessex' may have had its genesis in *Far from the Madding Crowd*, but Hardy had no clear or coherent vision of it at this early stage of his writing career. There is not only some confusion as to who lived where in Weatherbury – the Upper and Lower Weatherbury *for admission.*   3-34

& the sixpence which he had got ready, half an hour earlier, having become so reeking hot in the tight squeeze of his excited hand than the woman in spangles, brazen rings set with glass diamonds, & with chalked face & shoulders, who took the money of him, hastily dropped it again from a fear that some trick had been played to burn her fingers. So they all entered, & the sides of the tent, to the eyes of an observer on the outside, became bulged into innumerable pimples such as we observe on a sack of potatoes, caused by the various human heads, backs, & elbows, at high pressure within.

At the back of the large tent there were two small dressing-tents. One of these, allotted to the male performers, was partitioned into halves by a cloth; & in one of the divisions there was sitting on the grass, pulling on a pair of jack-boots, a young man whom we instantly recognise as Sergeant Troy.

Troy's appearance in this position may be briefly accounted for. After embarking on board the brig in Budmouth Roads as a new man with a new name he had worked his passage to the United States, ~~had shortly settled in a back street~~ ~~performed~~ where he made a precarious living in various towns as Professor of ~~Gymnast~~ Gymnastics, Sword Exercise, Fencing, & Pugilism. A few months were sufficient to give him a distaste for this kind of life. There was a certain

Facsimile 12 'a new man with a new name' (MS 3–34)

3 - 35

animal form of refinement in his nature, & however pleasant
a strange condition might be whilst privations were easily
warded off, it was disadvantageously coarse when money was
short. There was ever present too the idea that he could claim
a home & its comforts did he but choose to return to England
& Weatherbury Farm. Whether Bathsheba thought him dead
was a frequent subject of curious conjecture. To England
he did return at least, but the fact of drawing nearer to
Weatherbury abstracted its fascinations, & his intention to
enter his old groove at that place became modified. It was
with gloom he considered on landing at Liverpool that if
he were to go home his reception would be of a kind very unpleasant to contemplate; for what Troy had in the way of
emotions was an occasional florid fitful sentiment which sometimes
caused him as much inconvenience as emotion of a strong &
healthy kind. Bathsheba was not a woman to be made a fool
of, or set to suffer in silence; & how could he endure existence
with a spirited wife to whom at first entering he would be
beholden for food & lodging? X Thus for reasons touching on
distaste, regret, & shame commingled he put off his return from
day to day, & would have decided to put it off altogether if
he could have found anywhere else the ready made establishment
which existed for him here.
At this time — the July preceding the September in which we

Facsimile 13 'he could claim a home' (MS 3–35)

farms are juggled around in revision – but Carrow Cove itself was of indeterminate location. The manuscript has the cove's location, determined by the direction of Troy's wanderings at the opening of Chapter XLVII, quite simply set on 'the coast'. Or that is how Hardy's handwritten words appear to me: 'Troy wandered along towards the coast'. However, the *Cornhill* compositors printed this as 'west' (they made, in fact, very few compositorial errors), so that Leslie Stephen's readers had, 'Troy wandered along towards the west'. For those readers familiar with Hardy's topography this is a conundrum, since the only bay region west of Weatherbury lies at Budmouth (Weymouth) and this is far too large a shore inlet to be termed a cove; nor does it fit Hardy's description of the Pillars of Hercules nor, indeed, his story-line.

Hardy must have had Lulworth Cove in mind from the outset – hence 'coast' and not 'west'. For this particular shore inlet lies almost due south of Weatherbury (Puddletown), just as Hardy later revised it in 1895 to: 'Troy wandered along towards the south', at which point he also changed the name from Carrow first to Lulstead then to Lulwind. This name change, incidentally, not only echoes Lulworth's first syllable, but departs in meaning very little from its etymon – its origins in 'Lulworth'. If we take 'worth' to derive from the archaic 'worthen' (ME) meaning woe-betide, and 'wind' to mean twist, curve or warp, then in both namings the juxtaposition of 'lul' (calm) and twisting tides co-exists ('Lulstead', by contrast, diverges from the etymon in so far as 'stead' derives from the ancient use of the word meaning 'unwavering'; perhaps Hardy momentarily enjoyed the deceit in this naming). No doubt in ancient times 'Lulworth' signified to warn seafarers of the hidden treachery coursing beneath the surface of this serene shore – the same currents that take Troy unawares at Lulwind.

But these speculations have taken me further than I intended. Returning to Hardy's extensive revision to 'Adventures by the Shore', my feeling now is that Stephen may well have been concerned with accelerating the action for periodical purposes, and that Hardy would have seen the sense in that. But, given his own cancellations and retrievals as outlined above, it seems just as likely that he saw and seized the artistic advantages to be gained by restructuring this episode, by truncating Troy's exploits and keeping his reader in the dark as to his whereabouts – despite his apparent urge, in his first conception of things, to follow Troy (for several manuscript pages) all the way to America.

With Troy's rescue from drowning and subsequent departure for America, Hardy appears finally to have resolved the ambivalence of his concern for his 'wicked soldier-hero'. His constant adjustments to Troy's characterisation cease, and, significantly, the young man who later returns seeking a reconciliation with Bathsheba bears a closer likeness to the seducer stereotype – the devil-may-care scoundrel of Victorian melo-drama – than to the bewildered antagonist who, in confronting Fanny's death and the ruination of her devastated grave, feels with utter self-loathing that he is no longer the hero of his own story.

Indeed, with his identity now concealed and his last appearances on the scene now rendered, by his own efforts, unrecognisable, we seem to have lost the wild 'Corinthian' altogether, and to have gained something of the 'Trickster', now pitching himself towards self-obliteration. He hovers, literally and figuratively, beyond recognition. At the literal level he appears incognito, disguised as Dick Turpin (and locally recognised only by the lesser thief, Pennyways), and then, on his fatal visit to Boldwood's house he cloaks himself in

> a heavy grey overcoat of Noachian cut, with cape and high collar, the latter being erect and rigid, like a girdling wall, and nearly reaching to the verge of a travelling cap which was pulled down over his ears.[14]

At the figurative level, Hardy's use of these devices of disguise and shrouded identity indicates a modal shift to melodrama where, in drawing attention to the machinations of plot, they limit our sense of identification with the character in focus. Thus, as far as Troy is concerned, Hardy has now succeeded in creating the full alienating effect. This reaches its apogee when Troy enters the hall of dancers to claim Bathsheba. Here, he is presented as a total stranger momentarily perceived as 'the impersonator of Heaven's persistent irony' before his rival recognises him, takes aim, and shoots him dead. By way of obfuscating Troy's identity in this oddly surrealistic sequence (the stranger impersonated by Troy doubles as the impersonator of that most estranging of aspects, 'Heaven's persistent irony'), Hardy contrives a kind of masquerade of his death in which all events and characters take on an unreal quality. Bathsheba sits with her 'dark eyes fixed vacantly upon him, as if she wondered whether it were not all a terrible illusion'. Boldwood's 'strange voice' sounds 'far off and confined, as if from a dungeon'. And Troy himself speaks and moves like a mechanical fiend.

No doubt Hardy, with his remarkable flair for playing free with different genres, is also pursuing modes of psychological realism here, in so far as the shock of the real creates a sense of unreality. Yet the idea persists that the move, in this episode, away from realism and towards melodrama compounds the shift in Troy's characterisation from individuation to depersonalisation. This, in terms of a modal shift, propels the narrative away from the mimesis of the one convention and allows Hardy to exploit the sheer sensationalism of the other. He is now released from any further need to regulate and distance himself from this most demanding and intriguing of his male characters.

These observations are well supported by Hardy's proof revisions of this scene which reveal one concern only: to accentuate the focus on Boldwood and to amplify his psychological condition above all else. Hence the 'impersonator' sequence, which I will now show in full.

In the revised version, Troy advances into the middle of the room, takes off his cap, turns down his coat-collar, and looks Boldwood in the face:

> Even then Boldwood did not recognise that the impersonator of Heaven's persistent irony towards him, who had once before broken in upon his bliss, scourged him, and snatched his delight away, had come to do these things a second time.

This is not in the manuscript. In fact, in Hardy's first conception of this climatic scene, Troy simply looks Boldwood in the face and:

> Even then Boldwood did not recognise him.

And if, in his proof revisions, the 'scourged' Boldwood now becomes the focus of Hardy's concern, so this is intensified as shortly afterwards a strange voice comes from the fireplace and,

> Hardly a soul in the assembly recognised the thin tones to be those of Boldwood. Sudden despair had transformed him.

This is the revised *Cornhill* version. There is no 'despair' and 'transformation' in the manuscript. These proof changes are particularly interesting for their sympathetic overtones which may well have been added, as I have already suggested, to assist the transition, now in process, from Troy's melodramatic death to the harsh psychological reality of Boldwood's manic-obsessive psychosis, which Hardy treats in close detail in the chapters that follow.

These perceived distinctions of mode, tone, focus, and so forth would remain, in terms of our appreciation of Hardy's heuristics and, indeed, in terms of a full and accurate appraisal of his text, largely inaccessible without the benefit of a comparative study of his manuscript and printed versions of *Far from the Madding Crowd*. They may not, of course, provide a reliable index to Hardy's deliberate intentions – intentionality being itself dogged with hypotheses. My hope is, rather, that they will reveal the complexity and variety of Hardy's approaches to the writing process, many of them endearing, many surprising, many amusing, many disarming, but all of them artistically illuminating.

3–90

whether it were not all a terrible illusion.

Then Troy spoke. Bathsheba, I come here for you.

She made no reply.

Come home with me: come.

Bathsheba moved her feet a little, but did not rise. Troy went across to her.

Come madam, do you hear what I say? he said peremptorily.

A strange voice came from the fireplace — a voice sounding far off & confined, as if from a dungeon. Hardly a soul in the assembly recognised the thin tones to be those of Boldwood.

Bathsheba, go with your husband!

Nevertheless, she did not move. The truth was that Bathsheba was beyond the pale of activity — & yet not in a swoon. She was in a state of mental gutta serena; her mind was for the minute totally deprived of light, at the same time that no obscuration was apparent from without.

Troy stretched out his hand to pull her towards him, when she quickly shrank back. This visible dread of him seemed to irritate Troy, & he seized her arm & pulled it sharply. Whether his grasp pinched her, or whether his mere touch was the cause, was never known, but at the moment of his seizure she writhed, & gave a quick low scream.

The scream had been heard but a few seconds when it was followed by a sudden deafening report that echoed through the room & stupefied them all. The oak partition shook

Facsimile 14 'Hardly a soul in the assembly recognised the thin tones' (MS 3–90)

3

'The proper artistic balance'

Hardy confesses, in the *Life,* that due to his impending marriage, the last chapters of *Far from the Madding Crowd* were 'done at a gallop'.[1] He posted them off to Stephen in August and was married to Emma in September. In line with this, it is interesting to note that a manuscript reading indicates a strong sense, in terms of narrative flow, thematic unity, stylistic coherency and consistency of characterisation, that the novel's natural ending occurs around the time of Troy's disappearance from Weatherbury.[2]

As we have seen, Hardy experienced some difficulty in creating Troy's departure, in letting him go, so to speak. Not only did closure of the Lulwind scene present problems of overextension but as the tone and content of his revisions indicate, leading up to Troy's departure, Hardy had to make a conscious effort to shift his wicked soldier-hero towards the background of the novel. Perhaps 'conscious' is too incautious. Maybe I should say a 'seemingly purposeful attempt' to shift Troy off the scene and towards a decisive exit. The episode in Chapter XLV, where Troy is planting Fanny's grave with flowers, for example, finds Hardy adding to his original text a sizeable paragraph in which his close-up focus on Troy gradually blurs to a haze of narrative generalisations in which all sense of his presence is lost. Up to this point, Troy's actions, gestures and facial expressions have been closely detailed by Hardy as the disconsolate lover arranges the flowers around Fanny's grave and places 'lilies and forget-me-nots over her heart'. And, in the first writing, Hardy follows this sequence by following Troy, in feeling and action, to his last waking moment just before he falls asleep in the church porch. On a revisionary manuscript reading, however, Hardy interpolates the following, marked in verso on the preceding leaf:

> Troy, in his prostration at this time, had no perception that in the futility of these romantic doings, dictated by a remorseful reaction from previous indifference, there was any element of absurdity. Deriving his idiosyncrasies from both sides of the Channel, he showed at such junctures as the present the inelasticity of the Englishman,

together with that blindness to the line where sentiment verges on mawkishness, characteristic of the French.

The interception of these prosy pieties has the effect here of dislocating Troy and of placing him at exactly that point of 'indifference' Hardy mentions early on and permits to resound (with the repetition of 'in', 'id', prefixes) throughout the paragraph. We no longer sense his intimate closeness, no longer have him vivid before our eyes. The mood is entirely broken.

Another revision of this kind (this time in proof), which further helps to see Troy off the scene, occurs in the next chapter XLVI entitled 'The Gurgoyle: its Doings'. In the manuscript Hardy has it that, discovering the devastation to Fanny's grave and the ruination of his planted flowers, Troy:

> slowly withdrew from the grave. He did not attempt to fill up the hole, replace the flowers, or do anything at all. He simply threw up his cards and forthwith vanished from the churchyard. Shortly afterwards he had gone from the village.

In proof for the *Cornhill*, Hardy makes the following adjustment to this last exit from Weatherbury:

> He simply threw up his cards and forswore his game for that time and always. Going out of the churchyard silently and unobserved – none of the villagers having yet risen – he passed down some fields at the back, and emerged just as secretly upon the high road. Shortly afterwards he had gone from the village.

The original manuscript version is not only more dramatic (and therefore more engaging) – its very terseness conveys Troy's absolute despair – but it is also, with 'vanish', a far bleaker picture of desolation and annihilation (and therefore more compelling). The revised *Cornhill* version ambles, by contrast. Moreover, with the introduction of 'game' now set in juxtaposition with 'cards' we have the subtlest hint of trickery, and thus lose all sense of the depth and sincerity of Troy's feelings who, in the manuscript version, appears genuinely lost to himself and the world.

As these revisions indicate, in line with those made to the Lulwind episode, Hardy seems aware at this point of having to move his story ahead and of having to reduce both the dramatic and the sympathetic focus on Troy. He had, after all, an enthusiastic audience as well as an ambitious editor to consider, and they were all eagerly anticipating a 'happy ending' marriage for the deserving hero, Oak, whose ascendancy will become brighter by the minute as Troy descends, in his harsh cruelty to Bathsheba, into fiendish brutality and heartlessness. Thus with some hasty despatches of one baddie to the grave, one lunatic to the asylum, and one 'rejuvenated' heroine to the altar, Hardy effects a fairly reasonable closure of sufficient ambiguity to satisfy his own sense of having to make a compromise.[3]

As he had earlier written to Stephen:

> The truth is I am willing, and indeed anxious, to give up any points which may be desirable in a story when read as a whole, for the sake of others which shall please those who read it in numbers. Perhaps I may have higher aims some day, and be a great stickler for the proper artistic balance of the completed work, but for the present circumstances lead me to wish merely to be considered a good hand at a serial.[4]

As a statement of Benthamite expedience, these words express the fervent rationalisation of one who is determined to render necessity less uncomfortable. 'But for the present circumstances lead me to wish . . .' says enough about his feelings of ambivalence here, and now that we know a little more about his relationship with Leslie Stephen, these 'circumstances' take on a more precise meaning.

Hardy and Stephen undoubtedly held each other in mutual, if guarded, respect. To wit, in the first instance, Stephen's importance to Hardy as 'the man whose philosophy was to influence his own for many years, indeed, more than that of any other contemporary',[5] by which I take him to mean the influence of Stephen's apostasy, his spiritual strength in agnosticism in an age when the existential orphan so often experienced the death of God as a spiritual injury too deep for healing. Then, in the second instance, we have Hardy's importance to Stephen as a trusted friend and intimate confidant who would be chosen as the sole witness to his deed renunciatory of holy orders. Perhaps Hardy's most critically guarded approach to his editor is best expressed in his later observation to Virginia Woolf that he had suffered Stephen's 'grim and severe criticisms of my contributions and his long silences' because he had 'a peculiar attractiveness for me'. This suggests an almost unresolvable conflict of head and heart, of reason and feeling, perhaps even, to use Hardy's own words in *Jude*, of spirit and flesh.[6]

Hitherto, taking Hardy's words at face value, the general consensus has been that he is speaking here (in the 'good hand' letter) not only as the frustrated poet and the reluctant novelist but also as the heartsick lover consumed with the 'present' concern of getting married to Emma Lavinia. But neither of these last contingencies offers a psychologically tenable explanation justifying his abdicating authority (to Stephen) over his own text.[7]

Stephen, naturally, wanted Hardy to be a 'good hand at a serial' but what about Hardy himself? The reality is that he had been struggling with 'higher aims' as early as *The Poor Man and the Lady*, and his struggle never ceased. So long and so devoutly did he struggle that even the 'poet' insisted, throughout twenty-odd years of novel-writing, on speaking through his own prose.[8] And did these 'higher aims' really give way to affairs of the heart? It appears not. When newly wedded life brought heavier financial responsibilities he did not pursue a reputation as a 'good hand' at a serial – he did not capitalise on the success of his newly published 'pastoral' novel but instead adopted less immediately popular modes, notably in his city-based novel, *The Hand of Ethelberta* (1875), and in his elaborately designed and purposefully artistic *The Return of the Native* (1878).[9] All the evidence points to the fact that Hardy's pursuit of 'higher aims' predominated over his 'wish merely to be considered a good hand at a serial'. So I think we can reasonably suppose that the 'circumstances' to which he adverts in his letter to Stephen have less to do with his supposed willingness to defer to his editor's judgement, or even to his supposed matrimonial concerns and need to make a good living, and have more to do with the power and stringency of Stephen's own editorial exertions to have Hardy submit to those 'grim and severe criticisms' of his. In short, 'circumstances' dictated.

Editorial pressure and his own agreement to be guided by Stephen on matters of form and propriety certainly did not leave Hardy sanguine.[10] Indeed, the reality of working under Stephen's censorious eye exacted enough unwilling compromises to warrant an effort, on Hardy's part, to recollect and reinstate (for volume publication) numerous specific words and passages that had been cancelled for the *Cornhill*.[11] This, despite the fact that his manuscript was never returned to him, which meant that such reinstatements had to be drawn entirely from memory. Certain lengthier passages, cut for the *Cornhill*, would however remain permanently lost to him – as would numerous original, single words that, no doubt, equally defied recollection.

These, then, are the signs of resistance; but ultimately the manuscript speaks for itself. There is no evidence in the manuscript, despite his sacrifices to the narrative conventions of the serial and the cultural prudery of the parsonage, that Hardy is ever actually willing to forgo 'proper artistic balance' and the 'higher aims' of literary art. Even minor substantive changes reflect these aims. The 'height' of Hardy's concerns here is considerable. His revisions are at once pedagogical, stylistic, structural, philosophical, ethical and always unerringly artistic.

For a fairly representative passage in the earlier part of the novel let us take a brief look at a few of the interlinear manuscript changes in the looking-glass episode, for example, in which, alone, there are at least thirty cancelled words. Many are illegible, but several are decipherable – sufficient, at any rate, for our purposes in examining Hardy's (present) 'higher aims'. We have, for example, with reference to Bathsheba: 'the girl on the top sat motionless surrounded by tables' – cancelled. Changed to: 'The girl on the summit of the load sat motionless surrounded by tables' –

The handsome girl waited for some time idly in her place, ~~[illegible]~~ & the only sound heard in the stillness was the hopping of the canary up & down the perches of its prison. Then she looked attentively downward: it was not at the bird, nor at the cat: it was at an oblong package tied in paper, & lying between them. She turned her head to learn if the waggoner *were* ~~was~~ coming: he was not yet in sight; & then her eyes ~~crept back~~ to the package, her thoughts seeming to run upon what was inside it. At length ~~[illegible]~~ *she* drew the article into her lap, untied the paper covering; ~~[illegible]~~ a small swing looking-glass was disclosed, in which she proceeded to survey herself attentively. Then she parted her lips, & smiled.

It was a fine morning, & the sun lighted up to a scarlet glow the crimson, *jacket* ~~[illegible]~~, she wore, & ~~[illegible]~~ *painted* a soft lustre *upon* ~~bright face &~~ her black hair. The myrtles geraniums & cactuses packed around her were fresh & green, & at such a leafless *season they* ~~[illegible]~~ invested the whole concern of horses, waggon, furniture, & girl with *the peculiar* ~~[illegible]~~ charm of rarity. What possessed the girl to indulge in such a performance in the sight of the sparrows, blackbirds & unperceived farmer, who were alone its spectators — whether ~~[illegible]~~ the smile began as a factitious one to test her capacity in that art — nobody knows: it ended certainly in a real smile; she blushed at herself, & seeing her reflection blush, blushed the more.

Facsimile 15 'a soft lustre upon her bright face' (MS 1–6)

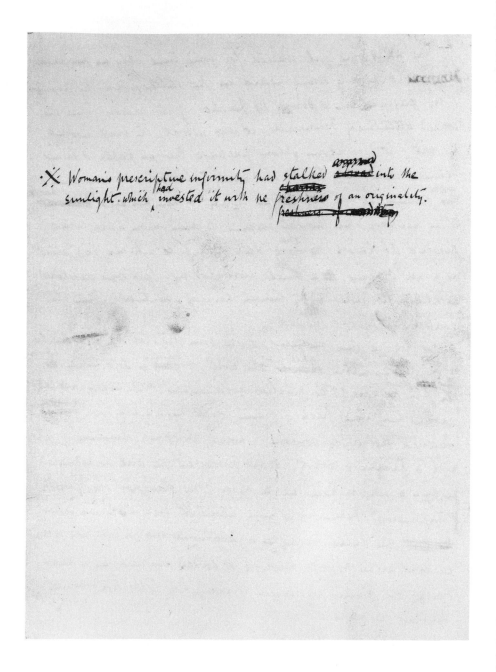

Facsimile 16 'Woman's prescriptive infirmity' (verso of MS 1–6)

clearly 'summit of the load' is more precise than 'top' and presents a more pictorial image. Then we have: 'her eyes returned to the package' – cancelled. Changed to: her eyes 'crept back' to the package. This is far more evocative! The altered performative, 'crept back', now extends the idea of a mere glance to include the slow inching back of Bathsheba's thoughts. The next word change is even more inspired – it subtly emancipates Bathsheba from the veil. Hardy alters his first description of her wearing a crimson shawl – a garment worn by women to cover the head and shoulders – to her wearing a crimson jacket.[12]

I should add, for the benefit of those readers interested in Hardy's painterly eye, that this 'eye' frequently develops latterly, so to speak. Or, put another way, the narrator who adopts the persona of the painter is not necessarily the first on the scene. For example, today we read:

> It was a fine morning, and the sun lighted up to a scarlet glow the crimson jacket she wore, and painted a soft lustre upon her bright face and dark hair.

However, in Hardy's first writing in the manuscript we have simply:

> It was a fine morning, and the sun lighted up to a scarlet glow the crimson shawl she wore, and gave a soft lustre to her black hair.

And just as the sun (through interlinear revision) now 'paints' a soft lustre and paints it more extensively not just upon her dark hair but also upon her 'bright face', so it serves to colour the picture 'a delicate one'. Unselfconsciously gazing into her looking-glass as she might at 'the dressing hour in a bedroom', it is as if the touch of the sun not only lights and 'paints' and 'blushes' her, but also adorns her nakedness – the nakedness of her innocent self-exposure to the reflecting eye of her author, to her own reflection in the mirror, and to the the peeping eye of the man hidden behind the hedge who will shortly elect to judge her vain, not 'fresh' and 'original':

> Woman's prescriptive infirmity had stalked into the sunlight, which had clothed it in the freshness of an originality.

That this image comes with hindsight to Hardy (possibly to differentiate the relative perspectives of author and principal), is indicated by its entry into the text as a verso addition, slightly altered in interlinear revision and marked for interpolation at 'The picture was a delicate one'. To this painterly scene, to this 'portrait' of blushing female arousal, Hardy brings an artist's perspective, thus legitimising the viewer's viewing of an act of unexpected intimacy – albeit that to Oak this is no original portrait but rather a commonplace act of typical female vanity.

By comparison, the first version (before interlinear revision) of this verso piece aims less high – in terms of aesthetic achievement and sexual suggestiveness. Here Hardy has:

> Woman's prescriptive infirmity had stalked into the sunlight which had invested it with the freshness of condition. A cynical inference ...

'Invest' clearly connotes more formality, a more public form of array, and 'condition' does nothing to carry forward the combined image of pristine form and original work of art, both of which exist in 'originality' in the revised version where they make vivid the artistic perception of a scene which is itself a tribute to Bathsheba's powers of self-transformation.

Typically, a painterly vision of the scene floods in on Hardy's consciousness with hindsight, as in the storm episode in Chapter XXXVI, entitled 'Wealth in Jeopardy – the Revel'. As Hardy originally conceived of it, in the manuscript:

> A hot breeze, as if breathed from the parted lips of some dragon about to swallow the globe, fanned him from the south, while directly opposite, in the north, hung a body of cloud.

A Turneresque image of latent grotesquerie now seems to flash across Hardy's imagination as he reads his proofs for the *Cornhill*, for he is suddenly urged onwards:

> A hot breeze . . . fanned him from the south, while directly opposite in the north rose a grim misshapen body of cloud, in the very teeth of the wind. So unnaturally did it rise that one could fancy it to be lifted by machinery from below. Meanwhile the faint cloudlets had flown back into the south-east corner of the sky, as if in terror of the large cloud, like a young brood gazed in upon by some monster.

None of this appears in the manuscript.

Earlier in the text, back in the manuscript, Hardy is struck, with hindsight, by another wonderful vision. This time, of Bathsheba, as she is halted by Oak and Coggan on her night ride to Bath. Interpolated between dialogue and marked in verso on the preceding leaf, Hardy writes:

> She turned her head – the gateman's candle shimmering upon her quick, clear eyes as she did so – passed through the gate, and was soon wrapped in the embowering shades of mysterious summer boughs. Coggan and Gabriel put about their horses, and, fanned by the velvety air of this July night, retraced the road by which they had come.

What an inspired vision! What more appropriate image could we have for this young, unknowing bride-to-be than to see her passing, clear-eyed, through a gate into 'embowering' darkness on her last journey as virgin and maid into the long night?

7

The change from the customary spot & necessary occasion of such an act — from the dressing hour in a bedroom to a time of travelling out of doors — lent to the idle deed a novelty it certainly did not intrinsically possess. The picture was a delicate one; A cynical inference was irresistible by Gabriel Oak as he regarded the; there was no necessity whatever for her looking in the glass. She did not adjust her hat, or pat her hair, or press a dimple into shape, or do one thing to signify that any such intention had been her motive in taking up the glass. She simply observed herself as a fair product of Nature in a feminine direction — her expression seeming to glide into far off likely dramas in which men would play a part — vistas of probable triumphs — the smiles being of a phase suggesting that hearts were imagined as lost & won. Still, this was but conjecture, & the whole series of actions were so idly put forth as to make it rash to assert that intention had any part in them at all.

The waggoner's steps were heard returning: she put the glass in the paper, & the whole again in its place.

When the waggon had passed on Gabriel withdrew from his point of espial, & descending into the road followed the vehicle to the turnpike gate at the bottom of the hill, where the object of his contemplation now halted for the payment of toll —

Facsimile 17 'The picture was a delicate one' (MS 1–7)

Most of Hardy's substantive revisions during the writing process clarify and heighten the significance of actions and objects, or enhance mood, thought and feeling with the most precise pictorial detail he can summon, which will enable the reader to picture the world in the imagination.

In terms of dramatic structure, he is equally painstaking. The art of story-telling depends largely upon not saying too much too soon: 'Make 'em laugh, make 'em cry', said Wilkie Collins, 'but make 'em *wait!*' Here is an example of Hardy at work doing just that. The chapter is the second (Hardy is nineteen pages into his manuscript) and the scene is Norcombe Hill where Gabriel Oak is to be found peeping into a hut where two women are at work tending two cows. The revised passage, the passage familiar to us today, is as follows:

> The place contained two women and two cows. By the side of the latter a steaming bran-mash stood in a bucket. One of the women was past middle age. Her companion was apparently young and graceful; he could form no decided opinion upon her looks, her position being almost beneath his eye, so that he saw her in a bird's eye aerial view, as [Milton's] Satan first saw Paradise.[13]

In this revised version, Hardy keeps Bathsheba's identity a mystery until the end of the chapter, while Oak's curiosity mounts and his fascination grows. Eventually, Bathsheba drops her cloak:

> and forth tumbled ropes of black hair over a red jacket. Oak knew her instantly as the heroine of the yellow waggon, myrtles, and looking-glass: prosily, as the woman who owed him twopence.

But, in the first writing, partly cancelled and largely amended by Hardy in the manuscript, the passage reads:

> The place contained two women and two cows. By the side of the latter a steaming bran mash stood in a bucket. One of the women was past middle age. Her companion was the black-haired girl Gabriel had seen upon the highway [then something illegible] her position being [almost] beneath his eye, so that he saw her perpendicularly as Satan first saw Paradise – but he knew her by the red shawl she wore which was freely flung over her head as a covering.

Well, we know that Hardy has already decided against shawls for Bathsheba, so the shawl goes and is here replaced not by a jacket but by a cloak. And we also now know that the moment of recognition goes with it. Out goes 'the black-haired girl' and 'but he knew her', and Oak no longer knows who he is spying on until his curiosity has mounted and his interest has intensified – a state of unresolved tension well designed to keep readers attentive also (particularly as Hardy decides, at this point,

19

slope reminded him that a shed occupied a place, the site being
a cutting into the slope of the hill, so that at its back-part the
roof was almost level with the ground. In front it was formed
of boards nailed to posts & covered with tar as a preservative.
Through crevices in the ~~roof and~~ side spread streaks & dots of
light, a combination of which made up the radiance that had attracted him. Oak
stepped up behind, where, leaning down upon the roof &
putting his eye close to a crack he could see into the
interior clearly.

The place contained two women & two cows. By the
side of the latter a steaming bran mash stood in a bucket.
One of the women ~~was past middle~~ second age. Her companion was
apparently young ~~& graceful. He could form no opinion upon her looks~~
~~her position being almost beneath his eye, so that~~
~~in a bird's eye aerial view~~
he saw her ~~~~ as Satan first saw Paradise.
She wore no bonnet or hat, but had enveloped herself in a large cloak,
which was carelessly flung over her head as a covering.

"There, now we'll go home," said the elder of the two, resting
her knuckles upon her hips & looking at their goings-on
as a whole. "I do hope Daisy will fetch round again now.
I have never been more frightened in my life, but I don't
mind breaking my rest if she recovers."

The young woman whose eyelids were apparently inclined
to fall together on the smallest provocation of silence, yawned

Facsimile 18 'as Satan first saw Paradise' (MS 1–19)

to wander off into matters philosophical and also has Oak wander off into vague romantic fantasies).

This device of delaying the moment of recognition maximises a dramatic climax that cannot take place at all in Hardy's first conception of the scene, where there is no mystery to unfold, therefore no unhooding of the hooded figure and no unloosening of her tumbling black hair. Moreover, this alluring unrobing, coming as it does at the end of the chapter (which in good serial form is the most appropriate place for revelations) now opens up the way for what is a very effective exit line: 'Oak knew her instantly as the heroine of the yellow waggon . . . prosily, as the woman who owed him twopence.'

Keeping, for the moment, to purely artistic aims on Hardy's part, it becomes evident that delaying the moment of truth was not a tactic that came easily to him at first. We have already noticed the extensive revisions made to Chapters XLVII and L, concerning Troy's disappearance and reappearance in Weatherbury, where Hardy eventually decides to keep the truth from his reader long enough to maximise the dramatic potential of his material. Similarly, with Chapter XLIII, entitled 'Fanny's Revenge', we find him still struggling not to reveal too much too soon.

The chapter opens with Liddy's concern for the tense and miserable Bathsheba, who is keeping night vigil beside Fanny's death-chamber. Having offered to relieve Bathsheba of her night watch, Liddy explains that she, herself, will not be troubled by morbid fears. Fanny, she says (in the manuscript version) 'was such a childlike innocent thing that her spirit couldn't appear to anybody if it tried'.[14] Bathsheba declines the offer and promises not to sit up after midnight, whereupon Liddy advises her that it is now half-past ten. The manuscript dialogue continues with Bathsheba's rather distracted response:

O is it. Fanny was very consumptive?
Well not very – she was rather
She has been away from us about eight months. Did anybody say before she left that she hadn't a twelvemonth to live?
I never heard anybody say so.
If she had lived to be an old woman nobody would have been surprised?
I don't think they would.
Have you heard today from anybody that she was not at all delicate in her chest?
No – have you ma'am?
O no no – I merely asked being interested in Fanny. She murmured then, People surely can't walk miles and miles the day before they die of consumption, inflammation of the lungs, or anything of the kind.
Why don't you sit upstairs ma'am?

Chapter **XLIII**

Fanny's revenge.

2–224

Do you want me any longer ma'am? enquired Liddy, standing by the door with a bedroom candle in her hand, & addressing Bathsheba, who sat cheerless & alone, in the large parlour beside the first fire of the season.

No more to night Liddy.

I'll sit up for master if you like, ma'am. I am not at all afraid of Fanny, if I may sit in my own room & have a candle. She was such a childlike innocent thing that her spirit couldn't appear to anybody if it tried, I'm quite sure.

O no, no. You go to bed. I'll sit up for him myself till twelve o'clock, & if he has not arrived by that time I shall give him up & go to bed too.

It is half-past ten now.

O is it. Fanny was *very* consumptive?

Well not very — she was rather.

She has been away from us about eight months. Did anybody say before she left that she hadn't a twelvemonth to live?

I never heard anybody say so.

If she had lived to be an old woman nobody would have been surprised?

I don't think they would.

Facsimile 19 'She was such a childlike innocent thing' (MS 2–224)

X ¶ Bathsheba was ~~miserable~~ lonely and miserable now; not lonelier actually than she had been before her marriage; but her loneliness then was to that of the present time as the solitude of a mountain is to the solitude of a cave. And ~~tonight~~ within the last day or two had come these disquieting ~~suspicions~~ thoughts ~~about~~ her husband's past. Her wayward sentiment that evening concerning ~~about~~ Fanny's temporary resting-place had been the result of a strange complication of impulses in Bathsheba's bosom. Perhaps it would be more accurately described as a determined rebellion against her prejudices, a revulsion from a lower instinct of uncharitableness, which would have withheld all sympathy from the dead woman because in life she had preceded Bathsheba ~~~~ in the attentions of a man whom Bathsheba had by no means ceased from loving, though her love was sick to death just now from the gravity of her misgivings.

Facsimile 20 'Bathsheba was lonely and miserable' (verso of MS 2–224)

None of this (except the very first and very last phrase) appears in the *Cornhill*. Aside from the oblique, and seemingly inadvertent reference to Fanny's pregnancy ('she has been away . . . about eight months'), there appears to be nothing about this passage that Stephen could find indecorous. Possibly, the impact of the whole unexpurgated chapter, in which the overall focus on the baby looms larger than it does now (after his cuts), caused him to overreact to this hint at pregnancy and babies. If so, and if Stephen did express any uneasiness over this passage, it could well be that Hardy agreed to cancelling it – but, I would think, for artistic reasons, not prudery. For one thing strikes me about its dramatic force, it is a fraction over-exposed: it reaches too deeply, too disturbingly and too inquiringly into an issue which is far better left in tight, unresolved suspense until the moment of climax arrives when Bathsheba finally looks into the coffin. Having said that, the disadvantages of this over-exposure seem very slight indeed when weighed against the purely advantageous quality of tenderness and understanding Hardy infuses into this sisterly relationship between mistress and maid. The delicately quiet way Liddy says 'Why don't you sit upstairs ma'am?', seems to occur in the manuscript version at that most sensitive moment when Bathsheba's thoughts are beginning to torture her in a way that is clearly unbearable to the loving Liddy. And this – this profound, unspoken intimacy between women that Hardy understands and portrays so well – is completely lost in the version we read today.

This dialogue is not, however, exemplary in terms of wasting dramatic potential. On the waste-scale it rates pretty low. I include it here simply to indicate, prefatorily (I shall be treating with this episode in depth later) the extensiveness, the whole range of changes, Hardy made in reworking this chapter. Some were made, perhaps, to accommodate Stephen's moral squeamishness about illegitimacy, sex and babies – or his moral squeamishness about Hardy's lack of moral squeamishness – and some were no doubt made for artistic reasons, to magnify the dramatic tension already mounting.

To this end, to enhance the tension of this episode in delaying the moment of truth, Hardy's next major proof revision makes a marked contribution. This concerns the dialogue between Bathsheba and Liddy, which follows the previous one by approximately ten minutes, when Liddy returns to report some strange news. In the revised version we have:

'I mean that a wicked story is got to Weatherbury within this last hour— that—' Liddy came close to her mistress and whispered the remainder of the sentence slowly into her ear, inclining her head as she spoke in the direction of the room where Fanny lay.
Bathsheba trembled from head to foot.

2—225

Have you heard to day from anybody that she was
at all delicate in her chest,
~~not consumptive or so~~

no — have you ma'am?

O no no — I merely asked, being interested in Fanny.
She murmured then, People surely can't walk miles & miles
the day before they die of ~~inflammation~~ ^{consumption, inflammation} of the lungs, or anything
of the kind.
~~Why don't you sit upstairs ma'am?~~

Why don't I? said Bathsheba desultorily. It isn't
worth while — there's a fire here. — Liddy, she suddenly repeated
in an impulsive & excited whisper, have you heard anything
strange said of Fanny? The words had no sooner escaped
her than ~~her face~~ an expression of unutterable regret crossed
her face, & she burst into tears.

no — not a word! said Liddy, looking at the weeping
woman with astonishment. What is it makes you cry so
ma'am, has anything hurt you? She came to Bathsheba's
side with a face full of sympathy. ~~for a paragraph...~~

no Liddy — I don't want you any more. I can hardly
say why I have taken so to crying lately; I never used
to cry. Good night.

Liddy then left the parlour & closed the door X
∧
In five or ten minutes there was another tap at
the door. Liddy reappeared & coming in a little way
stood hesitating, until at length she said, Maryann

Facsimile 21 'Why don't you sit upstairs ma'am?' (MS 2–225)

By contrast, Hardy's first impulse, in the manuscript version, to catch up with Bathsheba's frantic anxiety to know the truth, had been much at the expense of his literary art: he reveals far too much far too soon. He divulges to the reader what is being divulged to Bathsheba, and thus we are deprived of that tiny shred of uncertainty that lends a frisson here to the unravelling of the tale. This, then, is Hardy's manuscript version:

> I mean that a wicked story is got to Weatherbury within this last hour—that—there's <u>two of 'em</u> in there! Liddy as she spoke, slanted her head in the direction of the hall, delivering the words in a slow low tone.
> Where?
> In the coffin.
> Bathsheba trembled from head to foot.

So now that we know that she knows, will we follow her to the coffin with the same tense interest? It would seem that Hardy decided not to take the risk.

An even greater risk attaches to the next section, which for reasons which will become obvious demanded immediate revision. Returning to the same scene in the *Cornhill* we find Bathsheba now hotly denying the truth of the news she has just been told:

> 'I don't believe it!' she said excitedly. 'And there's only one name written on the coffin-cover.'
> 'Nor I, ma'am. And a good many others don't.'

However, in the manuscript, Hardy pursues Liddy's loyal denials with:

> I thought I'd just tell you. We shall be sure to learn the rights of it to-morrow. Oak was heard to say that that story belongs to another poor girl, and I believe him, for we should surely have been told more about it if it had been true – don't you think so ma'am.

In revision, the reference to Oak is cancelled. Oak has, of course, just a few hours earlier, taken it upon himself to rub out the incriminating last two words on the coffin-cover which had read: 'Fanny Robin and child'. Thus, to have him putting it about that the 'story belongs to another poor girl' makes him nothing less than a liar.

This is a rare instance of conceptual error on Hardy's part. Or I should say 'rare' in general but not quite so rare in Oak's particular case. As I shall go on to show in the next chapter, Oak undergoes no character transformation under Hardy's revising pen, but he does, frequently, blur at the edges in what appears, at times, to be a rather hazy focus on the part of Hardy, who tends to lose sight of him altogether – as here with

2—226

has just heard something very strange, but [I know] it isn't true. And we shall be sure to know the rights of it in a day or two.

What is it?

O nothing connected with you or us, ma'am. [It is about Fanny.] Not same thing you have heard.

I have heard nothing.

I mean that [a wicked story] is got to Weatherbury within this last hour—that there's two of 'em in there! Liddy, as she spoke, slanted her head in the direction of the hall, delivering the words in a slow low tone.

Where?

In the coffin.

Bathsheba trembled from head to foot.

I don't believe it! [she said excitedly.] And it is not written on the cover.

Nor I ma'am. And a good many others don't, but I thought I'd just tell you. We shall be sure to learn the rights of it to-morrow. Oak was heard to say that that story belongs to another poor girl, & I believe him, for we should surely have been told more about it if it had been true — don't you think so ma'am.

We might or we might not

Bathsheba turned & looked into the fire that Liddy might not see her face. Finding that her mistress was going to say no more Liddy glided out [softly] closed the door & went to bed.

Facsimile 22 'a wicked story' (MS 2–226)

'Oak was heard to say that the story belongs to another poor girl', which no honest Oak would ever be heard saying!

In contrast to other proof revisions and Hardy's higher literary aims within the manuscript itself, this cancellation of Liddy's words bears no ideological, pedagogical, ethical, stylistic, aesthetic or artistic imprint. It quite simply corrects an inconsistency in characterisation: Oak is not a liar. Indeed, his fundamental virtue, as both a character and an object of Hardy's art in characterisation, is plain, steady, uncomplicated consistency. And perhaps one of his fundamental virtues, as far as Hardy was concerned, is that of all his central characters in *Far from the Madding Crowd*, Oak exercises his revisionary powers, at the manuscript and proof-writing stage, the least.

4

'A rich mine of quaintnesses and oddities'

In contrast to the developmental complexity of Troy's characterisation, Oak demands very little of Hardy's revising pen. Some minor adjustments are made to reinforce his integration into the central action of the story, particularly at points where his role in the secondary action, which deals with farming life, assumes peripheral proportions slightly distanced from the major issues of Bathsheba's relationships. But, in the main, he emerges evenly and consistently from a solid, labouring man with simple tastes – even at his most affluent possessing no proper accommodation for visitors – to grow from his troubled experiences a little stronger, a little wiser, and a little more refined in thought and feeling.

We can trace this progression in the manuscript by examining the few substantive revisions Hardy does make in his characterisation of Oak, although, strictly speaking, most of these bear more closely upon the development of the plot than upon the delineation of Oak's character. The first significant change is a title change to Chapter IV. The original reads:

Short account of Gabriel Oak's love affair till a crisis came.

Hardy alters many of his chapter titles, presumably as and where the chapter content veers off in a direction different from the one planned, and Chapter IV is not atypical. The original title is cancelled in interlinear revision and replaced with:

Gabriel's resolve: the visit: the mistake.

In other words, the 'crisis' goes. As far as his manuscript changes go, in this chapter, Hardy seems fairly clear about the love affair and Oak's 'resolve' to claim Bathsheba, but, in his original conception of things, as indicated in the cancelled title, he evidently had some kind of crisis in mind that preceded the farming episode. Could it have been that the proposal scene, which renders Oak's love affair of short account, was originally intended as a more emphatic turning point in the action than actually transpired in the writing process?

One striking characteristic of the compositional process in *Far from the*

Madding Crowd is the occasional divergence of its directional flow – as we saw with Troy's characterisation. In some circumstances, Hardy checks this flow in midstream and either cuts off the diverging passage visibly with his pen, or simply severs the written page, which he may leave as a fragment or may paste on to a new section. In other circumstances, he (and in some cases Stephen) will abridge the passage in proof or, alternatively, will allow for the continuance of the directional flow according to its ultimate convergence with the mainstream of the plot. This last occurs, for example, in the description of the 'Great Barn' which Leslie Stephen thought should be allowed to run, despite certain misgivings on Hardy's part that he should perhaps shorten the piece or even omit it altogether.[1]

It is quite possible then that as the proposal episode grew in the writing process to be in fact something more of a *divertissement* than a dramatic climax, Hardy decided to let it stand. All that is required now is a different chapter title. Hence the cancellation of 'crisis' in the title to Chapter IV. As his alterations to Chapter V suggest, the crisis would now be the farming episode, later enlarged and intensified to become the 'pastoral tragedy' referred to in the new chapter title. This 'pastoral tragedy' treats with the destruction of Oak's flock by his sheep-worrying dog, George-the-Younger. The idea now is that the destruction of Oak's sheep (not the 'mistaken' marriage proposal) will render his love affair of 'short account'.

However, a love affair is certainly on the cards, and Hardy takes some pains in revision to ensure that it is comically mistaken, if not a little absurd. Having established Oak's infatuation in the original, wherein his thoughts turn from his newly acquired taste for black hair to the problem of how to find the opportunity to make a marriage proposal, Hardy now interpolates the following, marked in verso on the preceding leaf:

> Love is a possible strength in an actual weakness. Marriage transforms a distraction into a support, the power of which should be, and happily often is, in direct proportion to the degree of imbecility it supplants. Oak now began to see light in this direction, and said to himself, 'I'll make her my wife, or upon my soul I shall be good for nothing!'

As if the added touch of light irony in this afterthought does not quite satisfy Hardy's purpose in highlighting the absurdity of the situation, he now goes on to amend his commentary on Bathsheba to emphasise that in terms of education, class and modernity she may not be quite the Nymphean milkmaid Oak had taken her for. Accordingly (a few passages later), as Bathsheba's aunt artfully muses that her niece has,

> ever so many young men. You see, Farmer Oak, she's so goodlooking

Hardy decides (in interlinear revision) to have her add:

and an excellent scholar besides – she was going to be a governess once, you know, only she was too wild.

And to accentuate further the element of comic absurdity, the disparity between the bright young miss, a little wild at heart, and the stolid young farmer whose 'special power, morally, physically, and mentally, was static', Hardy makes yet another interlinear revision. Nearing the climax of the proposal scene where Bathsheba protests that,

> nobody has got me yet as a sweetheart, instead of my having a dozen, as my aunt said

Hardy augments this in the manuscript to have his modern young miss protest still further, this time against marriage, and this time with all the verve of her sister activists of the 1870s:

> I <u>hate</u> to be thought men's property in that way – though possibly I shall be had some day.[2]

Evidently the romance, as Hardy presents it at this stage, is meant to be serio-comic: the pursuit of an uppity young miss by a country swain in the classic, pastoral style of youthful insouciance with a touch of nonsense and swagger.

All in all, Chapter IV is a hardworked chapter. The manuscript reveals several subtle revisions all tending, it seems, towards accelerating the division of hearts. This division subsequently occurs in the following chapter, entitled in the manuscript, 'Departure of Bathsheba: a farming episode', but latterly altered (as aforementioned) to 'Departure of Bathsheba – a Pastoral Tragedy'. Hardy had many afterthoughts at this stage of writing, many adjustments to make to the original, as events and characters took life in his imagination, and most of these take the form of intensifying the action and drawing Oak into it more centrally. That 'Oak was an intensely humane man', was one such afterthought – a lengthy one. This reinstates him in the reader's sympathy following his laxity in feeding a dead lamb to his sheepdog, George-the-Younger, and leaving the dog unattended on the hillside overnight. Stimulated by bloodlust, George now sets about sheep-worrying and overdrives the flock to its death over a precipice.

> The ewes lay dead and dying at its foot – a heap of two hundred mangled carcases, representing in their condition just now at least two hundred more.

As the full horror of this tragedy dawns upon the reader – that every mangled ewe is carrying an unborn lamb – so it must have dawned upon Hardy, with hindsight, that he could not leave things as they are. As, for example, with this extraordinarily lethargic reaction on Oak's part:

> Oak raised his head, and wondering what he could do, listlessly

surveyed the scene. By the outer margin of the pit was an oval pond, and over it hung the attenuated skeleton of a chrome-yellow moon, which had only a few days to last

This is Hardy at his poetic best – engendering in the physical world a correlative lunar 'carcase' – but it does nothing whatsoever for Oak. If Hardy has a problem at all with Oak, it is one of diffidence. And this seems to concern him now as he interpolates, between the 'two hundred mangled carcases' and 'Oak raised his head', the lengthy piece about his humaneness which is marked in verso on the preceding manuscript leaf:

Oak was an intensely humane man: indeed, his humanity often tore in pieces any politic intentions of his which bordered on strategy, and carried him on as by gravitation. A shadow in his life had always been that his flock ended in mutton

And so on for some two dozen lines right down to his last words on the catastrophe:

Thank God I am not married: what would she have done in the poverty now coming upon me!

Hardy's verso augmentations are invariably thoughtful and reflective and are rarely designed to accelerate narrative pace or dramatic action. More often than not the narrative voice of the afterthought is endowed with an objective tone, as in this particular instance which does not depart from the text in any way but rather serves to close the chilling gap between the mangled carcases and Oak's listless appraisal of the scene. Hardy appears (in the first writing) to have lost sight of Oak's centrality to this scene. Thus the need to reinstate him, at any rate as the central consciousness, at a point in the tale where events tend to show him in an unfavourable light.

Simultaneously, the rejected marriage proposal has significantly paled by contrast as the farming episode intensifies, in the writing process, into a pastoral tragedy. This eclipse is thus amended as Oak's thoughts now turn, in the verso passage, upon his sorrowful thanks that he is not married after all! This last would seem to be a very necessary requirement of the plot. For as it stands in the manuscript, the trajectory of the plot, with Oak's journey to Weatherbury and, by way of the rick fires, back to Bathsheba, does not veer from the story's prevailing theme of love's romantic ideal repeatedly frustrated by the prosaic, unpalatable real. As far as Oak's story goes, this remains consistent: frustrated in love and pitting his strength against adversity, his fortunes gradually improve, his sensibilities become more refined, and the prospect of a companionate marriage to Bathsheba looks distinctly more favourable at the end of *Far from the Madding Crowd* than at the beginning. No doubt this was the plot-line Hardy originally had in mind when he outlined his story to Leslie

Stephen as a pastoral tale concerning 'a young woman-farmer, a shepherd, and a sergeant of cavalry'. That he had to struggle to keep Oak in focus and subdue his interest in Troy was not a problem he could have foreseen at the outset.

As Hardy has it in the first writing and in the early stages of the novel, Oak's romantic interest in Bathsheba, his inclination to continue in pursuit of her – and that it is she who acts 'as an inducement to him to travel' to Weatherbury – is more clearly defined than we have it now, in its revised form. For example, in the chapter entitled 'The Fair: the Journey: the Fire' (Chapter VI) where we are told in all versions from the manuscript onwards that,

> Bathsheba had probably left Weatherbury long before this time, but the place had enough interest attaching to it to lead Oak to choose Shottsford fair as his next field of enquiry.

the manuscript alone continues with:

> He resolved to walk half the distance overnight, sleeping at Weatherbury. Making a hasty meal, and with a portion of his bread and cheese still under his arm he struck out into the country by a footpath, which had been recommended as a short cut to the village in question. Although Bathsheba thus acted as an inducement to him to travel that way, Oak resolutely determined to keep out of her sight – a familiar contradiction

This is one of Hardy's narrative divergences. The manuscript leaf is cut off here, and the paragraph left unfinished. It looks as though Hardy decided at this point to curtail any further heartfelt speculations about love, for the present, and to push ahead with the plot; as it happens this new directional impetus adds considerable force to the internal tension of the following chapters.[3] For now we have, in interlinear revision and by way of replacement of the 'inducement' segment,

> Bathsheba had probably left Weatherbury long before this time, but the place had enough interest attaching to it to lead Oak to choose Shottsford fair as his next field of inquiry, because it lay in the Weatherbury quarter. Moreover, the Weatherbury folk were by no means uninteresting intrinsically. If report spoke truly they were as hardy, merry, thriving, wicked a set as any in the whole county. Oak resolved to sleep at Weatherbury that night on his way to Shottsford, and struck out at once into the high road which had been recommended as the direct route to the village in question.

It is fairly evident, aside from nudging him a little closer to independence and a little further back into pastoral comedy (in style and tone, reminiscent of the opening passages of the book), that a revision of this nature scarcely affects Oak's character or role, in contrast to the modifying tonal, focal and modal adjustments made to Troy's characterisation. In terms of plot – which this revision does improve – it makes far better dramatic sense to have the subsequent scene of the rick fires conclude with a meeting between Oak and Bathsheba that is entirely fortuitous. To have offered the reader too strong an impending sense of Oak's conscious or unconscious gravitation towards her (as in the original) would have pre-empted this marvellous climax in which Hardy makes strange the shocking moment of recognition and estrangement:

> Gabriel and his cold-hearted darling, Bathsheba Everdene, were face to face.
> Bathsheba did not speak, and he mechanically repeated in an abashed and sad voice, –
> 'Do you want a shepherd, ma'am?'

Incidentally, with regard to Oak's marriage proposal and his continuing gravitation towards Bathsheba, I should mention, in passing, that 'his cold-hearted darling' was originally 'his cold-hearted sweetheart'. In his first conception of things, Hardy invokes a stronger sense (as also at the last where Bathsheba uses the word 'sweetheart') of Oak's continuing consciousness of Bathsheba as his lover, despite her adamant refusal of him.

In view of these narrative tendencies, it seems that Oak is destined for a dogged romantic pursuit from the outset, including a dogged marriage proposal.[4] And despite his proving his true worth and achieving prosperity as time goes by, he remains relatively unchanged in characterisation from first to last. The denouement is indicative enough: when the 'rejuvenated' Bathsheba seeks him out to discover the reasons for his departure for California,[5] he mentions the subject of marriage once more. 'Things', he says, 'have been said about us':

> The top and tail o't is this – that I'm sniffing about here, and waiting for poor Boldwood's farm, with a thought of getting you some day.

The same blunt indiscretion; the same trusty faithfulness; in fact the same story: he is even still waiting for a farm! But there are one or two differences in his attitude to Bathsheba. These are (and Hardy makes no significant revisions to this scene) that he has learned a more tactful caution, a more endearing reserve and a certain skill in reading Bathsheba's contradictory signals.

Hardy's revisionary endeavour with Oak is, then, to realign him, where necessary, with the central characters and major events of the story.[6] This proves to be consistent throughout the manuscript, as for instance, with the rumours that Fanny had followed 'the Eleventh from Casterbridge through Melchester and onwards' (Chapter XLII), where the narrative continues with the news of her death but does not include Oak's know-ledge of her circumstances:

> But, thanks to Boldwood's reticence very little more was known than this bare fact of her death.

On second thoughts, Hardy alters this, in interlinear revision, to include Oak:

> But, thanks to Boldwood's reticence and Oak's generosity, the lover she had followed had never been individualized as Troy.

This is an imperative revision. After all, from the very beginning, Oak is the only character (aside from Troy) to be involved with Fanny. He encounters her destitute and cold outside Weatherbury church when, overwhelmed with compassion, he offers her his last shilling. Later, when Bathsheba summons her men to search for Fanny, Oak keeps silence on her behalf as he had promised he would, having fruitlessly hunted for her at the Buck's Head – where she had earlier indicated she would be staying.[7] And later still, Fanny sends him a letter of explanation, concerning Troy, and returns the borrowed money. It is therefore crucial that Oak should be numbered among those who had known something of her situation; and it is certainly appropriate to cite him as a man true to his promise – that he would never mention having met her (although he does fall from grace in the reader's eyes when he betrays this promise by showing Boldwood that same letter).

Earlier, in Chapter XLI, we find a change of a similar kind. The first writing in the manuscript has Boldwood approach Poorgrass to tell him the news of Fanny's death:

> The farmer stopped when still a long way off, and held up his hand to Joseph Poorgrass who was wheeling a barrow of apples up the hill to Bathsheba's residence. Boldwood spoke to him for a few minutes, and Joseph then took up his barrow again and came on

But Hardy strikes out this entire passage. He replaces it, in interlinear revision, with the following lines in which Oak, *not* Poorgrass, now becomes the recipient of Boldwood's news:

> The farmer stopped when still a long way off, and held up his hand to Gabriel Oak who was in another part of the field. The two men then approached each other and seemed to engage in earnest conversation. Thus they continued for a long time. Joseph Poorgrass now passed near them, wheeling a barrow of apples up the hill to Bathsheba's residence. Boldwood and Gabriel called to him, spoke to him for a few minutes, and then all three parted, Joseph immediately coming up the hill with his barrow.

This makes far better sense in terms of protocol: if the socially correct and gentlemanly Boldwood cannot speak with the mistress herself on such a grave matter (and certainly cannot speak with the master), he would no doubt seek out her first-in-command rather than a farm labourer, as in Hardy's first conception of things. As I shall go on to show in the next chapter, this kind of heightened awareness of 'manners', protocol or middle-class class codes and conventions, became a matter of special concern to Hardy in the writing of *Far from the Madding Crowd*. But there is an additional consideration here: that the inclusion of Oak at this point helps to draw him back into the plot and into the closer association with Bathsheba which the looming denouement will require, if Hardy is to contrive any kind of 'happy ending'. Thus, this small revision fulfils two functions: it corrects a minor slip in correctness on Boldwood's part, and it draws Oak back into Fanny's story at a point where, featuring in the secondary action of farming matters, he has become peripheral to the central action.

Likewise, in Chapter XXXIV, Hardy makes another small adjustment to keep Oak's involvement with Fanny in line. Where Boldwood attempts to bribe Troy and tells him that, as regards his attachment to Fanny:

> I believe I am the only person in the village, excepting one, who does know it

this is changed in interlinear revision in the manuscript to, 'excepting Gabriel Oak'. Again, this adjustment maintains the clarity and coherency of action and plot rather than adding depth, complexity and subtlety to Oak's characterisation.

The only revisions of any significant interest concerning Oak occur in Chapter LV, entitled 'The March Following – Bathsheba Boldwood'. Some of these were very late revisions made long after the composition of the novel in 1874, and were incorporated into the Wessex edition first issued by Osgood, McIlvaine in 1895. And Hardy at this late stage appears to have been completely confused about this chapter, and to have lost sight of Oak as a self-consistent, coherent character altogether. For example, he makes a grossly misconceived change in substituting Oak for Troy, who with Bathsheba, 'alone of all others . . . had momentarily suspected' mental derangement in Boldwood. This is an appalling oversight! But to explore fully its implications, I would like to look at the larger issue of Boldwood's insanity.

Returning to the manuscript and proof revisions for the *Cornhill*, we discover that Hardy had taken pains to insert a whole section in which, following the bribery scene and Boldwood's violent outburst, Troy questions Boldwood's sanity. The episode occurs in Chapter XXXV, entitled 'At an Upper Window'. Here Troy is discussing his ideas for modernising Bathsheba's farmhouse when (in proof revision) he suddenly changes the subject:

'Oh, Coggan,' said Troy, as if inspired by a recollection, 'do you know if insanity has ever appeared in Mr Boldwood's family?'

Jan reflected for a moment.

'I once heard that an uncle of his was queer in the head, but I don't know the rights o't,' he said.

'It's of no importance,' said Troy lightly.

There is no mention of insanity in the manuscript.

The new segment serves several purposes. First and foremost it lends insight into Boldwood's extraordinary behaviour the previous night when, armed with a cudgel, he had lain in wait for Troy and had tried to bribe him into marrying Fanny: with a sudden *volte face* and working on the assumption that Bathsheba has already been dishonoured by this 'juggler of Satan', this 'black hound', the maddened Boldwood then springs at Troy's neck to throttle him, only finally to attempt to settle five hundred pounds on that marriage instead. In short, he is dangerously out of control.

In the second place, the new segment on insanity also lends insight into Troy's triumphant and cruel baiting of his rival in this scene. Boldwood, in the normal course of events, is Troy's social superior and for all his insolence the young sergeant is not, to our knowledge, fool enough to 'lord it' over his superiors. But he does now. He is, of course, secure in the fact of his marriage to Bathsheba, which puts him in the ascendant over his rival, but nevertheless, his prolonged hounding of the maddened Boldwood is so manipulative, so vicious and so self-assured that if it is not overdetermined and melodramatic, it can only reflect the schematic bullying of a male absolutely assured of his dominance over an abject weakling. And why this absolute assurance, this relish in kicking the underdog? Because, in Troy's eyes, Boldwood is crazy. And this un-leashes – from his first contemptuous sneer to his last derisive peal of laughter – the compulsive drive of the sadist. This is a streak, in Troy, that we have already encountered in 'All Saints' and All Souls'' and will encounter again in the coffin scene. Thus, in all aspects, Hardy's proof revision of endowing Troy with a perception of Boldwood's derangement enhances theme, characterisation and plot and adds coherency to all three.

In Oak's case the situation is altogether different. His first inkling that something is awry with Boldwood does not occur until after the storm scene in Chapter XXXVIII, entitled 'Rain – One Solitary Meets Another', at which point he feels some concern for the farmer's unprecedented neglect of his cornstacks. But it is not in the first writing that Oak displays even this much awareness of what is obvious to Troy. Nor is it in the second – in interlinear revision. This is, in fact, a verso addition of Hardy's – a hindsight augmentation (as with the 'humane' segment), which bridges yet another unfortunate gap, but this time not between mangled ewes and listless eyes. Instead, this verso piece bridges Oak's practical observation to Boldwood that not a tenth of his corn will come to measure and the sympathetic, if cool thought, on Oak's part, that:

> A few months earlier Boldwood's forgetting his husbandry would have been as preposterous an idea as a sailor forgetting he was in a ship. Oak was just thinking that whatever he himself might have suffered from Bathsheba's marriage, here was a man who had suffered more

Now Oak by this time (late summer) is not only Boldwood's confidant but is also well on the way (in the late autumn) to becoming a profit-sharing partner in his farm. His immediate concern for Boldwood's interests must then, surely, be made a little more emphatic. Hardy evidently thinks so and inscribes the verso revision accordingly, now emphasising the effect on Oak of Boldwood's neglect of his ricks:

> It is difficult to describe the intensely dramatic effect that announcement had upon Oak at such a moment. All the night he had been feeling that the neglect he was labouring to repair was abnormal and isolated – the only instance of the kind within the circuit of the county. Yet at this very time, within the same parish, a greater waste had been going on, uncomplained of and disregarded.

But, and this is the important point, there is mention of suffering and dullardness ('a sailor forgetting he was in a ship'), but absolutely no mention, or rather no perception on Oak's part, of Boldwood's derangement.

Moreover, when at proof-reading stage, Hardy returns to Chapter XXXV and inserts Troy's insinuation of insanity, he also revises the end of the same chapter to include an extra line or two indicating Oak's puzzlement at the idea. Catching sight of Boldwood's approach on horseback, Oak is reminded of Troy's words:

> 'There's Mr Boldwood,' said Oak. 'I wonder what Troy meant by his question.'

Quite clearly then, Troy, not Oak, should be credited with the first suspicion of derangement. In fact, by contrast, Oak notices nothing unduly alarming in Boldwood's behaviour, and not only tries to persuade Bathsheba that she should marry him out of duty – 'to repair a wrong', as he puts it – but is also, as I mentioned previously, busily working towards going into partnership with him.

Possibly, over the years, Hardy came to feel the inadequacy of his hero's status – the 'dumb, devoted' Oak as Henry James called him – and felt he should amplify his role as and where he becomes marginalised by the central action. But was his heart in it? As he once told Leslie Stephen, on the topic of textual cuts and subsequent restoration, he would never 'have taken the trouble to restore them in the reprint'.[8] This is not always the case, in fact, but it does reveal something of Hardy's reluctance to return to a finished work to make substantive revisions once his visionary powers have been transferred to new scenes, new characters, new worlds.

Certainly, this late post-publication revision imputing prior knowledge of Boldwood's insanity to Oak instead of Troy utterly confounds Hardy's original conception of things and worse: it openly contradicts a proof revision he made to Chapter LV for the *Cornhill* publication.[9] This is where we have, in the original, in the manuscript, a perfectly sensible report from Oak to the villagers on his return from Casterbridge gaol:

> 'No tidings,' Gabriel said, wearily. 'And I'm afraid there's no hope. I've been with him more than two hours, and his mind seems quite a wreck. However, that we can talk of another time. Has there been any change in mistress this afternoon?'

So Oak is now fully established as Boldwood's confidant and sees the mental 'wreck' for himself. But, in proof revision for the *Cornhill*, Hardy changes this account to read:

> 'No tidings,' Gabriel said, wearily. 'And I'm afraid there's no hope. I've been with him more than two hours.'
> 'Do ye think he really was out of his mind when he did it?' said Smallbury.
> 'I can't honestly say that I do.'

This revision does tend to render Oak rather 'dumb', and possibly reflects a thoughtless change on Hardy's part as he was rushing his last chapters to Stephen at 'a gallop'. After all, if Boldwood is to be reprieved on the basis of 'a petition addressed to the Home Secretary' by a few 'merciful men', Oak must surely number among the 'merciful'? Moreover, he is one of the most reliable of recent witnesses to the 'wreck'. Among all of Boldwood's male acquaintances and friends, Oak is the one who had latterly been the most 'intimate with him'. It was Oak who, on the night of the party, had had to fasten Boldwood's tie because the wretched man's hands were too shaky. It had been he in whom Boldwood had confided, on the fatal night of the shooting, 'I have not been well lately, you know'. And what of the 'pathetic evidences of a mind crazed with care' – that 'extraordinary collection of articles' comprising expensive silks and satins, sables and ermines, lockets and rings, gathered in secret by Boldwood and labelled, on each package, 'Bathsheba Boldwood'? Oak, who is blind to none of this, who is not grossly obtuse, and who is at no point irresponsible or callous, is now implausibly attributed with views which suggest that he is all of these things. At the same time, Hardy has designated him the man deemed responsible to the authorities in Casterbridge for giving notice of the tragic shooting – for, after all, without his supportive evidence would Boldwood be granted a reprieve at all? And even if, after all of this contrary evidence, Oak does feel that Boldwood was in his right mind and fully responsible for his actions, would he so severely jeopardise his tenuous position by broadcasting those doubts when the man's life is hanging in the balance?

This proof revision creates a complete anomaly as far as events go, and a glaring inconsistency as far as Oak's characterisation goes – the more glaring now with Hardy's late, post-publication change, earlier in this same chapter, where he singles out Oak (instead of Troy) as the one man who had 'momentarily suspected' some 'symptoms of mental derangement' in Boldwood. It is hard to know what could have been afflicting Hardy that he so confuses his characterisation of Oak not in the first writing in the manuscript (which would be understandable), but in contradictory revision after contradictory revision.[10]

There is one further anomaly here which compounds the falsifying nature of these late revisions. This is where Hardy has, in the manuscript, a tense and sympathetic Oak awaiting news of Boldwood's sentence, but revises this in proof to show an altered emphasis. The manuscript version tells us that:

> Gabriel's anxiety was so great that he paced up and down, pausing at every turn and straining his ears for a sound. At last, when they all were weary . . .

This becomes, for the *Cornhill*:

> Gabriel's anxiety was great that Boldwood might be saved even though in his conscience he felt that he ought to die; for there had been qualities in the farmer which Oak loved. At last, when they all were weary . . .

Could the Oak we know, who suffers pity at the thought that his flock has to end in mutton, and who urges Bathsheba to promise herself to Boldwood because his 'case is so sad and odd-like', actually harbour feelings such as these? Can we really believe that Hardy's newly accentuated *humane* Gabriel Oak would himself believe that a lonely man, an honest friend, sick and tormented as he is who, in a fit of maddened passion, shoots his rival and then attempts to shoot himself, *'ought to die'*?

This all rings so false that one can only think that either Hardy's 'gallop' towards the end concluded in some kind of mindless bolting, or that this is Stephen's work. But why would Stephen tamper with Oak's characterisation at this stage? To shape Oak in yet more moralistic colours than he already owns? To nudge him towards the *Cornhill*'s establishment wing and its conscientious preference for capital punishment? Or simply to point to Oak as the moral arbiter of all things, to set a final moralistic seal on the serial? None of these provides satisfactory answers. Not one justifies bowdlerisation in this instance. And not one answers the most vexed question of all: why did Hardy overlook this gross distortion of Oak's character – his last-minute failure in honesty, in mercy, in good faith?

The only clear indication we have, in this case, of fault or unintentional error, is given by Hardy's manuscript revisions to Oak overall. Typically, Oak simply does not come under his revising pen in this way at any other point in the text. His development, as a character, is steady, consistent, uncomplicated and predictable; and, as we have seen, the only adjustments he undergoes tend towards realigning his role with the plot, not towards individuation or psychological complexity. Chapter LV is thus an exception and an aberration; and the only help we have from Stephen's letters at this time consists of his suggestion that Oak speaks rather too good English towards the end.[11] It is hard to imagine that Hardy would have responded to this by condensing the 'no tidings' passage and revising Oak's rather literary-sounding:

> However, that we can talk of another time. Has there been any change in mistress this afternoon?

for reasons of 'too good English', without attending to the internal logic of the revision at the same time. But this may be the only explanation we have, aside from the 'gallop' and the possibility of editorial interference.

One or two critics have claimed that Hardy does standardise some of the dialectal formations in Oak's speech.[12] And in pursuit of this claim, it has been argued that this is an attempt, on Hardy's part, to render Oak more sophisticated.[13] Alternatively, where dialect is added, the argument is that this is an attempt at consistency, following Leslie Stephen's criticism that the 'rustics – specially Oak – speak rather too good English towards the end'.

But the truth of the matter is that Hardy revises, amends and experiments with dialectal formations on a wholesale basis throughout the entire script and with all his rustics, not just Gabriel Oak. For example, on the night of the rick fires Maryann refers to Bathsheba's thick woollen headgear as 'that black cloth with holes in it'. This is a revision of her speech in the manuscript where she refers to 'that black cloth with holes in 'en'. The word ''en' is also common usage among the other rustics, serving as a general-purpose pronoun where it is not cancelled by Hardy in favour of the more conventional 'it' or 'him'. Likewise, 'you' and 'ye'; 'she does' and 'she do'; 'whether' and 'whe'r'; 'think of' and 'think o''; 'meaning' and 'maning'; 'going' and 'gwine'; 'he was not' and 'he wadn't'; and so on and so forth. These all undergo numerous changes in the manuscript, as do such verbal constructions as 'I saw', which alternate in Hardy's revisions with 'I seed'.

Poorgrass, in his progress with the bottle and contemplating the onset of his multiplying eye, turns to his companions with the words: 'the parish might lose confidence in me if I was seed here'. This, in the manuscript, stands as the more conventional 'if I was seen here'. Alternatively, when the Maltster offers Oak the gritty bacon sandwich with the apology, 'I let the bacon fall in the road as I wer bringing it along', this is changed in revision to: 'as I was bringing it along'.

With remarkable attentiveness to these forms, Hardy alternately standardises and localises the speech of his rustics in what appears, at first sight, to be a purely arbitrary process. Hardy would be one of the first to claim that a well-developed 'first sight' (or what he called variously 'seemings' and 'impressions'), is worth as much if not more than the accumulation of facts in grasping the instrinsic value and meaning of things. But in this instance, what appears at first sight to be 'arbitrary' disappears at second sight. This is no 'arbitrary process': this is one occasion where we can speak, with absolute confidence, of deliberate intention on Hardy's part. Not only did he take pains to instruct his editor that, with regard to any representations, his rustics should be made to appear intelligent 'and not boorish at all', but the issue remained of such importance to him that he puts the matter on record for all time in his autobiography. He enters it into the *Life*, explaining that he had written to Stephen to say that,

> 'the rustics, although quaint, may be made to appear intelligent, and not boorish at all'; adding in a later letter: 'In reference to the illustrations, I have sketched in my note-book during the past summer a few correct outlines of smockfrocks, gaiters, sheep-crooks, rick-"staddles", a sheep-washing pool, one of the old-fashioned malt-houses, and some other out-of-the-way things that might be shown. These I could send you if they would be of any use to the artist, but if he is a sensitive man and you think he would rather not be interfered with, I would not do so.'[14]

Hardy had no response to this, although his concern not to have his rustics misrepresented in any shape or form does seems to have been realised, as I will go on to show.

But first let me return briefly to the question of artistic balance and Hardy's higher aims – for there is every indication here that Hardy is striving for balance, an almost exquisite balance between idiomatic and vernacular modes which will preserve the individuality of his characters while accentuating the rich heritage of their shared rural culture and common tongue. This kind of focus and emphasis has the touch of the poet – a singularly Hardyan touch whose verses constantly tread unusual measures in balancing conventional and unconventional forms and modes.

But I do not think artistic balance alone warrants the effort and industry that Hardy puts into these numerous dialectal revisions. There is more to it than that. One of the discoveries yielded up by this study of the manuscript of *Far from the Madding Crowd* is that ethical concerns also inspire many of Hardy's revisions. The fact that he wrote to Stephen at least twice on this matter, clearly demonstrates his determination to break the Hodge stereotype so fondly patronised by sophisticated Victorians and so deplored by himself.[15] Hardy's method was to incorporate as much dialect as possible to give local colour and a salty forthrightness to his country folk, while at the same time ensuring, by standardising some of these speech forms, that his rustics do not degenerate into the Hodge mould.

And as it transpired, if his contemporaries are to be believed, Hardy succeeded in ensuring that no such Hodge lives or works in his Wessex. In July 1876, Charles Kegan Paul, writing for the *Examiner*, was one of the first to commend Hardy for the authenticity of his portrayal of country folk in Wessex. Kegan Paul praises Hardy's evocation of:

> the very last country in England whose sacred soil was broken by a railroad, and those which now traverse it leave the very heart of the shire untouched. The narrow provincialism of the squires, which is in some measure the bane of all the more distant counties, is accentuated there; and though charity and kindliness are not wanting, the labourer and squire feel towards each other as though they were of different races.

The article also observes that Hardy's Dorset labourer,

> is no fool in his own line, but rather very shrewd, racy, and wise, full of practical knowledge of all natural things, and of considerable powers of thought. Words are now and then lacking to him in which to clothe thought, for the vocabulary of those who live apart from books is everywhere restricted, but the dialect is yet vigorous and especially English.[16]

And R.H. Hutton in the *Spectator*, goes one step further. He actually criticises Hardy's rural characters for being too articulate and philo-sophical:

> if any one society of agricultural labourers were at all like that which we find here, that class, as a whole, must be a treasure-house of such eccentric shrewdness . . . as would cancel at once the reputation rural England has got for a heavy, bovine character, and would justify us in believing it to be a rich mine of quaintnesses and oddities all dashed with a curious flavour of mystical and Biblical transcendentalism.[17]

All of this prompts the thought that when Stephen complained that the rustics speak 'rather too good English', he was touching on an issue that, for Hardy, passed beyond the question of typological consistency, or artistic balance, and entered the equally exigent realms of pedagogy.

A few further examples of Hardy's experimentation with dialect will demonstrate well enough the comprehensiveness of his technique. On Bathsheba's night ride to Bath in Chapter XXXII, when Oak protests: 'We thought the horse was stolen', this is revised to become, 'we thought the horse was stole'; and when, in Chapter XXXVI, he approaches Troy drinking at the harvest supper on the night of the storm, his words in the manuscript – 'I only came to say that a heavy rain is sure to fall soon' – are changed to, 'I only stepped ath'art to say that a heavy rain is sure to fall soon'.

In similar vein, in Chapter XLI, Poorgrass, when questioned by Bathsheba about the cause of Fanny's death, answers in the original, in Hardy's first conception of things:

> I don't know for certain; but I believe it was from inflammation of the lungs, though some say she broke her heart. She was soon gone, it seems. She got worse in the morning

Aside from giving away too much at this point in the story, Poorgrass does sound rather too polished here. So his words are changed, in interlinear revision in the manuscript to:

> I don't know for certain; but I should be inclined to think it was from a general weakness of constitution. She was such a limber maid that 'a could stand no hardship even when I knowed her. She was soon gone, it seems. She was taken ill in the morning

Finally, with one more change in proof, Hardy achieves precisely the colloquial quality he is searching for, and the *Cornhill* has:

> I don't know for certain; but I should be inclined to think it was from a general neshness of constitution. She was such a limber maid that 'a could stand no hardship, even when I knowed her, and 'a went like a candle-snoff, so 'tis said. She was took bad in the morning

In fact, Poorgrass comes in for a good deal of vernacular change; he does, after all, have a rather sophisticated vocabulary. As Bathsheba continues to question him about Fanny's death, he is so unnerved by what he calls her 'promiscuous like' manner that he can barely speak, let alone speak plainly. Certainly he becomes a little plainer in revision where, in proof for the *Cornhill* version, 'promiscuous' is changed to 'judge-and-jury like':

> Really, mistress, now that 'tis put to me so judge-and-jury like, I can't call to mind, if ye'll believe me!

And whereas, in the manuscript, he would 'name the fact of her death', in revision he would 'name a hent'; and where he would go on to speak of Fanny's 'exposure to the night wind', he now speaks of her '*biding* in the night wind'. In a similar manner, his reference to Oak as a 'rather curious man' is changed to a 'rather curious item'; and whereas Oak had been 'very gloomy' that morning, now he is 'terrible down'.

The examples of cancelled words where dialectal formations occur are numerous. The lively old gossip, Jan Coggan, who is given to telling *risqué* stories, and who makes a good pretence at nonchalant disinterest when (in Chapter LVII) Oak tells him he is to wed Bathsheba the next day, starts out in the manuscript by protesting ' 'tis no business of mine', but ends up in the *Cornhill* by protesting ' 'tis no consarn'. And shortly afterwards, he supposes that all efforts at secrecy 'will be throwed away' since 'Labe Tall's old woman will horn' the news all over the parish – 'throwed' being originally 'thrown', and 'horn' being originally 'spread' in the manuscript. The ancient Maltster, on the other hand, who, in Chapter VIII, greets Oak with the words, 'I knowed yer father when he was a chiel', has his 'chiel' standardised to 'child' for the *Cornhill*, and also has his past tenses adjusted: 'I were fourteen times eleven months at Millpond St Jude's', becomes 'I was . . .', and 'I were disabled', and 'I were three-year at Mellstock', both take the standard form in revision. However, in his description of Bathsheba as 'not at all a pretty chiel', Henery is allowed to keep to his dialect, although he is not allowed to keep to it for 'sheulim'. The manuscript goes:

> The news is, that after Miss Everdene got home she . . . found Baily Pennyways creeping down the granary steps with half a bushel of barley. She collared 'en like a sheulim – never such a tomboy as she is

'Collared' then becomes 'flewed', in interlinear revision, and finally becomes 'fleed' in proof; and the linguistical star of the piece – sheulim – changes to 'cats'.

And so it goes! Hardy's work on dialectal forms is exhaustive and by no means exclusive. Not a single character, however minor, escapes his notice: even Boldwood's factotum and the thieving Pennyways come under his revising pen.

'Close inters...

If *Far from the Madding Crowd* stru...   ...as evoking
'an idyl or a pastoral poem'[1] pleas...   ...narsher realities
of life, and if recent criticism finds h...   ...arly stage of his career,
less the social critic than the romance...   ...a distanced perspective from
the culture he describes,[2] this may be justified on several textual and
extratextual counts. But it is less easily justified by Hardy's manuscript
account and a close study of his epistemology.

For an appreciation of the 'pastoral-idyl' reading of *Far from the Madding
Crowd*, the first point we have to consider is that for Victorians living in
what one contemporary called 'an age of transition',[3] when the last vestiges
of a long-established agrarian order were giving way to the onrush of
industrial capitalism, and when the clash between the old world and the
new brought the 'ancient and modern into absolute contact' as 'in a
geological "fault"' (as Hardy put it), there was no more appealing vision
than that of pastoral England's green and pleasant land. This was the
partly recollected, partly legendary and frequently romanticised world of
the ancestral village; a world in which space and time were measured by
nothing more crushing and pounding than the rising and the setting of
the sun, and the rhythmic ebb and flow of the seasons. This world existed
for some in the memory of 'better days', and for others, particularly
second-generation urbanites, as much in custom and tradition as in an
actively fostered nostalgia for the much-eulogised world of antiquity: old
Albion.[4]

Most aspects of daily life were pervaded, in one way or another, by this
shaping force which, in turn, created a design for living. Whether this
manifested itself at the tea-table with willow-pattern plates and sugar-
bowls replicating thatched cottages, or in the arabesque ornamentation of
water-closets, or in the municipal work of the Gothic revivalists, or in the
baroque architecture of railway stations, it held firmly to the intrinsic
value of a fellowship with Nature: Nature with its seasonal rhythms, its
wildlife flora and fauna, its crystalline rushing brooks – in short, a para-
disial world where the 'hard-worn heart' could wander far and free.[5]

Bearing a loose correspondence to the American dream, in so far as it was less regressive than mythic, the Victorian dream, in its aspirations and optimism, also looked forward to a world which, according to J.S. Mill, had not yet advanced beyond the unsettled state.[6] While this meant looking forward with uncertainty, there was always the hope for reconstruction. Nostalgia provides ballast against the isolation of the new and unsettled state as well as opening porous boundaries for the deracinated masses searching for a common horizon.

For his pastoral novel then, Hardy would seem to have had a captive audience only too eager to cherish dreams of an idyllic rural existence where the old ways still flourished unspoiled by the new, and where 'the essentials of Arcadian felicity' still prospered, as one writer for the *Daily Telegraph* expressed it in 1872.[7] Just as Leslie Stephen had approached Hardy, originally, for a story bearing the freshness and charm of *Under the Greenwood Tree*, so readers clamoured for tales of country life set in a condition of rural tranquillity and timelessness. 'No condition of society', wrote Andrew Lang in response to *Far from the Madding Crowd*, 'could supply the writer who knows it well with a more promising ground for his story.'[8] And no condition of society could so predispose Victorians towards the pastoral idyl as well as their own.

A twentieth-century perspective, however, tends to focus less on the idyllic and more on the romantic idealism of Hardy's Weatherbury world. While recognising Hardy's transfer of identification away from his labouring-class origins, it identifies too a certain disengagement from contemporary realities, a predisposition to choose a setting with a 'deliberate eye to its remoteness from the current unrest'.[9] Here, we have to recall Hardy's aims (under pressure and duress) to please his editor and to be considered a good hand at a serial. Rural unrest and peasant revolts may have been notorious in the Wessex region in the 1830s and 1840s; and, closer to Hardy's time, the discontented rural labourer of the 1870s may have been participating, under the leadership of Joseph Arch, in the movement towards the unionisation of labour. But for what good reason would the author of *Far from the Madding Crowd*, whose editor is looking to him for an evocation of rural quaintness and charm, whose reader is anticipating pleasant scenes of country life, make yet further representations of real-life unrest and discontent in his first major serialised novel?[10] Evidently, for no good reason at all, if Hardy's experience in writing for Leslie Stephen and his *Cornhill* reader is anything to go by.

For the truth is that *Far from the Madding Crowd* (if Stephen's letters are indicative) is by no means regarded by Hardy's editor or by his more Grundyist reader as in the least disengaged with contemporary realities.[11] The situation of the unmarried mother, a veritable victim of social and economic forces, is real and harsh enough. Struggling for a meagre living as a seamstress (the most exploited class of female skilled labour), hiding out in a distant town during her pregnancy, and finally destitute and homeless, Fanny Robin literally crawls to her death in her attempt to find shelter and aid in the Casterbridge Union. Less tragically but no less realistically in contemporary terms, there is the situation of the married woman whose hard-worked earnings are appropriated (or misappropriated) by her husband as part of his legal entitlement upon marriage. And, no doubt, the tyranny of the dutiful marriage-made-in-penance, as Bathsheba sees her prescribed role in relation to Boldwood, struck a bitter chord in many a Victorian woman's heart:

> I hate the act of marriage under such circumstances, and the class of women I should seem to belong to by doing it!

To be sure, Hardy's critical focus rests more keenly upon the condition of women in *Far from the Madding Crowd* than upon the condition of the rural labourer. Nevertheless, it was enough for Leslie Stephen that Hardy had already gone this far! Far beyond the traditional boundaries of the pastoral novel – a fact Stephen was never to forget, and maybe never to forgive. Some years later, reading through the first chapters of *The Return of the Native*, he refused to go ahead with publication. He claimed, no doubt with the wisdom of hindsight, that there were already signs, in the relationships between Eustacia, Wildeve and Thomasin, of something too dangerous for a family magazine.

Having played devil's advocate in plying *Far from the Madding Crowd* as a pastoral idyl, as a novel which glosses over the contemporary realities of Dorset life or, more precisely, glosses over the agricultural distress and discontent of the rural labourer, I shall now go on to show that all is not what it seems. What the Victorian critic regarded as a tale of rural tranquillity refreshingly free from social conflict, class struggle and economic strife, and what has been regarded, more recently, as Hardy's avoidance of the actual conditions of the day, is not so clearly indicated to the reader of his manuscript.

We have looked at Hardy's rigorous attempts to keep his rustics untainted by any bovine, boorish or clodhopping slur upon their characters. And I think we could say that such a scrupulously annotated rendering of the rustic 'voice', such an effort on Hardy's part to write a social class in its own language and idiom, evinces both sympathetic observation and a sensitive attempt at imaginative identification. At the same time, I think we could also say that however sympathetically Hardy dedicated himself to this task, he is also concerned to retain for his rustics a Fieldingesque air of mixed anarchy and wit, which he exploits to the full for light relief.[12]

He records in the *Life*, with ill-concealed resentment at the idea that *Far from the Madding Crowd* had been taken for George Eliot's work, that, though not a born storyteller by any means – she had never touched the life of the fields: her country-people having seemed to him, too, more like small townsfolk than rustics; and as evidencing a woman's wit cast in country dialogue rather than real country humour, which he regarded as rather of the Shakespeare and Fielding sort.[13]

'Real country humour', for Hardy's rustics, expresses itself frequently as a sheer delight in the absurdity of the human condition, especially their own. In the best of comic traditions, they become narrators of their own folly. And their lovability, which Hardy preserves for them as if it were their birthright, largely rests in their marvellous capacity for laughing at themselves. They utter their grievances, their anxieties, their forebodings and mishaps with an unmistakable relish for the absurd; and they treat the superstitious, the sacred and the profane (sometimes in the same breath), with a tongue-in-cheek dolorousness pitched to a mischievous mock-seriousness which is, in turn, directed at the mystifying ways of the world and Almighty God.

I wish to make two distinct approaches here. The first will be to take a look at some further examples of cancelled words, where these show, in the manuscript, Hardy's deeper commitment to the condition of rural labour than may be apparent in the *Cornhill* and its offspring editions of *Far from the Madding Crowd*. And the second will be to examine some of Hardy's revisions as and where these reflect his concern to represent, with the utmost accuracy and contingency, the subtle divisions of class, rank and status. These revisions link with Hardy's annotation of dialectal forms in so far as both signal his determination to write an age in its own idiom of regional and class consciousness. But in this case, the emphasis is upon distinctions of class; upon the subtle markings of class separation between the several ranks in the social hierarchy, rather than, as with dialectal forms, simply upon individuating his rustics and distinguishing them from the Hodge stereotype.

Both orders of revision appear to aim at striking the correct balance in representing the status quo: that is to say, both accentuate, with the scrupulous accuracy we have already discovered in Hardy's imaginative representations, the differences between individuated characters to enhance the subtlety and variousness of their separate social types and degrees of class status. But whereas Hardy's approach to annotating dialect appears to be pedagogical (the point being that too heavy a dialect may imply boorishness and too light may mute the salt-of-the-earth quality Hardy wishes to retain), his approach to the language of class seems of purely anthropological interest. It is almost as if he must and will make a correct record of the tribal markings – the codifications and demarcations of rank and status – of the class society for whom he is writing. As I shall go on to show, or as Hardy's manuscript and proof revisions will make quite plain, these precise demarcations of class and status barely feature in *Far from the Madding Crowd*, as Hardy originally conceived it. In this sense, their actual significance as revisionary adjustments to the text for the benefit of *Cornhill* readers opens up a whole new realm of understanding for Hardy scholars. To begin with, as epistemological indicators, they lay waste most arguments about Hardy's disengagement with contemporary realities. Class difference, class consciousness, class separation, class conflict – the entire spectrum of this new and complex social structure now emerging in Victorian society – constitutes for Hardy an issue to be confronted as a historical reality. And in this he assuredly demonstrates his sense of the contingency of the real world.[14]

But before coming on to Hardy's revisionary treatment of class, let us return for a while to the issue of the rural novel and his engagement with the contemporary realities of labour. The ultimate irony here is that Leslie Stephen recommended cuts that were, in the end, to reduce the rustic scenes more drastically than any others. He had wanted a *Greenwood Tree*-type tale, but he also wanted 'incident' and a 'well-arranged plot'. As it happened, he got a good deal less of the former and a good deal more of the latter than he had bargained for.

If we return to the holograph manuscript and Hardy's revisions to the shearing-supper chapter (rewritten for Stephen from an early draft submitted before the book was fully in progress and subsequently considerably reduced at his behest), we find that he makes very few additional changes for the *Cornhill*. There are some interlinear revisions, but none of any major significance. Coggan reassures Poorgrass, as he creakily renders his ditty, that he will:

> help ye to flourish up the shrill notes where yer wind is rather wheezy

which, in the first writing, had read: 'where yer voice is rather feeble'. And at the supper table, where the shearer's 'lower parts' were,

> becoming steeped in embrowning twilight while their heads and shoulders were still enjoying day

this originally went:

> the shearer's lower parts [were] enveloped in embrowning twilight while their upper halves were still enjoying day

('Steeped' is preferable to 'enveloped', but overall the original version with 'upper halves' has the edge on compositional wit.) Of marginally more interest, there is the single word change describing Gabriel's entry

87

into Bathsheba's parlour to accompany her song on his flute. In interlinear revision, Hardy now has it that Oak 'hastened up into the coveted atmosphere', whereas in the first instance this stands as 'the charmed atmosphere'. This is a subtle change in that it places the emphasis on Oak's point of view and feelings (covetous), rather than upon Bathsheba's powerful emanations – the 'charmed atmosphere' she generates. This revision, in turn, accentuates the continuing drive, in Oak's unconscious pursuit, to occupy her space – a drive first stressed by Hardy in the proposal scene, where Oak slowly circles and closes in on her person.

If we move to Chapter XV, however, which is entitled. 'A Morning Meeting – The Letter Again', we encounter some of the most extensive changes made to the entire work. This is the second Malthouse scene, and it originally ran to just under twenty manuscript pages, considerably longer than we now have it. At this stage of his relationship with Stephen, Hardy is still having trouble with instalment length: 'Chap X', Stephen writes, 'is judiciously reduced and I think is now satisfactory', but 'Chap XVI is rather a long one', could it be divided in order to end the March number 'at some possible halting-place' of Hardy's devising?[15] As it happened, the March number eventually ended with Chapter XIV with the arrival of Bathsheba's valentine and Boldwood's reaction to it. Hardy does appear to have made the division as required – Chapter XVI then being the section on Boldwood in the market-place and later in 'meditation' – both incidents now occurring in Chapters XVII and XVIII respectively. But in making these changes to accommodate instalment length, he now creates and inserts the present two-page Chapter XVI ('All Saints' and All Souls''), while also agreeing to an abridgement of the second Malthouse scene in Chapter XV.

The second Malthouse scene contains precisely the kind of lengthy rustic interchange that Stephen found the least satisfactory for the *Cornhill*. But, for our purposes in retrieving some of those original passages denoting Hardy's effort to record certain characteristic feelings and responses of his labourers, it is more than satisfactory.

The first major cut to this chapter occurs just after the entry of Matthew Moon, Joseph Poorgrass and other carters and waggoners who had just come 'from the cart-horse stables where they had been busily engaged since four o'clock that morning'. The manuscript has:

I be as feeble as a thrush, said Joseph Poorgrass. A straw-mote would throw me down. Maltster, I'll have a thimbleful of cider before going any further.

I be'ant much to boast of, neither, sighed Matthew. Such a pain as I've got in the small of my back and round my lines, words don't know – really they do not. My back seems to open and shut – that 'a do. I'll have a drop of summit too, maltster: coffee will do.

from the cart-horse stables, where they had been busily ... since four o'clock that morning.

I be as feeble as a thrush, said Joseph Poorgrass. A straw-mote would throw me down. Maltster, I'll have a thimbleful of cider before going any further.

I bean't much to boast of, neither, sighed Matthew. Such a pain as I've got in the small of my back and round my loins, words don't know — really they do not. My back seems to open & shut — that 'a do. I'll have a drap of summat too, maltster: coffee will do.

The maltster pointed to a small barrel in the corner, & to the pipkin in the ashes. Whichever ye be a-minded to, he said. And here's a few taties [raking them out of the ashes] Come have one — they be clane

Morn' t'ye, old blades! & how is it this morning? said another person in the doorway. And how is it yer back is so much worse Matthew Moon? The speaker stalked in, & proved to be Mark Clark.

O I've been sitting up with poor Pleasant, you know. I don't know what to make of her, I'm sure. The poor thing were very tranquil in the early part of the night, & had a little sleep, but 'a got restless again & quite light headed towards the morning.

Facsimile 23 'I be as feeble as a thrush' (MS 1–149)

The maltster pointed to a small barrel in the corner, and to the pipkin in the ashes. Whichever ye be a-minded to, he said. And here's a few taties [raking them out of the ashes] Come have one – they be clane.

Morn' t'ye, old blades! And how is it this morning? said another person in the doorway. And how is it yer back is so much worse Matthew Moon? The speaker stalked in, and proved to be Mark Clark.

O I've been sitting up with poor Pleasant, you know. I don't know what to make of her, I'm sure. The poor thing was very tranquil in the early part of the night, and had a little sleep, but 'a got restless again and quite light headed towards the morning.

Five and thirty pound – that's what mis'ess will lose if that horse should die, said Mark Clark.

And how is she getting on without a baily?

The *Cornhill* (in which this segment is omitted) picks up at this point, losing nothing in the way of entertaining dialogue but something, rather muted and understated, in the way of the weariness and the long hours of labour and the physical pain and stress of the farmworker's lot.

The next segment to be excised from this chapter for the *Cornhill* involves a superstitious interchange which again appears, at first sight, to contain little of importance. The rustics, anxious about Bathsheba's angry dismissal of her bailiff, the thieving Pennyways, are clearly worried that she will not be able to manage alone now that she has taken on the role of bailiff herself:

Ay – there's some sorrow going to happen, said Matthew Moon. I've had three very bad dreams lately and Sally put the bellows upon table twice following last week.

A sure sign that sommat wrong is coming, said Joseph Poorgrass. I had a white cat come in to me yesterday breakfast-time. And there was a coffin-handle upon my sister-law's candle last night.

And I've seed the new moon two months following through glass. I was told, too, that Gammer Ball dreamed of bees stinging her.

Horrible. O depend upon it there's something in all this, said Joseph Poorgrass, drawing his breath fearfully with a sense that he lived in a tragedy.

Our mis'ess will bring us all to the bad, said Henery. Ye may depend upon that – with her new farming ways. And her ignorance is terrible to hear. Why only yesterday she cut a rasher of bacon the long ways of the flitch!

Ho-ho-ho! said the assembly, the maltster's feeble note being heard amid the rest as that of a different instrument: heu-heu-heu!

150

Five & thirty pound — that's what mis'ess will lose if
her horse should die, said Mark Clark.

And how is she getting on without a baily? the maltster
enquired.

Henery shook his head & smiled one of the bitter smiles,
heaping all the flesh of his forehead into a corrugated heap in
the centre.

She'll rue it — surely, surely! he said. Benjy Pennyways
were not a true man or an honest baily — as big a betrayer
as Joey Iscariot himself. But to think she can manage
herself! He allowed his head to swing laterally three or
four times in silence. Never in all my creeping up — never!

This was recognised by all as the conclusion of some
awful speech, which had been expressed in thought alone
during the shake of the head. Henery meanwhile retained
several ~~marks~~ of despair upon his face, to imply that
they would be required for use again directly he should go
on speaking.

All will be ruined & ourselves too, or there's no meat
in gentlemen's houses! said Mark Clark in the manner
of a man ready to burst all links of habit & rear
his dusty race at the shortest notice.

Ay — there's some sorrow going to happen, said Matthew
Moon. I've had three very bad dreams lately; & Sally put
the bellows upon table twice following last week.

Facsimile 24 'there's some sorrow going to happen' (MS 1–150)

A head-strong maid – that's what she is – and won't listen to no advice at all.

The *Cornhill*, which has none of this, resumes at this point.

Where these dialogues might have struck Hardy's metropolitan reader as rather longwinded and boring, Stephen might have viewed them as crassly superstitious and uncomfortably heathen. Superstition is anti-rational and unscientific. And certainly Stephen had a loathing of irrationality. In his work on English thought, he provided sophisticated arguments to show the intellectually retarding effect of belief in such things as the literal truth of miracles, supernatural intervention and divine revelations.[16] In his own belief in the developmental imperative of progress in science and reason, and what he felt to be the social and philosophical necessity of a 'growing conformity between the world of thought and the world of facts', Stephen had no room for superstition which, to his way of thinking, exemplified a savage stage of intellect.[17]

But what is discerned by Hardy, who tends to perceive human behaviour in psychological rather than scientific terms, is that superstitions communicate dread. In the world of nature and country folk, the only reliable signs alerting change, portending threat or ominous circumstances – all of which might require advance practical preparation – are those signs which indicate some deviation from the normal course of events. Some interpretations of these signs may be regarded as rational, such as the 'heated breeze from the south', the 'lurid metallic' look of the moon, and the sheep trailing homewards 'head to tail', which Oak interprets as ominous signs of an impending storm. Other interpretations of, say, the new moon seen through glass, or Gammer Ball's dream of stinging bees, are more likely to be regarded as completely irrational: they conform to none of the laws of inductive or deductive logic. Hardy's rustics are not concerned with logic; they are concerned with dread. Their superstitious feelings, which are neither rational nor logical, communicate very real fears of matters which may turn out to be perfectly rational and logical. They may make no sense, but they are demanding that sense be made of them.

What they *are* communicating is the very real fear that Bathsheba will fail as farm-manager, bailiff and their employer, and that they will lose their livelihood. And what Hardy is communicating is his recognition of their feelings, their shadowy fears, their new and uncomfortable sense of insecurity, their instinctive recoil from change. Shaping their fears in the form of superstitious omens, his rustics filter these fears through an associated assortment of household objects and natural phenomena, thus externalising them and articulating them in a way that makes them seem less intangible, less strange, less unknowable, and more accessible to other members of the community. This much is evident from the sheer quantity

151

A sure sign that sommat wrong is coming, said Joseph Poorgrass. I had a white cat come in to me yesterday breakfast-time. And there was a coffin-handle upon my sister-law's candle last night.

And I've seed the new moon two months following through glass. I was told, too, that Gammer Ball dreamed of bees stinging her.

Horrible. O depend upon it there's something in all this, said Joseph Poorgrass, drawing his breath fearfully, with a sense that he lived in a tragedy.

Our mis'ess will bring us all to the bad, said Henery. Ye may depend upon that — with her new farming ways. And her ignorance is terrible to hear. Why only yesterday she cut a rasher of bacon the longways of the flitch!

Ho-ho-ho! said the assembly, the maltster's feeble note being heard amid the rest as that of a different instrument: hee-hee-hee!

A head-strong maid — that's what she is — & won't listen to no advice at all. Pride & vanity have ruined many a cobbler's dog. Dear, dear, when I think of it I sorrows like a man in travel!

True Henery — you do — I've heard ye, said Joseph Poorgrass, in a voice of thorough attestation, & with a wire-drawn smile of misery.

What, & do she dress so high? inquired the maltster.

Facsimile 25 'her new farming ways' (MS 1–151)

93

of superstitions they have collected and shared as anecdotes. Each one is referential and looks to the inside, the inexplicable irrational interior of the mind, and each opens up an element of wonder and fear uniquely real to that same world of the mind. Each one compounds the portentousness of the others, but each also names the sign of hitherto nameless fears which, in turn, being shared and generally understood, carries the potential to soothe and reassure. It is of some comfort to know that one is not alone and that everyone understands the meaning of a 'new moon seen through glass'! In this sense, as in all others, event and context become integrated, producing the effect of real disturbance needing to be laid to rest.

The structure of feeling and the sense of contingency underlying Hardy's comic touches in these anecdotes re-creates the everyday nagging anxieties of labouring men who are dependent, for their livelihood, upon the goodwill and competence of a management over which they have no control. But as this chapter now stands in its abridged form, all we are offered from this interchange is Henery's protest that Bathsheba will never manage alone, followed by Mark Clark's comment that:

> All will be ruined, and ourselves too, or there's no meat in gentlemen's houses!

From this we can infer a cynical humour, sexual prejudice even. What we no longer have is the larger dimension provided by dreams and cats and candlegrease. These bring us the feel of everyday life. These are the material details which convey to us that Hardy's working folk have been anxiously watching out for their interests, morning, noon and night, week after week, for as long as two whole months.

These are minor points in themselves, but in the aggregate they shape a certain tone and focus to this chapter which reflects a greater distress and discontent in Weatherbury's labour force, a greater sense of their feelings of precariousness, than is apparent in the abridged version for the *Cornhill*.

Let us look at some more examples. The Malthouse gathering is still harping on the ominous changes taking place up at the House, where Bathsheba has replaced all her old uncle's things with 'everything new' – an event which her workfolk view with some alarm. The manuscript reads:

> Yes, said Henery Fray. Then the next thing t'will be as tis always with these toppermost farmers as they grow grand; the parlour will have to be a drawing room, the kitchen must then forsook be a parlour. The wash-house is wanted then for the kitchen, and the pig styes is turned into a wash-house. Then says they to the landlord, if ye'll believe me my poor pigs haven't a roof between their heads and the

sky, and tis shameful of ye! Up springs a row of outhouses – and so they get lifted up like. . . . Lacking a comparison Henery cast his eyes around, seemingly under the impression that one might be found somewhere against the walls.

That's the right o't, as the maid said, cried Mark Clark.

Henery allowed his wrinkles of irony and despair to remain a few moments longer – then as he could think of nothing further to say that might require them, he smoothed his face and sat down.

None of this reaches the *Cornhill*.

Henery's grievance is slight. Hardy's rendering of it is, of course, serio-comic, and in a sense this sharpens the bitter truth of the matter which is that any and all such protests against class privilege are utterly futile. Henery's dolorous words reiterate the general resistance to change, but with an added emphasis on the caprice of modernisation; and in their small way these words also contribute to the overall sense Hardy conveys here of discontented labour feeling somewhat at odds with the 'top-permost' – albeit rendered in overtones of light irony.

Or perhaps it is not such a slight grievance after all. Indeed, of all passages in *Far from the Madding Crowd*, this comes closest to expressing Hardy's own sentiments on the capriciousness of change in his 1895–1902 Preface to the book:

> The change at the root of this [destruction of the rural community] has been the recent supplanting of the class of stationary cottagers, who carried on the local traditions and humours, by a population of more or less migratory labourers, which has led to a break in con-tinuity in local history, more fatal than any other thing to the pres-ervation of legend, folk-lore, close intersocial relations, and eccentric individualities.

Hardy is not talking along precisely the same lines as Henery (he is talking some twenty years later for a start), but he is talking about an age ushered in by the non-indigenous modern in which a new class of ambitious tenant farmers have uprooted the old class of stationary cottagers of which Henery is clearly one in *Far from the Madding Crowd*. And although Henery and his fellow workers may feel some assurance in the fact that the younger Everdene, having inherited her uncle's farm, is less likely to break up local traditions and 'intersocial relations' than might an outsider of the 'toppermost', there is no doubt that she represents, to all her workfolk, the greatest threat to stability and the greatest affront to tradition any one of them has ever known. Hardy may well be illustrating here the sexual prejudice with which Bathsheba has to contend, but if progress shows up this ugly warp in the social fabric, it also shows up the wretched condition of insecure dependency on the underside.

In the next segment excised from this chapter, Henery's final grievance about lambing profits can be seen as equally relevant to the labouring conditions of the day. Certainly, it offers convincing material detail in evidence of Hardy's imaginative re-creation of contemporary realities in Dorset life. To Poorgrass's complaint that the new mistress does not allow her shepherd the 'skins of dead lambs', Henery adds that in her uncle's day the practice was otherwise:

> If they died afore marking . . . the skin was the shepherd's – if afterwards, the farmer's. And every live lamb of a twin the shepherd sold to his own profit – yes, every immortal one to his own profit at a shilling a piece, if so be there were no ewes that had lost their own and wanted 'em.
> Ye be very badly used, shepherd.

The *Cornhill* has none of this.

Hardy was not, of course, writing a novel of agricultural unrest. Nor do I wish to give the impression that this lies dormant in his manuscript; rather that his local historian's concern for contemporary realities is manifestly more apparent in the original text of *Far from the Madding Crowd* than modern readers will find in the Wessex edition.

The extent of this concern, which suggests itself as convincingly in these cancelled passages of dialogue as in his thoroughgoing annotated reproduction of dialect, now broadens to encompass the equally vexed issue of class. This, as we will go on to discover, presented Hardy with many revisionary hours of labour, of close-detailing, of annotation in making minute adjustments to his manuscript and proofs as his relatively classless group of characters who originally inhabit Weatherbury and its environs are reshaped to take on the subtle markings of a more class-bound, class-conscious society.

Much is made of Hardy's class consciousness, and in this respect he was very much a man of his time. In an age of accelerated social mobility, the definitions of one's station-in-life, one's rank, one's class status and identity, were conceptually and ideologically complicated by conflicting codes and mystifying conventions of social acceptability. Most familiar to us are the continuing dialogues, throughout the nineteenth century, on what it meant to be a gentleman, and, of course, for Mrs Ellis's wives and daughters of England, on what it meant to be a lady.[18]

The extent of the class struggle, for Hardy, becomes nowhere so apparent as in his struggle to establish a correct social hierarchy for his fictional characters; his struggle to establish the conventional codes, manners, modes of address, and so on, which denoted class difference and all the complicated little nuances of rank, status and social identity. I have touched on the gentrification of Troy and the minute changes to dialectal speech, but I should also include Boldwood here, for although his rank in the Weatherbury hierarchy is firmly established by his occupation as gentleman-farmer, Hardy is still concerned to hunt out those subtle details and tonal markers that will assure readers, not only that a proper distinction exists between the classes in his world, but also that he himself knows how to make that distinction. Therefore, where his first impulse in the manuscript is to describe Boldwood quite simply as having 'full and distinctly outlined Roman features' (the stereotyped features of nobility), on second thoughts, in proof for the *Cornhill*, he decides on a more precise emphasis: 'He was a gentlemanly man, with full and distinctly outlined Roman features.' So far so good. Then along comes Boldwood in his carriage, overtaking Bathsheba on the way home from Casterbridge cornmarket. 'Another gig', Hardy writes in the manuscript, 'bowling along still more rapidly, overtook and passed them.' But that is not what the *Cornhill* readers received. They have:

A low carriage, bowling along still more rapidly behind a horse of unimpeachable breed, overtook and passed them.

At another point, when Bathsheba is quizzing Liddy about Boldwood and receives the reply that he is:

Forty, I should say – very handsome – rather stern-looking.

Hardy adds in proof, 'and rich'. Liddy's perception of Boldwood's status is evidently shaped by her attitude to wealth. To her way of thinking, wealth is synonymous with gentlemanliness. Hardy, at any rate, seems to feel that this is characteristic of her class and clime, and revises his text accordingly.[19]

Thus we also have the following. Nettled by Boldwood's lack of attention, Bathsheba discovers that Liddy, too, is surprised that her head-turning mistress is not turning Boldwood's head. With some indignation, Liddy exclaims:

But everybody else was noticing you, and it was odd he didn't. There, 'tis like him.

In the manuscript version Liddy stops there, but in the *Cornhill* she adds: 'Rich and gentlemanly, what does he care?'

In the space of a few minor but subtly revealing revisions, Hardy has clarified Boldwood's gentlemanly status: he now has the correct physiognomy of a 'gentlemanly man, with full and distinctly outlined Roman features'; he now has the correct thoroughbred horse of 'unimpeachable breed'; and, by virtue of his wealth, he has now the correct air – according to the maidservant, Liddy – of blithe indifference to the rest of the world.

Hardy now makes a further adjustment – this time to Chapter XIV, entitled 'Effect of the Letter – Sunrise'. This adjustment subtly enhances Boldwood's leisurely status as a gentleman-farmer (a prosperous farmer not obliged to work). The chapter opens, in the manuscript, with:

> At dusk on the evening of St Valentine's Day Boldwood sat down to supper as usual after coming in from the farm.

But with the omission of the last phrase, which rather suggests a working role, and the addition of a new image evoking luxurious fireside warmth, we now have in proof revision for the *Cornhill*:

> At dusk on the evening of St Valentine's Day Boldwood sat down to supper as usual, by a beaming fire of aged logs.

So prosaic a change yet so palpably different an implication!

Now, I am not quite sure about the relative standing of gigs and chaises, and which of them topped the bill in the Victorian scale of high-class carriages, but I suspect it is the chaise. To begin with, if we measure these things by horsepower, a gig is an open, one- or two-horse carriage, whereas a chaise may be drawn by a four-horse team and may also have a collapsible top. Hardy does not describe Boldwood's carriages in detail, but he does make the following revision which persuades me that the chaise is the superior carriage, in this instance.

The scene is the sheep-washing in Chapter XIX, and Boldwood, with agonising persistence, is yet again in the throes of begging Bathsheba to marry him:

> I will protect and cherish you. . . . You shall have no cares. . . . you shall never have so much as to look out of doors at haymaking time, or to think of weather in the harvest. I rather cling to the gig because it is the same my poor father and mother drove, but if you don't like it I will sell it.

But, for the *Cornhill*, it is out with the 'gig' and in with the 'chaise' (we now have, 'I rather cling to the chaise'), just as in the earlier passage cited above a 'low carriage' comes bowling along for the *Cornhill* reader in place of the 'gig' in the manuscript.

In an earlier episode, we find Hardy making another miniature change. Scrupulously intent in matters of class upon clarifying the tiniest of details, he has it (in revision) that poor Andrew Randle (the stammering man) speaks plainly just once in his life – to the squire – and promptly loses his job! But the squire does not feature in Hardy's original conception of things, in the manuscript. According to Henery (in the first writing),

> they turned him away because the only time he ever did speak plain he said his soul was his own, and other iniquities.

'Said to the squire' only turns up in a proof revision, where it not only

raises an element of class consciousness but also openly ironises 'iniqui-
ties': Andrew's iniquitous 'abuse' of his rank in speaking his mind to a
superior is nothing to the squire's iniquitous abuse of his rank in dis-
missing him! The change is minor. Possibly it provides a little amusement
at the expense of the squire, but I include it here mainly to illustrate the
close particularity of Hardy's annotations, and his impulse to extract every
ounce of sympathy for his underdog.

With Bathsheba and her working men, matters are more complicated.
The first significant revision occurs in Chapter VII in which, following the
rick fires, Bathsheba offers the men refreshment after their labours. 'Men',
says Bathsheba in the revised version.

> '. . . you shall take a little refreshment after this extra work. Will you
> come to the house?'
> 'We could knock in a bit and a drop a good deal freer, Miss, if so
> be ye'd send it to Warren's Malthouse,' replied the spokesman.

This is a more authoritative Bathsheba and a more deferential rustic
spokesman than we find in the manuscript, where Bathsheba says instead:

> Will you come to the house, or shall I send out something?

Her tone here is clearly less commanding and her instinct is to offer the
men the option of either coming to her or having her deliver to them. And
their original response reflects this felt level of social parity:

> 'Send it out please ma'am, to Warren's Malthouse', they replied,
> almost as one man.

Totally absent here is the suggestion that the men would feel constrained
up at the house, as the revised version has it: 'we could knock in a bit and
a drop a *good deal freer*, Miss, if so be ye'd send it to Warren's Malthouse'.
And, moreover, the reply, in the first writing in the manuscript is forthright: 'Send it out please Ma'am'. This has no overtones of servility as in
the later revised version. Then, of course, in the first instance, in the
manuscript, there is their unanimous response: 'they replied almost as
one man'. This has a noticeably less diminished quality of voice! In fact,
the necessity for a spokesman, as in the revised version, points not only
to a sense of decorum among the men – that they should not all burst out
with their spontaneous feelings before the mistress of the house – but also
(and this is the most subtle point of all), that there should exist (as Hardy
sees it), an internal hierarchy within the group of working men themselves.

These revisions and their emphasis on class difference are nicely done,
and with Hardy's customary economy of words. Perhaps their most
interesting aspect is that they reveal a less instinctive class consciousness
in Hardy, at the manuscript stage, than we might have expected. Certainly,
there is a far greater tendency, on the part of the menfolk in the manuscript

this Ashtoreth of strange report was only a modification
of Venus the well-known & admired, retired with him
to talk over the necessary preliminaries of hiring.

The fire before them wasted away. Men, said Bathsheba, you shall take a little refreshment after this
after work. Will you come to the house, or shall I send
out something?

Send it out please ma'am, to Warren's Malthouse,
they replied, almost as one man.

Bathsheba then rode off into the darkness, & the
men straggled on to the village in twos & threes — Oak
& the bailiff being left by the rick alone.

And now, said the bailiff finally, all is settled I think
about yer coming, & I am going home-along. Goodnight
to ye, shepherd.

Can you get me a lodging? enquired Gabriel.

Than I can't indeed, he said moving past Oak as a
Christian edges past an offertory plate when he does not
mean to contribute. If you follow on the road till you
come to Warren's Malthouse where they are all gone to
have their bit & drop I dare say some of 'em will tell
you of a place. Good night to ye, shepherd.

The bailiff who showed this nervous dread of losing

Fascimile 26 'Will you come to the house …?' (MS 1–65)

version, in Hardy's original conception of them, to speak openly, directly and without undue deference to Bathsheba. At Fanny's disappearance, Jacob Smallbury asks in a noticeably straightforward manner:

Had she any young man courting her in the parish, ma'am?

But in the *Cornhill* version this is altered to read:

I beg yer pardon, but had she any young man courting her in the parish ma'am?

Alternatively (Jacob again – in the original):

And you mean, ma'am, that a young woman would hardly go to see her young man without dressing up?

Not so in the *Cornhill* where we have:

And you mean, ma'am, excusing my words, that a young woman would hardly go to see her young man without dressing up?

The added words of deference speak for themselves.

Later, Bathsheba calls in her men for payday and Hardy, a little forgetful perhaps of the raised status she is supposed to exemplify, has her arrange the meeting in her kitchen. This never reaches the *Cornhill*. Here, instead, in all her dignity and due sense of occasion, Bathsheba commands her position as Mistress of the Purse at the upper end of the old hall!

Tiny pointers in Bathsheba's dialogues with Liddy show a similar effort on Hardy's part at establishing a fine class distinction between them. In 'Sortes Sanctorum – The Valentine', when Liddy remarks that Boldwood seems to have ignored Bathsheba at the church service, Hardy has, in the first writing:

'Why should he?' Bathsheba asked again, wearing a nettled look.

But this is altered in interlinear revision to:

'Why should he?' again demanded her mistress, wearing a nettled look.

First Bathsheba 'asks' Liddy a question but, upon reflection, Hardy has her 'demand'. He then marks in her status as 'mistress'. In similar vein, when Bathsheba mentions a Valentine and Liddy exclaims, 'Valentine! who for?', Hardy amends this to, 'Valentine, who for, miss?' Of additional interest here is the indication that these newly added emphases on class are introduced by Hardy in this scene at just the point where mistress and maid are at their most intimate and sisterly – perhaps too intimate and sisterly to be proper? Hardy appears to think so. Why else does he trouble to alter such paltry details as Bathsheba's frolicsome gesture in throwing the letter *across* the room to Liddy, which becomes in proof for the *Cornhill*, the more decorous, 'throwing down the letter frolicsomely'?[20] As with the Mistress-of-the-Purse sequence, it is almost as though Hardy is at first forgetful of, or even completely unconscious of the kind of class-specific roles and class-distinctive behaviours of which Bathsheba herself should, of course, be demonstrably aware. Or perhaps of which she should be *learning* to be aware?

No doubt, when it came to general matters of propriety and decorum, Leslie Stephen was right to accuse Hardy of having no more 'consciousness of these things than a child'. But if Hardy's manuscript and proof revisions point anywhere at all, it is to the certain fact that the man became father to the 'child' long before the day was out.

6

'A man's Damn'

The revisions we have examined so far have told us something about the 'good hand' of the early Hardy at work, notably his literary achievements in creating a finer artistic balance, a stronger coherency and autonomy of characterisation, a sharper precision of realistic details, and not least, a more fully developed consciousness of class codes and practices. Simultaneously, many of these textual changes have also told us something about the 'good hand' of Leslie Stephen. On matters of propriety he certainly kept Hardy on his toes, and despite his assertions that he was anything but a prude, which Hardy seems, at first, to have believed, his editorial principles could not have fostered many a libertarian among his readers.[1]

A fervent Darwinist,[2] Stephen saw promise in evolutionary progress and was never far in his thinking from the concept according to which 'certain gifted individuals act as instruments for the realization of the potentialities of the race'. These 'gifted individuals' should, in Stephen's view, offer the ignorant masses models of virtue, of moral propriety, and of transcendence over the 'baser emotions'. 'Only by suppressing the baser emotions can we move steadily upward away from the beast. . . . the ultimate value of art is dependent upon the moral qualities of the artist.'[3]

I should add in fairness to Stephen, that as the editor of a first-class periodical – the most influential medium in Victorian society – he would have seen it as his moral obligation to exercise the strictest censorship of all material accepted by him for publication. Indeed, he would have held it to be his mission. Holding that the new and powerful press was the strongest of controlling forces upon public opinion, and firm in his conviction that the nation[4] sorely needed an intellectual élite to exercise authority over the masses, it was particularly important to Stephen that the newly enfranchised classes should have their opinions and moral sensibilities shaped by freethinking, progressive minds.[5] He firmly believed that, in its articulation of certain ethical codes that would advance society towards a greater social order and a higher civilisation of existence,

103

the moral force of art should provide just such a shaping force. Likewise, it was his duty and social responsibility, as an editor and a man of letters, to equip himself as the moral conscience of his fellow men.

In his account of Stephen's life and work, Noel Annan explains that,

> Society, whether through the sanctions of the State or through the pressures which can be exerted by the market, will always impose some limitations on freedom of expression; and they will be most severe upon that medium which seems to be the most influential. In the eighteenth century Walpole thought the theatre was so potentially inflammatory that he imposed censorship on plays. In our time, first the cinema and then television was subjected to censorship, whether by the State or by public agencies or by commercial interests. In Victorian times it was the novel, and its medium for dissemination in monthly instalments, the periodical, which felt censorship most severely.[6]

And at the personal level also, Hardy felt it most severely.

He makes light of this in the early part of the *Life*, where he offers an anecdote or two concerning his dealings with Stephen. But, at the same time, apart from introducing a new air of diffidence, insouciance even, he adds virtually nothing to these ancedotes which are self-borrowings from an account he wrote earlier for F.W. Maitland's *The Life of Leslie Stephen*.[7] Given this duplication of earlier material in which the autobiographical self is reported upon and mediated by a purported past self which is, in fact, a rather defensive and self-protective present self, all of which inclines towards an act of exclusion (of the past) rather than inclusion, the thought occurs that this is a way of avoiding a narration of issues which remained painful and unresolved for Hardy. It could be that he would have glossed over these events even more than he does when it came to writing his own 'biography', had he not already committed himself in Maitland's biography of Stephen to putting them into print.[8] But include them he did, as a 'humorous illustration of the difficulties of "serial" writing in Victorian days':[9]

> Stephen had written to say that the seduction of Fanny Robin must be treated in a 'gingerly fashion', adding that it was owing to an 'excessive prudery of which I am ashamed'.
>
> I wondered what had so suddenly caused, in one who had seemed anything but a prude, the 'excessive prudery' alluded to. But I did not learn till I saw him in April. Then he told me that an unexpected Grundian cloud, though no bigger than a man's hand as yet, had appeared on our serene horizon. Three respectable ladies and sub-scribers, representing he knew not how many more, had written to

upbraid him for an improper passage in a page of the story which had already been published.

I was struck mute, till I said, 'Well, if you value the opinion of such people, why didn't you think of them beforehand, and strike out the passage?' – 'I ought to have, since it is their opinion, whether I value it or no', he said with a half groan. 'But it didn't occur to me that there was anything to object to!'

Hardy intervenes at this point to offer his own objections, that,

though three objectors. . . . might write their disapproval, three hundred who possibly approved of it would not take the trouble to write, and hence he might have a false impression of the public as a body.[10]

But Stephen is adamant: he should have cut the offending passage.[11] Driven on by a fierce compulsion to prove him wrong, Hardy even spoils his autobiographical chronology in his efforts to do so:

It may be added here, to finish with this detail (though it anticipates dates), that when the novel came out in volume form *The Times* quoted in a commendatory review the very passage that had offended. As soon as I met him, I said, 'You see what *The Times* says about that paragraph; and you cannot say that *The Times* is not respectable.'

(*Life*, p. 99)

Stephen is not amused. Nor, if the truth be told, is Hardy. Although he is ready enough (in the *Life*) to commend Stephen's influence, he remains astonishingly silent about his relationship with him, although it is evident that through the 1870s, but not beyond, these two men were in constant touch and plainly held each other in a kind of stern trust and guarded respect.[12] One aspect of that relationship to which Hardy never became reconciled and which commendation of Stephen's influence did not include, was censorship. This, to Hardy, was nothing short of 'paralysing'.

Possibly the inordinate privacy and pride of self-concealment that led Hardy, in the first instance, to write his own 'biography' under the pseudonym of his second wife, Florence Emily, also led to that suppression of hurt and rage that so often takes the form of jocular dismissal in his reminiscences. For, if we had not already detected in Hardy a certain resistance to his editor in *The Times* incident – in his efforts to re-establish authority over his own text – then we would almost surely perceive it in the defensiveness of his rationalisations in the *Life*. Recounting 'amusing' anecdotes of a past menace is, of course, one way of re-establishing the supremacy of the narrator over the story embodying the site of that menace. Another way is to affect that withdrawal of interest which flouts, or undercuts, the opposition (or authority) by means of adopting a remorseless attitude of indifference to it. This method of 'flouting' is familiar enough to most readers of the *Life*. In one breath, Hardy would, for instance, 'give up any points' in order to please his reader (indifference to the literary text) and in another, he cares nothing 'for a reputation as novelist' (indifference to public recognition and his own ambition). Suffice it to say that none of this remorseless indifference communicates itself in all those painstaking revisions!

Difficulties arose for Hardy because he cared too much about his reputation as a novelist. At the expense of becoming repetitious, it cannot ever be forgotten how inordinately sensitive he was to criticism. A good example of this arises in the case of Boldwood with whom, in general, Hardy had surprisingly few problems of characterisation. I say 'surprisingly', because Boldwood enters the book in Chapter IX as a gentleman-farmer in Weatherbury, and grows increasingly central to the plot as it progresses, but does not feature at all in Hardy's outline of the story as first told to Leslie Stephen. This is a remarkable growth from non-existent beginnings.[13] Uncharacteristically of Hardy, even Boldwood's farmstead remains indeterminate in his first imaginative conception of things: in the manuscript it is Upper Weatherbury Farm, in the *Cornhill* it is Lower Weatherbury Farm, and in the Wessex edition it becomes Little Weatherbury Farm.

But indeterminacy was not really the problem. The problem was outside criticism. Hardy tends, as we have seen with Troy, to over-expose his focus on individual characters who fire his imagination. And it was this over-exposure, this over-stimulated psychological and philosophical interest in Boldwood, which one or two critics found a little too overdetermined, a little too contrived and pretentious in style.[14] Hardy was cut to the quick! Now revising for a new edition, and inflamed, it seems, by an accusation that his treatment of Boldwood in a rather verbose section of Chapter XVIII resembled a caricature of George Eliot's style, he instantly abridged it.[15]

The offending passage, as it stands in the manuscript, reads as follows:

The phases of Boldwood's life were ordinary enough, but his was not an ordinary nature. Emotionally and mentally, no less than socially, a commonplace condition by itself affords no clue whatsoever to the potentialities of a nature. In all cases this state may be either the mediocrity of inadequacy, as was Oak's, or what we will venture to call the mediocrity of counterpoise, as was Boldwood's. The quiet mean to which we originally found him adhering, and in which, with few exceptions, he had continually moved, was that of neutralization: it was not structural at all. That stillness, which struck casual observers more than anything else in his character and habit and seemed so precisely like the rest of inanition, was the perfect balance of enormous antagonistic forces – positives and negatives in fine adjustment.

Clearly rather engaged with these ideas, Hardy sets about embellishing this passage in proof. For the *Cornhill* he now has his second phrase read:

> Spiritually and mentally, no less than socially, a commonplace general condition is no conclusive proof that a man has not potentialities above the level.

But it is this very elaboration in proof that he later desperately abbreviates in response to critical adversions to his affected style. He promptly cancels three entire sentences, and in the 'phases' section we are now left with a mere nine-line paragraph.[16] Perhaps, in the end, we lose little of significance in this cut other than evidence of Hardy's inordinate sensitivity to criticism, his fascinated probing of Boldwood's psychological make-up (and, *en passant*, his sense of Oak's 'mediocrity of inadequacy' – which, even at this early stage of the tale he cannot afford to let stand, given Oak's initial tendency as a hero to verge, in actual fact, upon mediocrity).

That this is an exceptional revision in Boldwood's case, and almost certainly provoked by outside criticism, is borne out by the fact that elsewhere Hardy's characterisation of Boldwood proceeds smoothly and virtually trouble-free from manuscript through proof to publication. As we have seen, Hardy does make certain detailed adjustments to reinforce Boldwood's class status, as is his practice with his *Madding Crowd* characters generally; and through Troy's perception of Boldwood's derangement, he emphasises the insanity issue – but nothing complicated or divisive or conflictive as far as authorial attitudes are concerned. We can, in effect, trace the simplicity of Hardy's characterisation of Boldwood, by mapping the route of his revisions through the text.

Beginning with his unattached status in Chapter XIV, entitled 'Effect of the letter: sunrise', Hardy says of him as he lingers over the Valentine:

> Here, his gaze was continually fastening itself, till the large red seal became as a blot on the retina of his eye

This is amended in proof for the *Cornhill*. We now find, with the addition of 'bachelor' a more subtle stress upon his solitary condition:

> Here, the bachelor's gaze was continually fastening itself till the large red seal became as a blot on the retina of his eye

Then comes the addition of a little artistic sanguinary touch:

> . . . till the large red seal became as a blot of blood on the retina of his eye

We now have a suggestive foreshadowing of things to come. Then, as the allure of the Valentine increases its hold on the solitary bachelor, so Hardy reinforces the impact of this on the reader. Thus Boldwood's consciousness that:

The same feeling that caused him to think it an act which had a deliberate motive

becomes (in proof revision):

The same fascination that caused him to think it an act which had a deliberate motive

And where he had risen the next morning and:

was noticing how the frost had hardened

now we find him (after revision in proof):

listlessly noting how the frost had hardened

The emphasis is now upon his torpor after tossing and turning all night.

As these added emphases begin to build a picture of a man suffering under pressure of mental and emotional disturbance, so Hardy ensures that every revisionary word will reflect this pressure, if only by virtue of its bearing a heavier stress than hitherto. For instance, he substitutes the word 'celibate' for 'bachelor' in the passage that reads in Chapter XVIII of the manuscript:

here, after looking to the feeding of his four-footed dependents, the bachelor would walk and meditate of an evening

So we now have (after proof revision) the more repressive-sounding or even unnatural-sounding:

. . . the celibate would walk and meditate of an evening

And as Boldwood is, in turn, overwhelmed by his incapacity 'to read a woman':

The cabala of this strange philosophy seemed to be full of the subtlest meanings expressed in commonest ways

So in proof this is altered to hint at some darkly hidden, perhaps even slightly sinister, mystery of sex:

The cabala of this erotic philosophy seemed to consist of the subtlest meanings expressed in misleading ways

Moving on to Chapter XXXI, entitled 'Blame – Fury', Boldwood has now become insanely jealous of Troy, at which point Bathsheba, trying to keep out of his way but accidently meeting him on her way to Yalbury, endures his miserable pleas and painfully guilt-making accusations:

even now I feel that the ignorant and cold darkness that I should have lived in if you had not attracted me by that letter – valentine you call it – would have been worse than my knowledge of you. But, I say, there was a time when I knew nothing of you

To this Hardy adds, in interlinear revision:

> . . . would have been worse than my knowledge of you, though it has brought me this misery. But, I say, there was a time . . .

First 'misery' is added and then, as Bathsheba tries to thrust away his words as they come,

> showering about her ears from the lips of the man in the climax of life

now we have, in interlinear revision, that she tries to thrust away his words as they come,

> showering about her ears from the lips of the trembling man in the climax of life

So 'trembling' is added to 'misery', and as Bathsheba 'fires up' with his furious accusations and perceives that, in his rage, 'Boldwood was nearly her own self', this, in interlinear revision becomes the more emphatic:

> Boldwood, in vehemence and glow, was nearly her own self

The scene is now reaching a climax. Boldwood, insensibly cursing and raging in whispered fury, swears he will horsewhip,

> the untimely stripling for this reckless theft of my property

But in revision Hardy alters this to:

> and I'll horsewhip the untimely stripling for this reckless theft of my one delight

This is certainly far more pathetic than the original which, with 'property' (given the political climate of the day) renders Boldwood less sickly and obsessed than something approaching the stereotypical patriarchal ogre.[17]

Thus, as Hardy intensifies Boldwood's drama, so his revisions reflect this intensification in tonal adjustments, and by the time we reach Chapter XXXV this revisionary practice has become fairly routine: Boldwood's 'struggle' becomes (in proof) 'the terrible sorrow'; the 'colourlessness' of his face, becomes his 'want of colour'; this 'troubled man' becomes 'this agonised man' – and so on in this vein. Finally, in Chapter XLIX, entitled 'Oak's Advancement – A Great Hope', we have one last significant change. Troy has now departed and it is spring again. Boldwood finds Liddy haymaking and enquires after Bathsheba:

> 'She is quite well, sir.'
> And cheerful, I suppose.'
> 'Yes, cheerful.'
> 'Fearful, did you say?'
> 'O no. I merely said she was cheerful.'

Now at this point in the manuscript when Boldwood mishears 'cheerful' as 'fearful', Hardy adds that 'Boldwood wished to get more involved in talk without seeming to attempt it':

> He was almost afraid to go further! Yet it suddenly occurred to him that if Liddy should notice his drift and report his words no harm would be done.

However, this section is omitted in the *Cornhill*. Possibly, in its rationality and self-awareness, it detracts from what is to come – an illustration of Boldwood's mental disorientation and Liddy's sudden thought: 'how stupid Mr Boldwood was getting'. So now we have, simply, Bolwood's interrogation of Liddy but nothing to indicate that he has ulterior motives or indeed any reasoning powers whatsoever:

> 'Tells you all her affairs?'
> 'No, sir.'
> 'Some of them.'
> 'Yes, sir.'
> 'Mrs Troy puts much confidence in you, Lydia; and very wisely, perhaps.'
> 'She do, sir. I've been with her all through her troubles, and was with her at the time of Mr Troy's going and all. And if she were to marry again I expect I should bide with her.'
> 'She promises that you shall – quite natural,' said the strategic lover, throbbing throughout him at the presumption which Liddy's words appeared to warrant – that his darling had thought of re-marriage.
> 'No – she doesn't promise it exactly. I merely judge on my own account.'
> 'Yes, yes, I understand. When she alludes to the possibility of marrying again, you conclude –'
> 'She never do allude to it, sir,' said Liddy, thinking how very stupid Mr Boldwood was getting.

With the omission of the manuscript piece pointing out his strategy in allowing Liddy to get his drift so that she might report back his solicitude to Bathsheba, we have in fact been left with no 'strategic' lover at all, but rather a pathetic and helpless mental wreck.

In this manner of tracing Hardy's revisions of Boldwood's character and situation, the clear pattern of his development emerges: the solitary recluse shaken from his protective and socially isolating cocoon turns obsessive bully, and the prosperous gentleman-farmer degenerates into a pathetic financial and mental ruin. Yet Boldwood remains, even in his crazed shooting of Troy and silent exit from the scene, assuredly a gentleman. And it is indicative of Hardy's achievement in writing this class and type that whereas some of his reviewers found fault with his style, Leslie Stephen had, for once, absolutely nothing whatsoever to complain about!

Returning to those matters about which Stephen probably did have some cause to complain, I now want to examine Hardy's use of oaths and blasphemies. In some cases, especially towards the latter half of the manuscript, there are signs that he is trying his hand at editing out the occasional swear-word himself. But Stephen must, surely, have been responsible for pointing him in this direction. Somebody, after all, attempted to 'clean up' Hardy's swear-words at the proof stage, and this looks to me very much like Stephen's touch with the 'buttocks'. But I can only substantiate this by citing a few instances of Hardy's reinstatement of one or two swear-words in his post-*Cornhill* revisions. Where these were cancelled for the *Cornhill*, they reappear in the first Wessex edition issued by Osgood, McIlvaine in 1895. For example, in the original manuscript version, in Chapter L,[18] Troy spies Bathsheba among the spectators at the travelling circus in which he is about to play the part of Dick Turpin. 'Here's the devil to pay!', he curses in the manuscript. The 'devil', however, disappears from the *Cornhill* version, and here we have instead, a d— blank. But in the Wessex edition the devil comes back again. From this I infer that Hardy wanted the 'devil' intact (so to speak), at any rate for Troy, and that this and most other instances of altered swear-words, made in proof, did not necessarily conform to his initial practice in the manuscript and may be laid at Stephen's door. I say 'most' since there are signs, as I say, of Hardy's curbing one or two swear-words in interlinear revision himself – at any rate, where Oak and the rustics are concerned. When, for instance, in Chapter XXXIII, 'In the Sun – A Harbinger', the impatient Oak tries to contain his frustration during Cainy Ball's incoherent account of Bathsheba's doings in Bath, but finally loses his temper and swears, 'Damn the boy!', this is truncated in both the manuscript and the *Cornhill* to 'D— the boy'. Then, like Troy's 'devil', it appears in uncurbed form in 1895. Likewise, when Poorgrass asks Cainy to swear on oath to Oak that his story is true, the boy replies, in the manuscript:

> 'Please no, Mister Oak!' said Cainy, looking from one to the other with great uneasiness at the spiritual magnitude of the position. 'I don't mind saying 'tis true, but I don't like to say 'tis d— true, if that's what you mane.'

Again, 'damn' appears uncurbed in 1895. So, no doubt Hardy, had he been given free rein in his text, would have avoided these coy truncations in the first place since they are inserted by him in uncurbed form in later revision, and simply do not conform either to his practice in general throughout the remainder of *Far from the Madding Crowd*, nor, more important in this particular instance, to his thematic line. For, in order to fulfil the immediate demands of the narrative, it has to be profanity, not coyness, that is vocally expressed. This, after all, is the issue:

> 'Cain, Cain, how can you!' asked Joseph sternly. 'You be asked to swear in a holy manner, and you swear like wicked Shimei, the son of Gera, who cursed as he came. Young man, fie!'

Poor Cainy bursts into tears.

With the exception of these few examples, however, where the d— blank truncation would have been visibly obvious to Hardy as he revised for the 1895 edition, the majority of his swear-words and oaths, cancelled for the *Cornhill*, were not retrieved and restored to his text at all. For example, where Hardy has Troy swear by these 'infernal' times, in the manuscript, this is cancelled in proof in favour of 'intolerable' for the *Cornhill*. And 'intolerable' remains with us today. The offending word crops up in Chapter XXVI, entitled, 'Scene on the Verge of the Hay-Mead'. Troy is assiduously trying to flatter his way into Bathsheba's good favour:

> I am afraid I have made a hole with my tongue that my heart will never mend. O these infernal times: that ill-luck should follow a man for honestly telling a woman she is beautiful!

Moreover, as he is about to swear by God in the manuscript: 'I said you were beautiful, and I'll say so still, for by G . . . so you are!', the *Cornhill* prints this as:

> I said you were beautiful, and I'll say so still, for, by — so you are! The most beautiful ever I saw, or I may fall dead this instant! Why, upon my —

Unfortunately, what these proof changes for Stephen's *Cornhill* reader again fail to take into account is that, in cutting out Troy's profanities, Bathsheba now has no real justification for responding: 'Don't – don't! I won't listen to you – you are so profane!'

Now Boldwood, on the other hand, is allowed to keep his oaths sworn by God, so possibly there is an element of class privilege to all of this cursing business. Perhaps by any double-standard of class and belief, a swearing gentleman is very different from a swearing barracks-man! At any rate, in Chapter XXXI, entitled 'Blame – Fury', it is Boldwood's turn to besiege Bathsheba, and here we have, in both the manuscript and the *Cornhill*:

> 'O, Bathsheba – have pity upon me!' Boldwood burst out. 'God's sake, yes – I am come to that low, lowest stage – to ask a woman for pity!'

However, when it comes down to things truly diabolical, at a point when

Boldwood comes as close to evil, premeditated evil, as he will ever get, his near invocation of things devilish, his 'D . . . !', is cancelled in favour of 'Hang!' for the *Cornhill*. This occurs in Chapter XXXIV, entitled 'Home Again – A Trickster' where, as we have already seen in the section on 'insanity', Boldwood, armed with a cudgel and lying in wait for Troy, accosts him on his way home to Bathsheba:

> 'I was engaged to be married to Miss Everdene,' said Boldwood, 'but you came and –'
>   'Not engaged,' said Troy.
>   'As good as engaged.'
>   'If I had not turned up she might have become engaged to you.'
>   'Hang might!'

No 'Damn!'s, then, for the *Cornhill* readers. Although at the climax of this episode, with Troy's jeering laugh in his ears, Boldwood is permitted a hellish curse or two: 'You juggler of Satan! You black hound!'

No character is permitted to swear by the devil, in the *Cornhill*, that is by direct naming. On the other hand, no character is denied this little liberty in Hardy's original conception of things. And clearly, Hardy harbours no superstitious fears, no taboos about naming the devil, nor does he appear to consider it unseemly or injudicious. The respectable Oak, for example, in tracking Bathsheba on her night ride to Bath, suspects that the gipsies have taken her missing horse. 'The devils!', he shouts in the manuscript. 'The villains!', he shouts in the *Cornhill*.

Alternatively, Coggan, in advising Oak not to show disrespect to Troy,

> For if he's married to her, mark my words, he'll buy his discharge and be our master here

further cautions that:

> 'tis well to say 'Friend' outwardly, though you say 'Devil' within.

Not so in the *Cornhill*, where 'Devil' is replaced by 'Troublehouse', and 'Troublehouse' is what we still have today.

It is no wonder Hardy did not restore all his oaths and 'devils' in revision for the Wessex edition. What a despairing task it would have been! No original manuscript to work with and a gap of more than twenty years of separation to overcome. And in any case, most cancellations and replacements of swear-words in *Far from the Madding Crowd* carry very little significance beyond the site of their expletive form and what they reveal about Stephen's views on literary decorum – or, by default, Hardy's! To my mind, their major interest lies in the fact that there appears to be a set of class and gender standards prescribing who can say what, when and how. Troy, as we have noticed, is debarred from swearing by the devil: another example occurs in Chapter XXXVI entitled 'Wealth in

Jeopardy – The Revel', where he is warned of the impending storm and scorns the idea with a 'Pooh!' in revision where originally he had sworn 'Damn!' or 'Dash!' (the word is almost illegible in the manuscript). But, unlike Boldwood, he is not permitted to swear by God either. In Chapter XXXIX, entitled 'Coming Home – A Cry', having very little money to give to Fanny on her last journey to Casterbridge, he offers everything he has, with the words:

> Good God! – I wish I had more to give you! Here's – wretched – the merest trifle. It is every farthing I have left.

But 'Good God!' is cut for the *Cornhill* and becomes 'Good Heaven' instead. And here the gender gap appears. For in Chapter XXXII, entitled 'Night – Horses Tramping', when Bathsheba cries out with 'Good Heaven!' (in the manuscript) upon discovering that Oak and Coggan have taken Boldwood's horses in order to track her, this becomes 'Goodness Mercy!' in proof revision for the *Cornhill*. Perhaps, to contemporary ears, 'Goodness Mercy' sounded more ladylike.

The rustics do not do much swearing, but neither are they instinctively reverent. A good example occurs in Chapter XLII entitled 'Joseph and His Burden – Buck's Head' where Joseph Poorgrass is expressing some qualms about his drinking and cursing,

> so I don't want to go too far for my safety. Your next world is your next world, and not to be squandered offhand.

At this point in the manuscript,[19] Mark Clark, extolling the virtues of having a firm doctrine with all matters properly 'printed aforehand', explains:

> or, dang it all, we should no more know what to say to God Almighty than to the man in the moon.

I suppose the problem lies with God Almighty's alignment with the man in the moon who is not only a nursery-tale joke but also something of a freak. At any rate, Stephen seems to have thought this too irreverent, despite the fact that Hardy had already altered 'God Almighty' to 'Providence' in interlinear revision, and now we have:

> or, dang it all, we should no more know what to say to a great gaffer like the Lord than babes unborn.[20]

And while I am on the subject of sacrilegious talk among the rustics, I should also include Mark Clark's little homily on martyrs, through which Leslie Stephen has actually drawn his censoring pencil in visible bowdlerisation of Hardy's manuscript. This occurs just after Coggan has waxed eloquent on Joseph Poorgrass's observation that 'Chapel-folk be more hand-in-glove with them above than we', from which Coggan concludes that getting to heaven is not everything; that putting your faith in someone like Parson Thirdly who had the goodness of heart to give away his last sack of seed potatoes, is what he would go by:

> D'ye, think I'd turn after that? No, I'll stick to my side, and if we be in the wrong, so be it: I'll fall with the fallen!
>
> The same here, said Mark. If anything can beat the old martyrs who used to smoke for their principles here upon earth 'tis being willing to smoke for 'em hereafter.
>
> 'Tis the old feeling in a new way,' said Coggan.
>
> 'Well said – very well said,' observed Joseph.

It is here that Stephen draws the line. He strikes out the entire dialogue – from Mark's old martyrs who used to smoke for their principles to Coggan's 'old feeling in a new way' – and, instead, moves directly to Joseph's observation 'well said – very well said', so that this now functions as an approving rejoinder to Coggan's 'I'll fall with the fallen'. And this is what we have today. If the difference between sacrilege and irreverence, as exemplified respectively by Hardy's original text and his editor's bowdlerisations, can be said to be marked by decree as well as by degree, Leslie Stephen seems, in the case of Hardy's rustics, to know exactly which and by how much!

Passing for a moment beyond conventional oaths to epithets relating to female sexuality, Stephen's bowdlerising touch here is indisputable. We are not in any sense left guessing. His characteristic pencil marks, denoting an intended cancellation within the manuscript proper as opposed to cancellations made in proof, are particularly useful in determining his mode of regard and focus of concern. And, in this instance, Hardy's use of vernacular phrases bearing references to female sexuality is 'marked' by both.

As we saw in the section on Hardy's characterisation of Troy, Stephen had struck out Liddy's reference to ruined maidenhood – her comment that Troy was 'a walking ruin to honest girls'. Likewise his pencil goes right through Matthew Moon's affectionate reference to those same girls as 'little rascals'. The phrase occurs in Chapter XXXIII, entitled 'In the Sun – A Harbinger'. Here, in the original, Matthew says:

> 'Twas only wildness that made him a soldier, and maids – little rascals – rather like your man of sin.

No 'little rascals' for the country parson and his daughters! The relish implicit in Matthew's words, together with the noticeable absence of any authorial censoriousness or any hint of moral consciousness on Hardy's part, would not have endeared Leslie Stephen to Matthew's sentiments – rustic innocence notwithstanding. In fact, I would venture a guess that 'man of sin' passed censure only by virtue of its smacking tone and curt, monosyllabic structure which brings the curtain down, so to speak, with a punitive ring.

Bathsheba, one of the 'little rascals' herself, also comes under Stephen's hand in a chapter showing signs that Hardy, too, is now aware of the need to exercise a little decorum. This is Chapter XXXVII, entitled 'The Storm – The Two Together', and Hardy's thoughts in revision are here directed towards that bodily contact between male and female that his critics were later to regard as one of his most flagrant violations of decorum. Bathsheba is mounting the stack with a reed-sheaf on her shoulder when a thunderbolt unnerves her and she clutches at Oak 'round the waist'. But on second thoughts (in interlinear revision in the manuscript), Hardy cancels this unseemly touching of the male body and now we have her clutching him 'by the sleeve'.

In the same chapter, Stephen's hand touches more upon silencing the female utterance – Bathsheba's act of naming her sexual thoughts. She is broaching the subject of her reputation and asks Oak if her standing within the community has become degraded by her association with Troy:

> 'I suppose you thought that when I galloped away to Bath that night it was on purpose to be married?'
> 'I did at last – not at first,' he answered, somewhat surprised at the abruptness with which this new subject was broached.
> 'And others thought so, too!'
> 'Yes.'
> 'And you blamed me for wantonness?'

Stephen, with his pencil, strikes out 'wantonness' in the manuscript with the result that we are left with something rather odd: 'And you blamed me for it?' The way this reads now completely fuddles Bathsheba's meaning. In the original meaning of her words, she fears that she will lose her dignity and reputation within the community if it is generally put about that she went running after Troy in 'wanton' (in Victorian parlance, sexually lustful) desire which, of course, she was not doing at all. Or so she would like to think, and certainly would have the community think. But this was too much for Stephen. So now we have simply the implication that she was galloping off to get a husband, which may be undignified or improper but certainly not an appalling transgression nor by any means 'wantonness'! And in truth, aside from its demeaning aspect, the proud Bathsheba herself might not think it worth mentioning at all, as far as fears about her reputation go. But if she is thought to be galloping off to Bath by night wild with desire . . . ? Maybe even she might have to set that rumour to rights.

Naming the thing is clearly taboo. And certain things that can be named by men cannot be named by women. Angered by Liddy's view of Troy as a 'fast man', in Chapter XXX, Bathsheba turns on her with rage and

2—163

said Gabriel. Every moment is precious now, & that would save a good deal of time. It is not very dark when the lightning has been gone a bit.

I'll do anything! she said resolutely. She instantly took a sheaf upon her shoulder, clambered up close to his heels, placed it behind the rod, & descended for another. At her third ascent the rick suddenly brightened like burnished silver — every knot in every straw was visible. On the slope in front of him appeared two human shapes, black as jet. The rick lost its sheen — the shapes vanished. Gabriel turned his head. It had been the sixth flash, which had come from the east behind him, & the two dark forms on the slope had been the shadows of himself & Bathsheba.

Then came the peal. It hardly was credible that such a heavenly light could be the parent of such a stygian sound!

How terrible! she exclaimed, & clutched him by the sleeve. Gabriel turned & steadied her on her aerial perch by holding her arm. At the same moment, while he was still reversed in his attitude, there was more light, & he saw as it were a copy of the tall poplar tree on the hill drawn in black on the wall of the barn. It was the shadow of this tree, thrown across by a secondary flash in the west.

Facsimile 27 'she . . . clutched him round the waist' (MS 2–163)

117

swears to her face that she is a 'hussy!' Stephen's pencil goes speedily to work and we now have, 'You graceless girl!'

Bathsheba's greatest verbal outrage to decorum never actually passes beyond the ancient walls of the Malthouse, in the largely excised Chapter XV. Here, as we have already seen in the section on the rustics and their anxieties and superstitions, they are gloomily predicting that Bathsheba's taking on the role of bailiff is bound to bring about some unnatural disaster. To be sure, there are all the signs: Matthew Moon's three bad dreams. Sally's bellows on the table, Poorgrass's white cat and his sister-in-law's coffin handle on her candle, not to mention the new moon seen through glass two months running and Gammer Ball's dream of stinging bees. And it is all to do with what Henery calls 'Mis'ess new farming ways'. But alarming as these new farming ways may be, the worst is the ferocity of the woman:

> Tis the toss of the head, the sweep of the shoulder, and the dare of the woman in general. Tis a word and blow with her, and the blow first, and 'tis got about that she said a man's Damn to Liddy when the pantry shelf fell down with all the jam-pots on it.

A 'man's Damn'! Needless to say, none of this gets into the *Cornhill*.

152

Well – not dress altogether, resumed Henery, listening attentively to the wisdom of his own words; though 'tis that too – a sort of spiritual dress as it were. 'Tis the toss of the head, the sweep of the shoulder, & the dare of the woman in general. 'Tis a word & a blow with her, & the blow first, & 'tis got about that she said a man's damn to Liddy when the pantry shelf fell down with all the jam-pots upon it. Only yesterday in this round world she rode all of a sudden up to me, & watched how fast $_\wedge$ I worked, rode away again & never said a friendly word. Yes, neighbours – in cold blood, without a moment's warning.

or how slow

Facsimile 28 'a man's Damn' (MS 1–152)

7

'The form of its manifestation'

Hardy wrote to the novelist and travel-writer, Kathleen Macquoid, in 1874:

> The question whether ordinary types should or should not be depicted as the heroines of novels, is such a nice one that it is difficult to discuss it in writing. I myself, I must confess, have no great liking for the perfect woman of fiction, but this may be for purely artistic reasons.
>
> As regards the woman of real life, the whole gist of the matter lies in what you summarise in the words 'true and simple'. . . . I had an idea that Bathsheba, with all her errors, was not devoid of honesty of this kind: it is however a point for readers to decide. I must add that no satire on the sex is intended in any case by the imperfections of my heroines, those qualities being merely portrayed in the regular course of an art which depends rather on picturesqueness than perfect symmetry for its effects.[1]

For the duration of his novel-writing career, Hardy was called upon to defend his unconventional heroines – their nonconformity, their sensuality, their lawlessness, their unrestrained passions, and what seemed to Victorian critics to be the sheer perversity of their ways, especially in protesting the status quo and scorning the ways of men. In reviewing *Far from the Madding Crowd*, Henry James saw it thus:

> The chief purpose of the book is, we suppose, to represent Gabriel's dumb, devoted passion, his biding his time, his rendering unsuspected services to the woman who has scorned him, his integrity and simplicity and sturdy patience. . . . But we cannot say that we either understand or like Bathsheba. She is a young lady of the inconsequential, wilful, mettlesome type which has lately become so much the fashion for heroines. . . . She remains alternately vague and coarse, and always seems artificial. . . . the only things we believe in are the sheep and the dogs.[2]

'Fashion' is a neat sleight-of-hand! No heroine of a best-selling novel (as *Far from the Madding Crowd* rapidly became) should be seen as a commonplace item found on every bookstall.

The reviewer in the *Westminster Review* is less subtle but equally hostile to Bathsheba:

> Whatever Mr Hardy may wish us to think of his heroine, the one leading trait of her character . . . is at the bottom – selfishness. She plays fast and loose with poor Gabriel Oak. She blows hot and cold upon Farmer Boldwood. . . . Her very selfishness makes her wayward and inconstant. When she is entrapped by Sergeant Troy with his scarlet coat and vulgar love-making we feel no pity for her. She never really cared a straw for Troy. She was fascinated by his swagger and flattery. Her behaviour, however, at his death seems to us most inexplicable[3]

In the final crisis of Troy's death, Hardy tells us that Bathsheba astonishes all around her with her powers of endurance. She proves herself to be, in the hermetic sealing of her heart and tender solicitude for her dead husband, 'the stuff of which great men's mothers are made'.[4]

The *Westminster* reviewer, with 'Whatever Mr Hardy may wish us to think of his heroine', evidently feels Bathsheba fails to make the grade in qualitative terms, as heroines go. Does he feel cheated of an edifying heroine? Or is it that Bathsheba does not conform to his expectations of conventional feminine virtue? Instead of steadfastly loving the bad man, should she punish him for his swagger and flattery by withdrawing her love if she cannot, as a good woman and a good heroine, reform him? Or is it that she shows no sign of penitence, that she is not bound upon reform, that she offers no epiphanic revelation – a revelation of unqualified love for the 'good' man? Or perhaps it is that sense of loss conveyed in that last grey morning of the book, that the spirited girl, the adventurous, daring Bathsheba is gone forever?[5]

It is possibly all of these things and more. To those who feel her behaviour over Troy's death is inexplicable, there is the frustration of irresolution – or what we have come to see as the ambivalence or the indeterminacy of the resolution. The truth is that Hardy is no 'reformist' of womankind in his novels, nor does he indicate in either his novels or personal writings that this kind of moral edification, incorporating a humbling, or even a demeaning, lesson or two which renders the heroine nicely fit for wifehood to a strong man, holds any value for him. The social mores of the day, particularly the prescriptive codes of behaviour for women, were not held high in his estimation. In line with John Stuart Mill,[6] he felt that with less social conditioning, less straitening into rigid gender roles and less social conformity, women would prove their own worth in a world that currently denied them the opportunity to do so.

If we return to the letter to Macquoid we find Hardy testing out one or two ideas in line with some of the above:

> The majority – or at any rate a respectable minority – of women are quite worthy enough in nature to satisfy any reasonable being, but I venture to think that they too frequently do not exhibit that nature truly and simply – and thus the nature is condemned by their critics when the form of its manifestation only is in fault.

'Its manifestation' – as perhaps, when Bathsheba displays her sexual interest in Troy by coquetry and provocative invitations of flattery. This is condemned by her critics, within and beyond the novel, but not simply because 'the form of its manifestation' is at fault. The form may appear superficially frivolous, capricious, vainly attention-seeking, egotistical – to the critic. But what Hardy perceives in Bathsheba (as does, perhaps, the more sexually anxious Henry James) is a 'nature truly and simply' expressing itself – that is, female desire testing out the desirability of the male, albeit in stylised cultural form: a little verbal parry and thrust, a little invitation and rebuff, a little taunting and flaunting, all designed to test the extent to which Troy is willing to please her. Clearly, if his flatteries are indicative, he is very willing indeed to please her. This is pure erotica.[7]

This is not the stuff of which good marriages are made, but it is the stuff in which Bathsheba is interested. It is also the stuff in which Hardy is interested, and it was not only Victorian critics who were alarmed. As recently as 1979, we are told that Bathsheba's 'moral growth . . . is always problematical':

> she is an un-deliberate, inadvertent, unconscious agent of evil. Her actions are not within her control. . . . She is vain, haughtily independent of spirit, and recklessly flirtatious

and so on and so forth.[8] As also with Gabriel Oak! This is precisely the 'vanity' and 'whimsy' that Oak also perceives.

If we were to differentiate between the narrative voices in the novel we would discover that characterisation is itself a composite of perspectives, of various alignments, of conflicting points-of-view. Inevitably, to identify with Oak is to identify with his experience of refusal, the refusal of his sexuality by the woman, which becomes in turn the shaping of his injured consciousness and his wounded manhood. All of this colours his moral perspective.

Oak's moral *purpose* on the other hand, is to shape Bathsheba a 'meek and comely woman' – a shaping which Hardy perceives as an injury of a different kind. For the meek and comely woman is the pale, subdued shadow of the proud, hot-tempered heroine – the 'Diana'-huntress of Hardy's imagination, as he perceives her at the peak of her matrimonial crisis:[9]

She chafed to and fro in rebelliousness, like a caged leopard; her whole soul was in arms, and the blood fired her face. . . . she . . . had been proud of her position as a woman. . . . Although she scarcely knew the divinity's name, Diana was the goddess whom Bathsheba instinctively adored. . . . O, if she had never stooped to folly of this kind[10]

This is the sexually exciting woman Oak must shame, but whom Troy, even at his most abusive, does not – which is more than one can say for the more shaming of Hardy's critics.

Hardy's redefinition of women in his novels, the sexually exciting woman openly seeking sexual compatibility in a world severely limiting her opportunity to do so, appears to arouse as much fear and hostility in the world beyond Wessex as within it. Having no liking for the 'perfect' woman in fiction, and having a preference for 'imperfection' in his heroines, Hardy has been accused, from Victorian days to the present, of misogyny. But, for the imperfections of the men in his fiction, he has not once been accused of misanthropy.

Blow for blow, it would be easy enough to explode this critical double-standard and to match any one of Bathsheba's imperfections with any one of Oak's, or Boldwood's, or Troy's, but the problem is less exegetical than ideological. In the simplest manner of speaking, we are looking at the intricate ramifications of gender construction and the structure of power. It is the view of these particular critics that Bathsheba should be *constructed* differently.[11]

Gender roles, being man-made and largely a product of cultural definitions, dictate that in her so-called vanity, which might otherwise be defined (as Hardy presents the case) as pure self-delight, she should submit to feelings of shame. In this, in her sexual power and pride, she transgresses the prescribed gender roles of her day. She challenges all of her menfolk (not only Troy) on the count of their sexuality: does Oak have the spirit (or the 'allure'!) to 'tame' her? Or will his dullness irk her into seeking challenges, into running fast and free? Can the silent and reserved Boldwood be roused by a lighthearted dare? Or will he turn out to wear 'in her eyes the sorry look of a grand bird without the feathers that make it grand'? (Chapter XXIII). Will the wild young soldier drive her sexually wild? Or is he 'a fast man' and 'as bad as they make out?' (Chapter XXX). Clearly, if these were the youthful activities of the male, they would be unremarkable – a little roguish, perhaps, but unremarkable and by no means a slight on desirability or lovability. But it was not for women to exert these kind of controls over sex-appeal. Indeed, the conventional Victorian suitor would have felt far safer being assessed on the grounds of his financial standing – what were called 'his prospects'.

According to one contemporary response to what Victorians called the 'strong-minded woman':

When a woman is so strong-minded as to suggest a resemblance to the stronger sex, men feel that they could not *love her,* and *accordingly do not like her.* This is a matter of instinct[12]

If, in his lifelong admiration for strong women, Hardy did not share these instincts, he was aware of arousing them in his readers.[13] But it was not until he had fully established his literary reputation that he felt free to dispense with that nod to the Grundyists, that proprietorial narrator who intervenes from time to time to wag a moralising finger at his 'inconsequential, wilful, mettlesome' heroine. In *Far from the Madding Crowd*, Oak himself provides much of the moralising; but at times, as he becomes marginalised from the central action, the proprietorial narrator steps in to take his place and this often comes as an afterthought to Hardy in so far as it takes the form, in the manuscript, of hindsight augmentation to the text inscribed in verso on the preceding page.[14] One of the very first of these verso augmentations, as we saw in the section on Bathsheba's first appearance sitting on the summit of her wagonload, occurs as she voluptuously gazes at herself in the mirror and then slowly parts her lips. At this point the proprietory narrator intervenes with 'Woman's prescriptive infirmity had[15] stalked into the sunlight'. To recapitulate for a moment, this intervening 'voice' subtly bridges the gap between two conflicting perspectives: the primary perspective of the 'painterly' observer who, in effect, creates the 'portrait' of blushing sensuousness and who sees the picture as 'a delicate one', and the alternative perspective of the keenly watchful Oak who now steps in to 'regard the scene' with 'A cynical inference' of woman's 'Vanity'. Not all such afterthoughts, or hindsight efforts at injecting a moralising tone, are overtly critical or censorious, but they do invariably help to ghost-in the approving 'nod-nod' or the disapproving 'tut-tut' of a ubiquitous but invisible Mrs Grundy. Even so, despite these emendations, Hardy's difficulties with his unconventional heroine are by no means over. The sensuous, sexually hungry, passionate Bathsheba is also an angry Bathsheba, and it is this, more than any other characteristic, that Hardy takes pains to modify in his revisions.[16]

In line with the manuscript changes Hardy later made to *The Return of the Native*,[17] in order to modify Eustacia's rage the better to minimise any suggestion of 'coarse' temper or 'witch-like' fury, so too with Bathsheba.[18] Aside from the episode of the 'man's Damn', most of these changes are minute: it is in their aggregation that the story is told.

Let us begin with the proposal scene in Chapter IV:

'Mr Oak,' she said, with luminous distinctness and common sense, 'you are better off than I. I have hardly a penny in the world – I am staying with my aunt for my bare sustenance. I am better educated than you – and I don't love you a bit; that's my side of the case. Now yours: you are a farmer just beginning, and you ought in common prudence, if you marry at all (which you should certainly not think of doing at present) to marry a woman with money, who would stock a larger farm for you than you have now.'

Gabriel looked at her with a little surprise and much admiration.

'That's the very thing I had been thinking myself!' he naively said.

Hardy, a little wrily, explains that it is Oak's 'superfluous moiety of honesty' that disconcerts Bathsheba. But no blunt clumsiness of mind ever acted on youthful high seriousness without utterly infuriating it:

'Well, then, why did you come and disturb me?' she said, almost angrily, if not quite, an enlarging red spot rising in each cheek.

'Almost angrily', but not quite! Then her temper fires as Oak blunders on:

'You have made an admission now, Mr Oak,' she exclaimed even more angrily

Or, yet again, not quite! For, in proof, Hardy changes 'angrily' to 'hauteur' and, consequently, his heroine departs the scene in the appropriate manner of 'feminine' pride and haughtiness.

Striking the correct balance between the aggressive and the passive, or the unfeminine 'bad' and the feminine 'good', evidently requires Hardy to adjust the genuine sensibility of anger to the more decorous, and more culturally acceptable, 'feminine' mannerism of haughtiness. Hauteur is decidedly more 'weak-and-wilful' (in the sense of being contrived, manipulative, undangerous) than anger which, for all its threat to loss of emotional control, is intimidating, endangering and empowering. Hauteur is merely a mannerism; it mimics, in socially acceptable form, a kind of leashed anger, or anger leashed to pride, to show that offence has been taken, or might be taken, or pretends to be taken, but will not be retaliated. And, bearing a modicum of repressed feeling, it cannot help but give off contradictory signals (like the hasty smile that covers hurt feelings), which then gives it the appearance of arrogance or wilful pride. Henry James may well have felt that wilfulness was now the fashion for heroines. But he clearly found it just as ludicrous, affected and as much to be scorned as did contemporary *Punch* satirists, who vacillated between representing wilful womankind on the one hand as the infantilised, spoilt, petulant doll-woman who, in rage, would pout her lips and stamp her pretty little foot, and on the other as the virago – the gross, overblown battleship-in-crinoline who, equipped with all the 'masculine' features of anger such as beetling brows and bristling moustachios, would bear down upon some inoffensive little man cringing wide-eyed with alarm at such a fright in nature!

The problem for Hardy is, then: if Boldwood can rage and curse fairly freely and remain a respected man of stature, dignity, integrity and honour – in sum a gentleman – but Bathsheba cannot behave likewise and retain like qualities and certainly cannot remain a lady, how then can she express her anger? Haughtiness does not adequately serve: as we have seen in 'Hot Cheeks and Tearful Eyes', with the substitution of 'you graceless girl!' for 'you hussy!', a single word change can introduce an element of artifice into what was originally a genuine explosion of feeling, thus subtly muting the authenticity of Bathsheba's voice. This, in turn, enfeebles her power. Painstaking as Hardy certainly is in these revisions, in struggling to avoid that coarseness imputed to his hot-headed heroine as he attends with scrupulous care to her every passionate utterance, he is rarely successful in striking exactly the right balance. If Bathsheba does not emerge artificial from the revision, she emerges disempowered. It would seem that the lady and her rage were too conceptually contradictory, too mutually exclusive in terms of their social acceptability, to be reconciled at any point within a single serious female characterisation (rage could always be acceptably laughable) with any degree of ease or credibility.[19] But Hardy is still determined to try.

Let us return to Chapter XXX for some more examples. Here Hardy has, in the original manuscript version:

O Liddy, are you such a fool!

which becomes, for the *Cornhill*:

O Liddy, are you such a simpleton?

Then as Bathsheba's frustration intensifies and she cries in exasperation:

Yes, you must be a fool, Liddy!

this becomes, in proof revision for the *Cornhill*:

Yes, you must be a blind thing, Liddy!

'Fool' is evidently the culprit – not a word to be heard upon a lady's lips. We have another example of Hardy's chasing out this offending word in Chapter XXVI, 'Scene on the Verge of the Hay-Mead' where Troy (in the manuscript) is urging Bathsheba to accept the gift of his gold watch:

'But, Sergeant Troy, I cannot take this – I cannot!'
she exclaimed with round-eyed wonder. 'A gold watch!
What are you doing! Don't be such a fool!'

This time Hardy catches it in interlinear revision, before his manuscript reaches Stephen's door, and 'fool' is cancelled in favour of 'dissembler'. This is perhaps one of those moments where Henry James's accusation of artificiality (in Bathsheba) can, I think, be fully justified. 'Don't be such a dissembler!' sounds horribly like a schoolroom exercise in language translation![20]

126

But that Hardy took such pains to make these minute changes says much about his awareness of their contingency, their social relevance, and the fine margins he felt he should observe between acceptable and unacceptable utterance in order to safeguard his heroine from opprobrium.

In our next example, in Chapter XXIV, the scene of the fir plantation, Bathsheba is, again, rather more powerfully ferocious in Hardy's first conception of her than she emerges after revision. With the rowel of his spur caught in the gimp of her gown, and a good deal of eye-catching and hand-touching to go with it as the unfastening process advances, Bathsheba finds herself doubly trapped as the dashing young sergeant also ensnares her with personal compliments. But in the manuscript she flushes with 'indignation,' and not, as in the *Cornhill*, with 'embarrassment'. And feeling more affronted than shy, in Hardy's first conception of things, she snaps at Troy, 'Go on your way Sir!', which is amended, in interlinear revision, to the more docile, 'Go on your way, please'. Similarly, but in a manner wholly out of keeping with the 'Diana'-huntress paradigm. Hardy reinforces this passive demeanour for the *Cornhill*. In his first conception of things, he had had Bathsheba retort, in response to Troys's regretful words, that,

> These moments will be over too soon!
> Not for my pleasure, she said, didactically rather than angrily.

The alteration for the *Cornhill* more than silences her controlled retort – it closes her mouth:

> 'These moments will be over too soon!'
> She closed her lips in a determined silence.

Hardy, though, does keep her 'high temper' in this segment as she insists upon trying to unravel the ensnared gimp herself. But he does show a certain anxiety about keeping it. First he writes it down, in the manuscript, then he cancels it, then he finally restores it in interlinear revision. 'High temper' observed by the narrator does, of course (safely and edifyingly) carry the potential for judgement in so far as any form of observation implies the presence and role of an observer capable of making a value judgement. Hardy detaches himself from this judgemental role by maintaining a neutral tone, an objective stance and a discreet narrative distance, established in the first instance by allowing the proprietory narrator a hearing (who will cast a Grundyan eye over things for the edification of Stephen's 'Young Ladies'), and, in the second, by backgrounding the omniscient narrator's point of view who will now be intercepted by the bystander narrator's conjectural point of view (who will observe that a thing 'may' be this or 'might' be that or 'could' be the other). These perspectival manoeuvres tend to shift the narrative into an evaluative mode of discourse in which no single point of view is clearly detectable, or concrete, or even fully graspable, yet in which the Grundyist might well find a sufficiently reassuring moral tone. This would not be the case if Bathsheba had uttered her own 'high temper' herself in vehement imprecations or hot curses. It may be, then, that Hardy vacillated over 'high temper' finally to let it stand precisely because of its relative safety in allowing for the free expression of his heroine's feelings without undue transgression of decorum. She is, one might say, 'being watched'!

As we saw in the last chapter, Hardy had already felt the need to adjust Bathsheba's curses; and as we discerned in 'Don't be such a dissembler!' (as in 'You graceless girl'), the difference in degree of authority, force and insult, together with the tonal and intentional differences between the original and revised versions, predicates a dramatic difference between spontaneous expression and sheer artifice. One is almost tempted, here, into the ultimate fallacy of saying that it is no wonder Bathsheba found it 'difficult for a woman to define her feelings in language which is chiefly made by men to express theirs' (Chapter LI).

It is worth noticing, in passing, that in paying close attention to Bathsheba's utterances, whether they are expletive or philosophical in kind, Hardy here rephrases her original words in the manuscript where she had initially observed that it is 'difficult for a woman to define her feelings in words made by men'. The alteration to 'language' far more aptly mirrors her deeper feminist concerns – her feelings of oppression at the idea of marriage, her repugnance at being 'thought men's property', her disgust at becoming the 'class of women' she would 'seem to belong to' by marrying a man out of penance.[21] Just as the Victorian institution of marriage circumscribes a way of life, ways of feeling, ways of regulating relationships and bonds (as Sue Bridehead is to explicate more fully later), so too with the institution of language. 'Language', as opposed to 'words' (which are merely units of language), is also a construct with many ramifications. Bathsheba is painfully aware of this. One of these ramifications (criticism) has already stripped her of her freedom and autonomy. As an object to be constantly evaluated, judged and admonished about 'rules' for women, she feels most acutely that 'a watched woman must have very much circumspection to retain only a very little credit'.

Thus, just as Hardy struggles, in his composition of *Far from the Madding Crowd*, to achieve a proper artistic balance between dialectal and standard forms of speech, or between the elements of expectation and surprise in his dramatic structures, so with his heroine he endeavours to strike the correct balance between the eidetic form – the flesh-and-blood woman he (and his reader) 'sees', 'touches', 'hears' and 'feels' – and the more stylised form who must enter the Victorian parsonage without flouting too many of the proprieties. Or perhaps it is simply a question, for Hardy, of not steering quite so close to the 'bad girl' of whom he is rather fond and a little closer to the 'good girl' the parson and reviewer are hoping to find.

Maintaining the correct balance apparently entails attending to a variety of small details to lay a more conventional 'feminine' stress upon Bath-sheba's characterisation, as in the scene of the cornmarket where, in the manuscript, Hardy has:

> Among these heavy yeomen a feminine figure glided, the single one of her sex that the room contained. She moved between them as a chaise between carts, was heard after them as a romance after sermons, was felt among them like a breeze among furnaces.

With the exception perhaps of 'glided', this is quite remarkably free of stereotypical associations, but it does not remain so. In a late, post-*Cornhill* revision Hardy interpolates, 'She was prettily and even daintily dressed', and instantly the 'feel', the 'sound', the 'sense' of her is undercut by the reductive invitation to view her as a decorative object, a 'dainty piece', a 'nice bit of skirt'. (Hardy's late revisions of a completed work are often extraordinarily out of synchronism with the original.) Similarly, with the substitution of 'shapely maid' in place of Hardy's original 'handsome maid' five paragraphs on. 'Handsome' is, of course, more impressive, more dignified, and signifies force of character and gracefulness of demeanour, if not a certain grandeur. All this we have lost in 'shapely' which points, as with 'daintily dressed', to the form or appearance exclusively, with some considerable loss of the essence or substance.

We lose as much again in Chapter XLIII, 'Fanny's Revenge', where, in Hardy's first conception of the scene, Bathsheba's sense of brutalisation is more intensely felt. We are told, for example (in the manuscript), that in her shock she feels 'the terrors of life' to be 'measureless', but in the *Cornhill* we are told that she feels 'the shames of life' to be 'measureless'. And of her earlier sudden longing 'to speak to someone stronger than herself' but 'there was nobody to help her', so her sense of isolation in need becomes (for the *Cornhill*) less a reflection of her own strength than a peculiarly 'feminine' lack of knowledge or wisdom or even capability: she longs to speak to someone stronger than herself but now we have it that 'there was nobody to teach her'!

Then (in the manuscript), back beside the coffin with Troy as he seizes her hand,

> [all] volition seemed to leave her, and she went off into a state of collapse.

In the *Cornhill* she goes off into a state 'of passivity'. Then, as Troy (in the manuscript) bends over the coffin to kiss Fanny with the tender words, 'darling . . . in the sight of Heaven you are my very, very wife', Bathsheba gives a wail of anguish:

'If she's–that,–what–am I?' she added, as a continuation of the same cry, and sobbing brokenly

But again, in proof for the *Cornhill*, we have a subtly 'feminised' version and Bathsheba sobs 'fearfully'. In similar vein, as she runs from the room and out towards the swamp, Hardy has it, in the manuscript, that she flings herself down in the thicket – altered for the *Cornhill* reader to her simply going in to hide.

In slow degrees, Bathsheba has become just a touch more vulnerable, a touch more pathetic, a touch more passive.[22] But there is yet more to come. Still more of the strong woman is lost in Chapter LV, 'Beauty in Loneliness – After All'. Here, Hardy cancels 'will' in favour of 'whim', a change which subtly undermines Bathsheba's strength of mind. This revision occurs at a moment when it best exploits the reader's sympathy for her vulnerability. In the manuscript, Hardy has it that,

Bathsheba's feeling was always to some extent dependent upon her will

but this is cancelled for the *Cornhill* where we now have,

. . . to some extent dependent upon her whim

And if 'whim' only partly enhances her mental lightness of being at a point where characterisation has to give way to plot, where we have to lose the feisty, strong-minded woman to gain a modicum of 'happy ending' sentiment, then a further miniature adjustment to this passage helps to reinforce this emphasis.

Something big came into her throat and an uprising to her eyes – and she thought that she would allow the imminent tears to come if they wished. They did come

For the *Cornhill*, Hardy changes one small word: 'come'. In its place he puts 'flow'. Instantaneously, we have moved from a voluntary act of will in allowing tears to shed from the ducts in the first place, to a concessionary act in allowing them flow freely now that they have already started to shed. The difference is very subtle, but it is the difference between control by the will and being controlled by the feeling.

Alternatively, structural alterations also play a part in Hardy's adjustments to Bathsheba's characterisation, as we see in Chapter XXXII, entitled 'Night: horses tramping'.

It is a warm July night. Oak and Coggan are in hot pursuit of Bathsheba in their belief that she is the robber they are chasing. As they halt her at the turnpike gate, she is justifiably annoyed:

> What, then, were you following me?
> We thought the horse was stolen.
> Well – what a thing! . . . How very foolish of you. Why I made a memorandum in chalk upon the coach-house door that I had taken the trap and horse and gone off with them.

And as her anger increases by the minute, so she also perceives that her workmen have acted in her best interests:

> 'True,' she said, and though angry at first she had too much sense to blame them long or seriously for a devotion to her that was as valuable as it was rare.

This, however, is the partly cancelled manuscript version. And if ferocity does not damage his heroine's credibility as far as Hardy himself is concerned, he is wary here. Or so it would seem as 'angry' now becomes 'vexed'. 'Vexed', with its admixture of petulance and irritability, most certainly diminishes the force and dignity of Bathsheba's emotional stature.

At the same time, in terms of structural alterations to this passage, a rather more interesting change occurs: Hardy cancels Bathsheba's explanation about the chalked message. Or at any rate, he delays it for the moment, and interpolates a new segment in interlinear revision: What we now have is Coggan's admonishment of her behaviour and his observations on what is right and proper for women:

> What, then, were you following me?
> We thought the horse was stolen.
> Well – what a thing! . . . How very foolish of you not to know that I had taken the trap and horse. I could neither wake Maryann nor get into the house, though I hammered for ten minutes against her window-sill. Fortunately, I could get the key of the coach-house, so I troubled no one further. Didn't you think it might be me?
> Why should we, miss?
> Perhaps not. Why those are never Farmer Boldwood's horses! – Goodness Mercy. What have you been doing – bringing trouble upon me in this way! What mustn't a lady move an inch from her door without being dogged like a thief?
> But how were we to know, if you left no account of your doings miss? expostulated Coggan, And ladies don't drive, at these hours, as a jineral rule of society.[23]

In the original version, Hardy makes Bathsheba's perfectly responsible behaviour apparent from the outset. She has taken the trouble to chalk a memorandum on the coach-house door and is therefore justifiably astonished to find herself 'dogged like a thief' in the night. But with the cancellation of her words of explanation in their original context, which

131

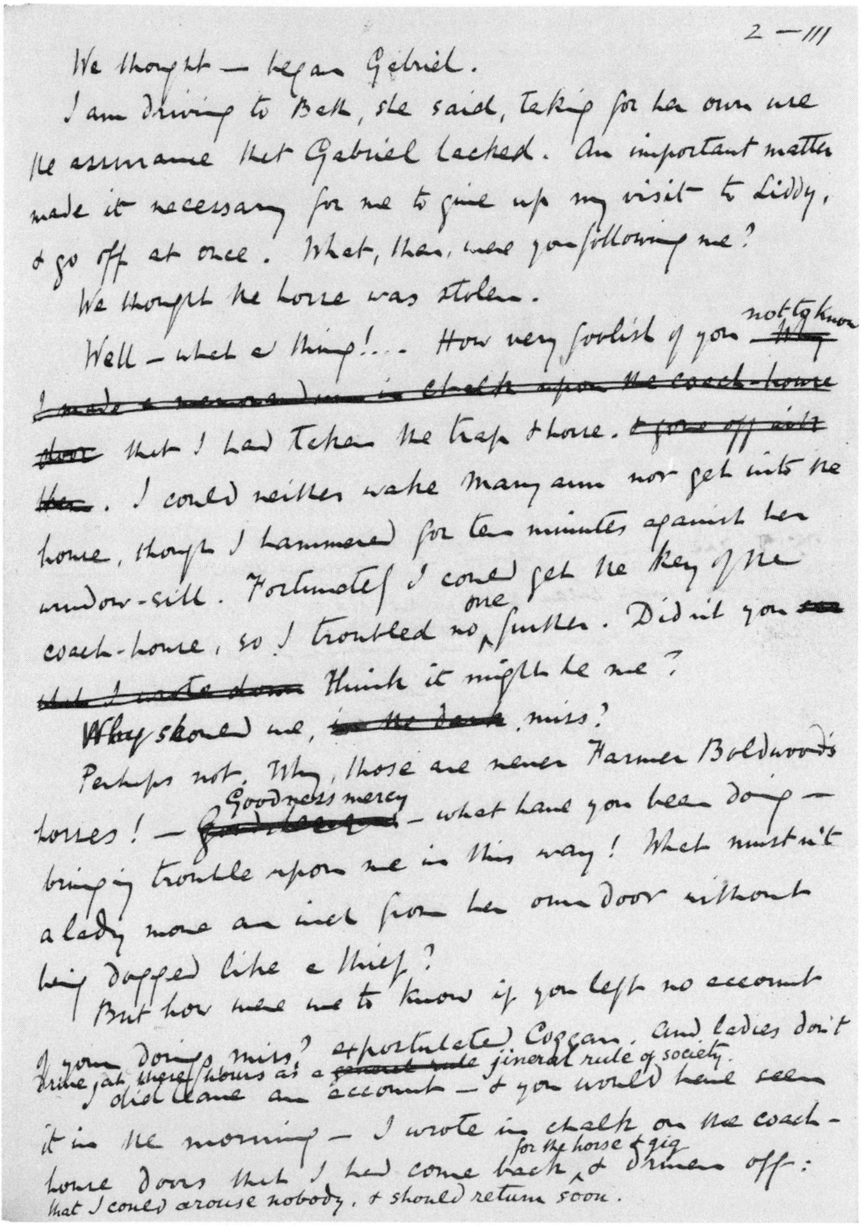

2 — 11

We thought — began Gabriel.

I am driving to Bath, she said, taking for her own use the assurance that Gabriel lacked. An important matter made it necessary for me to give up my visit to Liddy, & go off at once. What, then, were you following me?

We thought the horse was stolen.

Well — what a thing!... How very foolish of you not to know ~~Why~~ ~~I made a memorandum in chalk upon the coach-house door~~ that I had taken the trap & horse. ~~& gone off with the~~ ~~then~~. I could neither wake Maryann nor get into the house, though I hammered for ten minutes against her window-sill. Fortunately I could get the key of the coach-house, so I troubled no one further. Didn't you ~~see~~ ~~that I wrote down~~ think it might be me?

Why should we, ~~in the dark~~, miss?

Perhaps not. Why, those are never Farmer Boldwood's horses! — ~~Good heavens~~ Goodness mercy — what have you been doing — bringing trouble upon me in this way! What mustn't a lady move an inch from her own door without being dogged like a thief?

But how were we to know if you left no account of your doings, miss? expostulated Coggan. And ladies don't drive at these hours as a ~~general rule~~ jineral rule of society.

I did leave an account — & you would have seen it in the morning — I wrote in chalk on the coach-house doors that I had come back for the horse & gig, & driven off: that I could arouse nobody, & should return soon.

Facsimile 29 'What, then, were you following me?' (MS 2–11)

Hardy does not bring in until after Coggan's 'jineral rule', we are invited, for a moment, to stand in judgement of her with Coggan's connivance. With the first accusation – she should have left a message – the second follows easily enough, and we are momentarily caught in sympathy for Coggan and Oak, the exemplars of devotion and trusty service. But no sooner are we caught than Bathsheba explains:

> I did leave an account – and you would have seen it in the morning –
> I wrote in chalk on the coach-house doors that I had come back for
> the horse and gig and driven off; that I could arouse nobody, and
> should return soon.

Had Hardy left the original intact, there would be no cause for Coggan to adopt a defensive position and to accuse her of negligence and, consequently, Hardy would have no opening for the prescriptive 'jineral rule' for women. If this structural revision effects only this, that Bathsheba is yet again uncomfortably exposed to male judgemental attitudes, we might simply perceive something of the later champion in Hardy who more openly declares himself in opposition to the sexual double standard in *Tess*. But, taken in the aggregate, his revisions of Bathsheba's characterisation seem to indicate more than this. One can only hazard an educated guess on the basis of all these manuscript changes, but my impression is that they point, at once, to his commitment to her sense of oppression as a 'watched woman' constantly found wanting, constantly put in the wrong by exacting males, and at once to the dilemma that if, as he says, a woman cannot 'exhibit [her] nature truly and simply' without suffering condemnation by critics, neither can her male author exhibit her nature truly and simply without risking just as much.

But the greatest danger zone is babies! Not just illegitimate babies. Take the following conversation between Oak and Bathsheba in the proposal scene in Chapter IV. This is the manuscript version:

> 'You shall have a piano in a year or two – farmers' wives are getting
> to have pianos now – and I'll practise up the flute right well to play
> with you in the evenings.'
> 'Yes, I should like that.'
> 'And have one of those little ten-pound gigs for market – and nice
> flowers, and birds – cocks and hens I mean, because they are useful,'
> continued Gabriel, feeling balanced between prose and verse.
> 'I should like it very much.'
> 'And a frame for cucumbers – like a gentleman and lady.'
> 'Yes.'

'And when the wedding was over, we'd have it put in the news-
paper list of marriages.'

'Dearly I should like that.'

'And the babies in the Births – every man-jack of 'em!'

'Don't talk so!'

'And at home by the fire whenever you look up there I shall be –
and whenever I look up there will be you.'

Her countenance fell, and she was silent awhile.

Nothing of significance is apparent as yet, but if we go to the *Cornhill*
version, or to the copy we have today, a very small change with very large
implications will come to notice. The *Cornhill* version is virtually identical
with two exceptions:

'And when the wedding was over, we'd have it put in the news-
paper list of marriages.'

'Dearly, I'd like that.'

'And the babies in the Births – every man-jack of 'em. And at home
by the fire whenever you look up there I shall be – and whenever I
look up there will be you.'

'Wait, wait, and don't be improper!'

Her countenance fell . . .

In the manuscript version, Hardy (with obvious thoughtfulness, given
the augmentation at the caret) sees Bathsheba's response to 'babies in the
Births' to be properly and quite spontaneously, 'Don't talk so!' Why would
Stephen want to alter this – especially when Hardy had taken pains to
revise the first writing where there was no cautionary response from
Bathsheba at all? Evidently this emendation did not pass muster, and I
can only think that as a spontaneous response to Oak's words, perhaps it
draws too much attention to babies to be 'quite nice'. At any rate, out it
goes and since Hardy was apparently obliged to inject some tone of
decorum at this point, in comes 'Wait, wait, and don't be improper!'

Insignificant as this bowdlerisation may appear, it is actually one that
Sue Bridehead might call a literary enormity! Let us look at it a little more
closely. First, with the elimination of 'Don't talk so!', we have lost a certain
informality in the rejoinder and even a certain cheeky relish in the tone.
Its replacement, 'Don't be improper', effects a complete tonal change: it
is hard to say without sounding prudish or prissy or pompous and,
even if it is said lightheartedly, it is far more remonstrative. Second,
the relocation of Bathsheba's response completely alters her meaning.
Whereas pianos and gigs and cucumber frames and weddings come
within the compass of pretty fancies but talk of babies evidently does not,
with her remonstration now coming, not after babies but after 'there I
shall be . . . [and] there will be you', the whole point of her remark is lost.

"And the babies in the Births — every man-jack of 'em! And ¶ Don't talk so! 41
at home, by the fire, whenever you look up there I shall be — & whenever I look
up there will be you."

"_____." Her countenance fell, & she was
silent awhile. He contemplated the red berries between them
over & over again to such an extent that holly seemed in his
after life to be a cypher signifying a proposal of marriage.
Bathsheba decisively turned to him.

"No: 'tis no use," she said. "I don't want to marry you."

Try!

I have tried hard all the time I've been thinking; for a marriage
would be very nice in one sense. People would talk about me.
& think I had won my battle, & I should feel triumphant,
& all that. But a husband — _____

Well!

Why he'd always be there, as you say: whenever I looked up,
there he'd be.

Of course he would — I, that is.

Well, what I mean is that I shouldn't mind being a bride
at a wedding if I could be one without having a husband.
But since a woman can't show off in that way by herself
I shan't marry — at least yet.

"That's a terrible wooden story."

At this elegant criticism of her statement Bathsheba
made an addition to her dignity by a slight sweep away
from him.

"Upon my heart & soul, I don't know whether maid can

Facsimile 30 'And the babies in the Births' (MS 1–41)

In fact, it becomes nonsensical: there is nothing remotely 'improper' about Oak's picture of fireside intimacy. Third, and rather more important, is the fact that the spontaneous Bathsheba, who can spring, in a flash, from picturesque fancies to a quick sense of unwanted realism in the story (the arrival of babies) now appears, if we are to take her delayed response at face value, to be less feisty, less candid, less quick-minded and less responsive than we know her to be. Instead she comes across as the proper little miss we know she is not. Fourth – and most important of all in terms of Hardy's artistic aims, there is now the loss of dramatic irony as Bathsheba's countenance falls too late in the *Cornhill*. Her countenance no longer falls at the point where Oak's dream reaches (for him) the ultimate height of bliss – 'and whenever I look up there will be you' – which ironically marks Bathsheba's descent from the bliss (thus her countenance falls), but after her relocated protest 'Don't be improper'. The interpolation of this last phrase at this particular moment completely undoes the irony of her fall from pretty fancies to mundane realities in the very peaking moment of Oak's prettiest fancy. Small changes – large implications. This is certainly one instance where Hardy's original version has been badly mangled in the cleaning process.

Stephen's code of decorum is sometimes hard to decipher. To what extent was he representative of his peers in his dislike of the mention of babies? Was 'baby' a taboo word like 'pregnant', not quite nice to mention in mixed company, as, say, 'menstruation' was in our grandparents' day? It may be so, for when Stephen wrote to a friend to tell him that a 'young woman has just come into the world' he was referring not to some débutante but to the birth of his own baby daughter. And if the word 'baby', in certain circumstances, remained one of those Victorian unmentionables, so too, in certain circumstances, it remained one of those Victorian invisibles. I notice that in Helen Paterson's illustration to the September number of *Far from the Madding Crowd*, which depicts Fanny Robin taking her last sleep under a haystack before reaching the Casterbridge Union where she gives birth to her baby, the 'form of this manifestation' is one of a slender young woman with a waistline of about 19 inches!

8

'A curious frame of Nature's work'

And so to the issue of Fanny's baby and the most extensive bowd-lerisations of Hardy's novel. We are, by now, familiar with Stephen's editorial method of apologising to Hardy for having, on the one hand, to act censoriously on behalf of the more prudish among his readers, and on the other, for having to act censoriously on Hardy's own behalf because he has 'no more consciousness of these things than a child' (*Life*, p. 99). We also know that Stephen was making cuts in *Far from the Madding Crowd* as early as March 1874 (long before the arrival of Fanny's baby) when, as we have already seen, he wrote to Hardy to say that he had,

> ventured to leave out a line or two in the last batch of proofs from an excessive prudery of wh. I am ashamed; but one is forced to be absurdly particular.[1]

And we now know that a 'line or two' frequently turned out to be a paragraph or two and by the time Hardy had reached the final stages of his manuscript, a page or two!

I think we are also fairly assured by now that if we gauged Stephen's literary relationship with Hardy purely by epistolary measures we would be thoroughly misled. I have covered much of this ground in earlier chapters but have not yet touched on Stephen's own frustrations with his role of editor; for instance, his grumbles about *The Cornhill Magazine* itself, which had, he complained, a tradition of being,

> limited to the inoffensive. . . . exclud[ing] the only subjects in which reasonable men can take any interest: politics and religion.[2]

Yet, despite these grumbles about being 'limited to the inoffensive', Stephen himself, as we have seen, exercised the most rigorous censorship of all material that came his way for publication and excluded many 'subjects' in which 'reasonable' men and women of his day took an active interest: notably illegitimacy, sexuality, prescriptive behaviour for women, marriage codes, dissent and protest in the Victorian underclass, and so on. Moreover, such were his high principles that of all the major mid-

Victorian novelists, poets and critics who, at one point or another, passed through his editorial domain,[3] few could claim to have passed unscathed by the severity of his critical eye and toughness of mind. Possibly this 'improving' routine was itself so deeply ingrained in Stephen that he scarcely considered how far-reaching it had become in practice – that what he considered a helpful suggestion, a small exercise in caution, or the deletion of a 'line or two' frequently exceeded, in the view of his authors, the mildness of an intention yoked to an austerity of principle. That he seemed, on occasion, something of an ogre did not escape his own notice. Years after his connection with Hardy had been severed, he wrote that,

> The editor is regarded by most authors as a person whose mission is the suppression of rising genius and as a traitor who has left their ranks to help their natural enemy the publisher.[4]

Despite the ironic overtones, this is a defensive statement culled from years of exercising the patience and tolerance of expediency in setting limitations on freedom of expression. It needs no analytical subtlety to perceive in these words the speaker's deep-seated dislike of his own editorial self-image.

Stephen is clearly more comfortable with the idea of himself as a mere adviser, who, seeing himself as the 'slave' of his readers in his 'wretched concession to popular stupidity',[5] gently counsels his authors accordingly.[6] The letter about his 'excessive prudery' is the same in which he continues to say that Troy's seduction of Fanny,

> will require to be treated in a gingerly fashion, when, as I suppose must be the case, he comes to be exposed to his wife.[7]

How would Hardy have taken 'gingerly'? We may never know; but we do know that he did not take it as Stephen took it – Stephen who found the treatment of sex in French novels rather 'nasty'; who objected to 'the suggestion of a close embrace in the London churchyard' in Hardy's next novel, *The Hand of Ethelberta*; and who hotly denounced the Fleshly School of Poetry. 'Gingerly' is offered advisorily; excision of Hardy's text is what occurs.

As Stephen's words indicate quite clearly, he still has not yet had sight of the complete manuscript (now three months into publication), and still does not appear to know where Hardy is going with it; although to know that Troy has a wife, he must already have had Chapter XXXIV in which Bathsheba's clandestine marriage to Troy, at Bath, becomes known.

Hardy had already made some considerable adjustments to the Troy–Fanny relationship. We may recall that in the first instance, he had eliminated from the shearing-supper episode all mention of her gambols in town – that she was too well-off to be anything but ruined: attitudes that

138

were much in line, in tone and content, with Hardy's poem along a similar theme, 'The Ruined Maid'.

Second, he had capitulated to Stephen's censorship of all references to Troy's being a 'walking ruin to honest girls', and to the 'little rascals'– as Henery speaks of them – or indeed to any suggestion of sexual desire in women, including Bathsheba's use of the word 'wantonness'. These cancellations bear closely upon Hardy's treatment of Fanny in so far as his own sneaking affection for 'honest girls',[8] or (as his manuscript text alone testifies) his lack of condemnation of them, establishes an internal opposition within the narrative structures of his novel which is now virtually eclipsed. Fanny's pregnancy, in that it comes as a shock to the Weatherbury community, is kept a secret; this suggests, in turn, that her 'fallen' status and the opprobrium attending it are manifest in the invisible background of the novel; this is also evidenced by her occupation (in a distant town) of seamstress, which had traditionally become, in Victorian society, the last resort (short of prostitution) for homeless and destitute women, especially those in Fanny's condition. This silent moral con-demnation in the Victorian overworld of the novel, which I think we can undoubtedly infer from Fanny's situation, from her state of poverty and destitution and her quittal from her position as seamstress in late preg-nancy, establishes a clear opposition between implied internal moral atti-tudes – at any rate in the world beyond Weatherbury – and those of the original narrator from whom sympathy, affection and even respect flows, quite instinctively, towards the fallen woman. That these attitudes are essentially in conflict and radically opposed is the more readily apparent to the reader of Hardy's manuscript.

The implications of this internal opposition are such that, as with Henry Fielding's treatment of *Tom Jones*, the reader is invited to share in the wry benevolence of the author whose accommodation of youthful, healthy sexual instincts may not be universally shared by those on the inside of the story. This much then – this deeper engagement between writer and reader – we have now lost in losing the original narrator's insouciant attitude to 'honest girls' and 'little rascals'. Simultaneously, we have lost a (latent) benign order in which the Fanny Robins of this world find more room to manoeuvre – room perhaps for avoiding starvation, exhaustion, homelessness and eventual destitution. As we 'lose' this order in varying stages of elision and exclusion at the behest of Hardy's editor, and, more important, as Hardy, in the process of serial writing and the cancellation of his words, is repeatedly deprived of his benevolent narrator as his story proceeds, the world narrows down for author, reader and character alike to become a place in which Fanny's demise becomes inevitable – not ambiguous, outrageous, insufferable, pernicious or grossly unjust, but quite simply and quite tragically inevitable. And unlike the outrageous (as in Hardy's later novel, with the refusal of a sacred burial for Tess's infant, say), the 'inevitable' brings with it a certain passive acceptance of the tragic. This appears to go entirely against the grain of Hardy's original text, his holograph text, in which we sense his deeper allegiance to Fanny and thus experience a greater sense of injustice as her circumstances become increasingly insufferable. Yet despite the loss of his benign narrator (where 'little rascals' are concerned), who would, no doubt, have extended yet more tenderness, yet more warmth and yet more sympathy towards Fanny, Hardy resists this passive acceptance of the tragic to the bitter end. It is true that tragedy at this point, in Fanny's last chapter, turns upon melodrama in modular dramatisation of what we perceive quite plainly to be the sheer inhumanity of mankind, but it turns no less upon cruelty and pathos, symbolically exemplified by Hardy in the Union-house banishment of the only living creature to come to Fanny's aid:

> From the strip of shadow on the opposite side of the bridge a portion of shade seemed to detach itself. . . . It glided noiselessly towards the recumbent woman.
>
> She became conscious of something touching her hand; it was softness and it was warmth. . . . Night, in its sad, solemn, and benevolent aspect, apart from its stealthy and cruel side, was personified in this form. Darkness endows the small and ordinary ones among mankind with poetical power, and even the suffering woman threw her idea into figure.

Thus, 'resting her two little arms upon the shoulders of the dog', who 'thoroughly understood her desire and her incapacity', Fanny inches her way, painfully and pitifully, to the Union, where her last words hold the (benign) world in frame before it collapses about her ears:

> 'There is a dog outside. . . . Where is he gone? He helped me.'
> 'I stoned him away,' said the man.

But returning to Hardy's adjustments to the Troy–Fanny relationship, we should also take account of his hindsight invention of the very short chapter of a couple of pages, inserted as Chapter XVI entitled 'All Saints' and all Souls' '. This chapter treats with the marriage that does not take place between Fanny and Troy because she goes, mistakenly, to the wrong church.

Stephen's letters were, at this time, concerned with the uneven length of Hardy's instalments, so it seems reasonable to suppose that this very short chapter was written and inserted by Hardy at the proof stage to adjust the length of the March number. He had already sanctioned fairly extensive cuts to the previous lengthy chapter (XV), as we saw in 'Close intersocial relations, and eccentric individualities' (Chapter 5 of this volume). Chapter XV may well have been one of those chapters singled out by Stephen as causing a delay in the action – in his view, lengthy rustic interchanges were not suitable for periodical publication. If this were the case, Hardy may also have felt that there was a decided benefit in having this new abortive-wedding episode follow hard upon a lengthy rustic interchange in so far as it livens up the plot at a rather static point in the action.

The new piece, then, serves several purposes: dramatic, structural, thematic and, perhaps, even private and personal. For we know how fond Hardy was of hit-and-miss shots at marriage ceremonies, so perhaps this chapter satisfied not only the purposes of structure and plot, and of course his love of situational irony, but also his relish for playing fast and loose with matrimonials. On the other hand, the more important thematic change this additional chapter effects in terms of the Troy–Fanny relationship, is that it redefines Fanny's 'Ruined Maid' position. Whereas she no longer features in the manuscript as too well-off to be anything but 'ruined', she is clearly doing quite nicely by the time she returns Oak's shilling. The 'All Souls'' chapter rather reverses this position (foreshadowed in the barracks scene where she is 'out in the cold'), while at the same time showing 'good intentions' on Troy's part, even if those good intentions do not survive a rather nasty jilt at the altar. In turn, these 'good intentions' render more plausible his utter devastation at her death. Nor can we overlook the fact that with Stephen quietly intent upon striking out 'a line or two' at his own – not Hardy's – discretion, there is the added consideration (as Hardy, in all his mischievousness must have seen) that this interpolated 'All Souls'' chapter helps to shift a dangerous liaison a little closer to godliness – or, at any rate, a little closer to the church door.

However, by April, things are looking distinctly ungodly, and Leslie Stephen is feeling the part of Dr Bowdler rather acutely. Writing to Hardy, he says that he has to object, not as a critic but as an editor, having in mind 'the interest of a stupid public', that the cause of Fanny's death is 'unnecessarily emphasized'. 'I have some doubts', he writes,

> whether the baby is necessary at all and whether it would not be sufficient for Bathsheba to open the coffin to identify the dead woman with the person she met on the road .... It certainly rather injures the story, and perhaps if the omission were made it might be restored on republication.

He is anxious, he says, to be on the safe side and would be glad to omit the baby.[9]

Hardy would not omit the baby: by direct implication, with Oak's erasure of the last two words on the coffin, the baby remains; but he does appear to have sanctioned some massive cancellations. And these cancellations in the 'Babyhood' section have the effect of rendering the stillborn infant entirely invisible. As I shall go on to show, by being forced

141

to eclipse the baby, not partially but totally in terms of its visibility, Hardy cannot avoid eclipsing, in turn, Bathsheba's feelings of grief and compassion as the focus now rests primarily on Fanny – her rival – and less upon the stillborn infant at her side. Had it been merely a question of adjusting a word here and there simply to leave babies unspoken (as opposed to invisible), Hardy's characterisation of Bathsheba might have survived the cuts. But even this is doubtful. Just as with the changes previously noted, where 'terrors' in the manuscript become 'shames' in the *Cornhill*, 'collapse' becomes 'passivity', 'brokenly' becomes 'pitifully', so also the 'Babyhood' cancellations considerably reduce Bathsheba's stature and bring her closer to the 'feminine' weaker-vessel stereotype than is designated in the manuscript.

The first alteration is particularly subtle. Bathsheba has peered into the coffin and is in shock.

> Her head sank upon her bosom, and the breath which had been bated in suspense, curiosity and interest, was exhaled now in the form of a whispered wail: Oh–h–h!

This is the manuscript version. The *Cornhill* adds:

> in the form of a whispered wail: 'Oh–h–h!' she said, and the room added length to her moan.

For later editions, Hardy has 'silent room', but this alters nothing much, except perhaps atmospherically. Primarily, it simply enhances the rhythmic pace of the line.

The addition for the *Cornhill* has been introduced, I think, because the major cuts to this scene (of which more anon) have left us with a rather vague sense of Bathsheba's surroundings at this point. That she is now completely alone in the temporary morgue has been made quite clear in the manuscript, but is no longer quite so clear in the cancelled version. The alteration, then, for the *Cornhill*, which unobtrusively resets the 'morgue' scene for the reader, offers necessary information at the expense of dramatic focus. Just as in Hardy's first dramatic conception of Troy's departure from the churchyard, where he threw up everything and simply vanished, so in this instance, in the manuscript version, the dramatic force of action rests in its brevity. Bathsheba's whispered wail 'Oh–h–h!', is ghastly, haunting, and reverberative. It also has force of impact. We feel its hollow pain!

But the *Cornhill* has to do without, and that is not the only loss, not the only change this 'Babyhood' cut enforces on Hardy's text. To have Bathsheba's terrible moan now lengthened (in the *Cornhill* version) by the 'silent room' is, first, to shift the focus from her wail to her surroundings, thus away from the audible sound of her felt pain to merely the echo of it. And second, to use the 'room' in place of her emotional pain as the transmitter of utterance and intensifier of feeling is to depersonalise her at the very moment when she had been for Hardy, in his original conception of things, as vivid, as immediate, and as palpably real as his own flesh and blood.

In later speaking of censorship as 'paralysing', Hardy must have had such experiences (as this) in mind. His entire vision of mother and babe in the coffin is now obscured, and with this obscurity he momentarily loses sight and sound of Bathsheba – her 'voice' becomes a mere echo. As the 'silent room' adds 'length to her moan', her own utterance is both abbreviated and silenced. And something similar occurs in the next small revision which is not quite so subtle, although it does still 'cut off' the force and complexity of Bathsheba's feeling.

Now she is contemplating the 'measureless' terrors of life and the 'inconvenience and awfulness' of suicide:

> She glided rapidly up and down the room, as was mostly her habit when excited, her hands hanging clasped in front of her, as she thought and in part expressed in broken words: 'O, I hate them yet I don't mean that I hate them, for it is grievous and wicked – and yet I hate them a little! Yes, my flesh insists upon hating them, whether my spirit is willing or no. . . . If she had only lived I could have been angry and cruel towards her with some justification, but to be vindictive towards a poor dead woman and babe recoils upon myself.

But, of course, babies have to go, so we now have a pronominal change: 'I hate her yet I don't mean that I hate her . . . yet I hate her a little . . . but to be vindictive towards a poor dead woman recoils upon myself.' Here it is not only that Hardy cannot mention the baby, not even indirectly by use of the plural pronoun, but that Bathsheba cannot 'see' it! Yet, her intense mixed feelings of rage and pity, humiliation and regret, cruelty and sorrow are all bound up with that deepest sense in human nature of beholding, in a tiny stillborn baby, something unspeakably sacred. All of this we are now denied.

Later, when Troy arrives, there is still no actual mention of the baby for the *Cornhill* reader:

> The candle was standing on a bureau close by them, and light slanted down distinctly enkindling the cold features within.

This had originally read, in the manuscript, 'enkindling the features of the young girl and babe', and later, in post-*Cornhill* revision, Hardy did adjust this passage so that we now have, today: 'enkindling the cold features of both mother and babe'. However, by now, close to the chapter's end, much of what has been lost in censorship has already left its effect on Hardy himself, who no longer sees (or restores to his characterisation in re-publication), his original Bathsheba or the complexity of her

143

'excruciating' feelings. Gone are all her sisterly feelings for Fanny. Gone are her sorrows and pities for the dead infant. And gone too, is the subtle-souled woman who now emerges from Stephen's hand rather more pathetic and childlike than she emerged from Hardy's own.

The most extensively cut segment which now follows effects the most profound change in this context. By virtue of its omission in the *Cornhill*, Bathsheba's characterisation is manifestly 'redefined'. She emerges, as we will see, in a manner not only more pathetic and weak but also reshaped in such a way that she confounds Hardy's original conception of her. The proof changes he has to make to subsequent passages in order to accommodate the cancelled portions, actually take his narrative in quite a different direction. This is the cancelled section:

Bathsheba's eager eyes were not directed to the upper end. By the dead girl's side, enclosed by one of her arms, was the object of the search:-

A curious frame of Nature's work,
A flow'ret crushéd in the bud,
A nameless piece of Babyhood,

neatly apparelled in its first and last outfit for earth – a miniature wrapping of white linen – with a face so delicately small in contour that its cheeks and the plump backs of its little fists irresistibly reminded her, excited as she was, of the soft convexity of mushrooms on a dewy morning.

Fanny was framed in by that yellow hair of hers, just as she had slept hundreds of times in this house, with the exception of the fresh colour which had formerly adorned her. There was no longer any room for doubt as to the origin of the curl owned by Troy. She appeared rounder in feature and much younger than she had looked during the latter months of her life. Her hands had acquired a preternatural refinement, and a painter in looking upon them might have fancied that at last he had found the fellows of those marvellous hands and fingers which must have served as originals to Bellini.

The youth and fairness of both the silent ones withdrew from the scene all associations of a repulsive kind – even every unpleasant ray. The mother had been no further advanced in womanliness than had the infant in childhood; they both had stood upon the threshold of a new stage of existence, and had vanished before they could well be defined as examples of that stage. They struck upon the sense in the aspect of incipiency, not that of decadence. They seemed failures in creation, by nature interesting, rather than instances of dissolution, by nature frightful.

But what was all this to her who stood there? A thought of a few

2—231

more severed now by a reaction from the first feelings which Dick's example had raised in her, she paused in the hall, looking at the door of the room wherein Fanny lay. She locked her fingers, threw back her head, & strained her hot hands rigidly across her forehead, saying with a hysterical sob. "Would to God you would speak & tell me your secret, Fanny!..... O I hope, hope it is not true..... If I could only look in upon you for one little minute I should know all. A few moments passed & she added slowly, And I will!

Bathsheba in aftertimes could never guage the mood which carried her through the actions following this return to the house on this memorable evening of her life. At the end of a short though undefined time she found herself standing in the small room, quivering with emotion, a mist before her eyes & an excruciating pulsation in her brain, standing beside the uncovered coffin of the girl whose conjectured end had so entirely engrossed her, & saying to herself in a husky voice as she gazed within:

"It was best to know the worst, & I know it now."

She was conscious of having brought about this situation by a series of actions done as by one in an extravagant dream; of following that idea as to method, which had burst upon her in the hall with glaring obviousness, by searching about the house for something she required for her purpose, then by gliding to the top of the stairs, assuring herself by listening to the heavy breathing of her maids that they doze asleep, gliding down again, & turning the handle of the door within which the young girl lay, & deliberately setting herself to do what, if she had anticipated such an undertaking, would have frightened her,

Facsimile 31 'an excruciating pulsation in her brain' (MS 2–231)

2–232

but which, when done was not so dreadful as was the conclusive proof which came with knowing beyond doubt the last chapter of Fanny's story.

Bathsheba's eager eyes were not directed to the upper end. By the dead girl's side, enclosed by one of her arms, was the object of the search: —

A curious frame of Nature's work,
A flow'ret crushèd in the bud,
A nameless piece of Babyhood,

neatly apparelled in its first & last outfit for earth — a miniature wrapping of white linen — with a face so delicately small in contour & substance that its cheeks & the plump backs of its little fists irresistibly reminded her, excited as she was, of the soft convexity of mushrooms on a dewy morning.

Fanny was framed in by that yellow hair of hers, just as she had slept hundreds of times in this house, with the exception of the fresh colour which had formerly adorned her. There was no longer any room for doubt as to the origin of the curl owned by Troy. She appeared rounder in feature & much younger than she had looked during the latter months of her life. Her hands had acquired a preternatural refinement, & a painter in looking upon them might have fancied that at last he had found the fellows of those marvellous hands & fingers which must have served as originals to Bellini.

The youth & fairness of both the silent ones withdrew from the scene all associations of a repulsive kind — even every unpleasant ray. The mother had been no further advanced in womanliness than had the infant

Facsimile 32 'A nameless piece of Babyhood' (MS 2–232)

moments, which pity and a common sex insisted upon introducing. Then Bathsheba was in the real world again, and other than the highly poetical aspects of this scene returned upon her mind. Her head sank upon her bosom, and the breath which had been bated in suspense, curiosity and interest, was exhaled now in the form of a whispered wail: Oh–h–h!

Notice, in the first instance, that it is the baby, not Fanny, who is the 'object of her search', and in the second, that as she gazes down on the girl who had 'slept hundreds of times in this house', Bathsheba's feelings are of unmixed tenderness and compassion.

An interesting narrative dimension is also noticeable here, in the fusion of perspectives Hardy introduces as the omniscient narrator with a liking for Bellini stands side by side, so to speak, with the young woman who instantly perceives the 'origin of the curl'. If the plump backs of the baby's little fists 'irresistibly reminded her ... of the soft convexity of mushrooms on a dewy morning', we may be fairly certain it is not Bathsheba, but rather Hardy, who is reminded of the line and couplet describing the stillborn infant. But whose 'sense' is struck upon by that 'aspect of incipiency'? Who perceives that the girl-mother and babe had 'stood upon the threshold of a new stage of existence'? Is it upon Bathsheba's sense that these perceptions strike? Or upon both?

If that proves to be a slippery question, one thing is certain: the observer of the scene, and of the wounded Bathsheba's shock and misery, is as close to moving into her own consciousness and as close to identifying with her here as he will ever be. And the sympathy that flows from this close proximity and fusion of vision flows on and on, through all of the next few paragraphs as they stand in the manuscript. For example, we have:

> But even Bathsheba's heated fancy failed to endow that innocent white countenance with any triumphant consciousness of the pain she was retaliating for her pain with all the merciless rigour of the Mosaic law

However, due to Stephen's cancellation of the entire 'Babyhood' passage, the emphasis is now almost solely upon Fanny's presence as Bathsheba's rival. Whatever Stephen sent back to Hardy for final revision in the proofs for the *Cornhill* did not contain the 'Babyhood' section, and the directional flow of events, as well as Bathsheba's characterisation, take on, as a result, a completely different look, feel, tone and focus. And it is presumably this radical alteration, this new and strange emphasis, that drove Hardy to change – indeed to put into reverse – the whole 'Mosaic law' passage. This, revised for the *Cornhill*, now reads as follows:

> In Bathsheba's heated fancy the innocent white countenance expressed a dim triumphant consciousness of the pain she was retaliating for her pain with all the merciless rigour of the Mosaic law

2–233

in childhood; they both had stood upon the threshold of a new stage of existence, & had vanished before they could well be defined as examples of that stage. They struck upon the sense in the aspect of incipiency, not in that of decadence. They seemed failures in creation, by nature interesting, rather than instances of dissolution, by nature frightful.

But what was all this to her who stood there? A thought of a few moments, which pity & a common sex insisted upon introducing. Then Bathsheba was in the real world again, & other than the highly poetical aspects of this scene returned upon her mind. Her head sank upon her bosom, & the breath which had been baited in ~~the~~ suspense, curiosity, & interest, was exhaled now in the form of a whispered wail: Oh-h-h!

Her tears fell fast beside the unconscious pair – tears of a complicated origin, ~~of a~~ of a nature indescribable, almost indefinable [except as other than those of ~~simple~~ simple sorrow] Assuredly their wonted fires must have lived in Fanny's ashes when events were so shaped as to chariot her hither in this natural, unobtrusive yet effectual manner. The one feat alone – that of dying – by which a mean condition could be resolved into a grand one, Fanny had achieved. But even Bathsheba's heated fancy failed to endow that innocent white countenance with any triumphant consciousness of the pain she was retaliating for her pain with all the merciless rigour of the Mosaic law: "Burning for burning;

Facsimile 33 'Her head sank upon her bosom' (MS 2–233)

2—234

wound for wound; strife for strife."

Bathsheba indulged in contemplations of escape from her position by death, which, though it was an inconvenient & awful way, had limits to its inconvenience & awfulness which could not be overpassed; whilst the terrors of life were measureless. Yet even this scheme of extinction by death was but tamely copying her rival's method without the reasons which had glorified it in her rival's case. She glided rapidly up & down the room, as was mostly her habit when excited, her hands hanging clasped in front of her, as she thought & in part expressed in broken words; "O I hate them yet I don't mean that I hate them, for it is grievous & wicked — & yet I hate them a little! Yes, my flesh insists upon hating them, whether my spirit is willing or no. If she had only lived I could have been angry & cruel towards her with some justification, but to be vindictive towards a poor dead woman & babe recoils upon myself. O God have mercy — I am miserable at all this!

Bathsheba became at this moment so terrified at her own state of mind that she looked around for some sort of refuge from herself. The vision of Oak kneeling down that night recurred to her, & with the imitative instinct which animates woman she seized upon the idea, resolved to kneel & if possible, pray. Gabriel had prayed; so would she.

Facsimile 34 'wound for wound' (MS 2–234)

In other words, the massive cuts made here have enforced a completely different focus, a completely different tone, and a completely different perspective. As a result, we have a completely different response on Bathsheba's part.

It is a salutary thought that such was Stephen's power and influence as the arbiter of Victorian values, that both Hardy and his Bathsheba, one of his most compelling heroines, should have to suffer such a distortion in creation in order to ensure *Far from the Madding Crowd*'s safe admission to the country parsonage.

Afterword

A year later, Hardy promptly turned his back on the *Greenwood-Tree*-type tale so highly favoured by Stephen. Following the publication of *Far from the Madding Crowd* in 1874, he published his first city-based novel, *The Hand of Ethelberta* (1875), in which he resurrected the issue of class-warfare as a major theme – a theme which had gone underground with the demise of *The Poor Man and the Lady* but which resurfaced with *Ethelberta* subsequently to become an ascendant motif in the Wessex novels as Hardy's career progressed. Interestingly enough, with *Tess*, in the 1890s, the country parsonage (the epitome, in Leslie Stephen's view, of good taste, propriety and social respectability) finally comes to blows, in the form of Angel Clare, with 'honest girls' and all that they represent in terms of natural virtue, embodied by Tess herself. And equally fascinating in this context is the fact that the parson's son, renouncing his faith and turning to agnosticism ('communistic' readings), finds his new free-thinking, rationalist philosophy[10] less triumphal than assaulted (and ultimately punished!) in its collision with Tess's simple, pure and honest humanitarianism, exemplified by her own 'un-moralised' 'Babyhood' story. Do these subtle correspondences in *Tess* dimly echo in Hardy's literary imagination from distant haunts and unresolved conflicts of the past?

Returning to the 1870s and *Ethelberta*, Hardy then published his purposefully artistic novel, *The Return of the Native* (1868), which as we now know, Stephen declined to publish. Did Hardy ever seriously think that he would publish it? If Stephen had been perturbed that a woman might call her writings 'amours' (in *Ethelberta*), and had, at the same time, been poised 'pencil-ready' to stop any kissing going on in the churchyard, he would scarcely have blessed Hardy for offering him adultery-on-the-heath, barefaced and uncensored, in virtually the very first instalment of his next serial!

So, Hardy seems to be turning his back on more than just a prose genre (though *Greenwood Trees* are by no means abandoned, just seconded *ad interim*). Prohibition generates a counteractive force, and if Hardy had operated through repression with Stephen, he is now deploying the power of his oppositional stance and gaining incitement to discourse on his own terms.

Aside from this, aside from the schooled reaction to prohibition, culminating in the impetus towards experimentation and oppositional literary manoeuvres, as this reveals itself in Hardy's fiction over the next two decades, Stephen's influence appears to be as indeterminable as Hardy seems to have hoped to have kept it – if his equivocal and subversive anecdotes in the *Life* are at all indicative. Perhaps we come closest to an accurate evaluation of his schooling at his editor's 'good hand' by way of Stephen's own sardonic words to his friend, Frederic Maitland: 'that when one of our great schools is said to have "produced" one of our famous men, the word "produced" means "failed to extinguish" '.[11]

Appendix 1

*A survey of post-*Cornhill *substantive revisions*

Hardy's post-*Cornhill* revisions are scanty up until 1895 when he revised for the complete collected edition, issued by Osgood, McIlvaine – the first Wessex edition. Topically, he concentrates, in his later revisions, more upon scene than character or event, and tends to steer clear of his treatment of female sexuality – from sexual desire to 'babies' – as manifest in the manuscript and cancelled by Stephen for serial publication. There is no doubt that this topic gave author and editor more trouble than anything else and later contributed, with Stephen's refusal of *The Return of the Native*, to the ending of their professional relationship. Hardy was sensitive to criticism of any kind, and possibly had to suppress a good deal of rage and frustration with the Bowdlers and Grundys, including those who criticised his sexually daring heroine as unwomanly and coarse. Needless to say, his post-*Cornhill* revisions of *Far from the Madding Crowd* leave this vexed issue well alone, with the exception of a few small adjustments, such as reinstating a direct reference to Fanny's baby (discussed in Chapter 8) and introducing the word 'maternity' into the coffin scene: 'she had meditated on . . . eclipse in maternity by another'.

The influence of post-publication criticism was such that Hardy concentrated, in revision, upon modifying passages that reviewers found pretentious or derivative or too self-consciously ingenious, such as the segment concerning Boldwood, about which Hardy had already shown signs of indecision in the manuscript (see Chapter 6 of present volume). Alternatively, he concentrated upon reinforcing aspects of the novel which had found favour – such as his 'prose-idyl' of country life. Hardy's response to this general enthusiasm for his evocation of fresh pastoral scenes and nascent Wessex world, which has little more than an embryonic topographical design in the manuscript version, was vigorous and immediate and by 1895 with the Osgood, McIlvaine complete collected edition he had schematically created it (see Appendix 2).[1] But, of course, these topographical revisions – mainly the more precise, distinctive and coherent incorporation of place-names – were not unique to *Far from the Madding Crowd*.

Some single-word changes of a more general nature were introduced by Hardy in post-publication revisions, but they are fairly routine: 'barbarous' is changed to 'barbarian', 'believe' to 'worship', 'before' to 'afore', 'soldier' to 'sojer', 'refinement' to 'refinery' and 'luxery' to 'luxury' in Chapter XXXIII; 'Juggler' to 'Trickster' in XXXIV; 'help' to 'teach' in XLIII – and so on and so forth in that vein. Most of these word changes serve either to enhance meaning or to adjust dialectal and vernacular modes of speech. Some, though, are designed to simplify obscurities – Hardy, incidentally, has some interesting coinages and spellings in the manuscript: 'querelous' (Chapter XXII); 'tranquility' (Chapter XXIII); 'feminality' (Chapter XXXI); 'meridional' (Chapter XLII); and the rather curious use of 'parabolic' (Chapter XV) which Stephen dealt with peremptorily (with a pencil cancellation in the manuscript) and changed to 'hyperbolic'. These, however, are all extant in the manuscript. Further simplifications of obscure or pretentious-sounding words (including a couple of instances of Greek) take place in proof revisions for the *Cornhill*, although one or two do still remain to engage Hardy's attention in later years.[2]

An example of one such post-*Cornhill* alteration occurs in Chapter XL, where Fanny struggles on with the aid of forked sticks as crutches. Hardy now has it that 'the original amount of exertion was not cleared away'. This previously stood in the manuscript as 'the quantum of exertion was not cleared away' – which is not, in fact, quite as bad as Simon Gatrell[3] makes out with his misquoted: 'the original quantum of exertion'. This wrongly attributed phrase is more than clumsy and obscure, it is a negation of terms! To be fair to Hardy, nothing quite as lumpy as this arises in his manuscript – although compositors and editors do not always help. Where Hardy has it (in the manuscript), when the petitioners for Boldwood's reprieve[4] have delivered their evidence (Chapter LV), that 'The promoters were a few merciful men', the *Cornhill* compositors print 'prompters' (and this remains in print to the present day). And where he has, in his marvellous description of the Great Barn:

> The fact that four centuries had neither proved it to be founded on a mistake, inspired any hatred of its purpose, nor given rise to any reaction that had battered it down, invested this simple grey effort of old minds with a repose, if not a grandeur, which too curious a reflection was apt to disturb in its ecclesiastical and military compeers.

this, up to the Wessex edition, remained intact. But then someone mislaid the final conjunction and so now we have a curious (unhyphenated) compound of church and army:

> which too curious a reflection was apt to disturb in its ecclesiastical military compeers.

153

But this is not as remiss as 'lancelote', misprinted from the Wessex edition onwards. Hardy himself, as an erstwhile architect, had no such problems with architectural terminology: in his description of the ancient, narrow-pointed barn windows he has 'lanceolate' from first to last! Then too, where Hardy has 'martial' in the *Cornhill* to describe Oak's rising to the occasion 'with martial promptness and vigour' (Chapter XV), the Norton edition has 'marital'. This is a particularly regrettable error, since Hardy had actually taken careful pains to revise this phrase which stands in the manuscript as 'Gabriel . . . rose to the occasion though in the greatest good humour'. Presumably, 'martial promptness and vigour' (his revised version) is meant to add a little manliness to what almost verges on sheer buffoonery in this segment.

Hardy does fall into some grave errors himself, in post-publication revision, but not literary errors. His difficulties arise, it seems, when he tries, on a few hazardous occasions, to redraw his characters. It is true that he succeeded in gentrifying Troy with hindsight without damaging his coherency or his credibility or falsifying his nature. But his post-publication revisions of Oak go badly awry (as we saw in Chapter 4). Nothing quite so drastic in the way of character distortion occurs in his late, post-*Cornhill* revisions to Bathsheba, although he does fall into a minor pitfall at one point with a dislocated referent in a small revised passage in the coffin scene: this points to the loss of the object both on the page and in the mind. That is to say, the original creation, the living and breathing Bathsheba, is now lost from view as the object of both the grammatical sentence and the imagined vision. In the manuscript version, Liddy has entered the room a second time:

> the dark eyes which met hers had worn a listless weary look. When she went out after telling the story they had expressed wretchedness in full activity. This also sank to apathy after a time. But her thoughts, sluggish and confused at first, acquired more life as the minutes passed, and the dull misgiving in her brow and eyes suddenly gave way to the stillness of concentration.

This remains intact and unchanged for the *Cornhill*, with the exception of 'dark eyes' which become 'beautiful eyes'. However, for the Wessex edition, the section beginning 'This also sank to apathy' and ending 'stillness of concentration' is cancelled and replaced with the following:

> Her simple country nature, fed on old-fashioned principles, was troubled by that which would have troubled a woman of the world very little, both Fanny and her child, if she had one, being dead.

With the lack of a clear referent here, and an odd sense that Hardy is looking at the recently departed Liddy and not at all at the anguished Bathsheba now torn by bitter conflict, the narrative loses dramatic force

2—227

Bathsheba's face as she continued looking into the fire that evening might have excited solicitousness on her account even among those who loved her least. The sadness of Fanny Robin's fate did not make Bathsheba's glorious, although, *she was the Esther to this poor Vashti* *their fates might be supposed to stand in some respects* ~~~~ as contrasts to each other. When Liddy came into the room a second time the dark eyes which met hers had worn a listless weary look. When she went out after telling the story they had expressed wretchedness in full activity. This also sank to apathy after a time. But her thoughts, ~~from~~ sluggish & confused at first, acquired ~~~~ more life as the minutes passed, & the dull misgiving in her brow & eyes suddenly gave way to the stillness of concentration, ~~~~ ~~~~.

Bathsheba had *grounds for conjecturing a* ~~~~ connection *between* ~~~~ ~~~~ ~~her own history~~ *& the possible tragedy which may have ended Fanny's life* which Oak & Boldwood never for a moment suspected her of possessing. The meeting with the lonely woman on the previous Saturday night had been unwitnessed & unspoken of. Oak may have had the best of intentions in withholding for as *many* days as possible ~~away~~ the details of ~~~~ *what had happened; but* ~~had he known~~ that Bathsheba's *perceptions* ~~~~ had already ~~been~~ *exercised in the* ~~~~ *matter*, he would have done nothing to lighten

Facsimile 35 'the dark eyes . . . had worn a listless weary look' (MS 2–227)

155

as it drifts into discursive mode momentarily eclipsing the immediacy of Bathsheba's presence – in effect losing her living force! In the original manuscript version, Hardy had moved into her own consciousness to follow closely her various emotional and mental phases as she passes from worn listlessness and apathy through confusion to the sentience of 'the stillness of concentration'. But in the post-publication revised version this is entirely lost. In fact, by implying a rather dubious moral opposition of town and country, which seems spurious by any Hardyan standards, given his lifelong enthusiasm for 'country matters' and disparagement of citified prudery and pretence, the revised passage also acquires an oddly inauthentic voice. It seems to intervene between character and reader, forcing us to doubt our own judgement – after all, 'simple country nature' comes rather unexpectedly when the testimony has shown psychological complexity and an intriguing admixture of courage, daring, pride, weakness, ferocity and tenderness and a good deal more besides. Moreover this is a townborn woman, as Jacob testifies, and daughter of a 'gentleman-tailor' eccentrically inclined towards repeated bankruptcies, committing the 'seventh' with his own wife, and godfathering illegitimate children. So, where and when Bathsheba was 'fed on old-fashioned principles' remains a mystery. Even Uncle Everdene, Bathsheba's benefactor, kept a 'wet of a better class' for the likes of Jan Coggan, who enjoys a 'pretty tipple' and 'such lovely drunks' as were to be had in his house. Curiously, the only aspect that distinguishes this late, post-*Cornhill* revision and aligns it with the falsifying late revisions of Oak, *is* the moral aspect. While both sets of revisions mutilate text and characterisation, they also hint at an 'improving' moral tone – in this case, one that turns rather spuriously and rather vaguely on 'old-fashioned principles'.

Perhaps these late changes are no reliable index to Hardy's intentions. Could he be trusted with his novels at such a long distance from their origins? It is something of a paradox that as he was making these final changes in proof, in the 1890s, he felt that his closer attention should be devoted to proof-reading his poems. No printer, he said, could be trusted with verse.

Appendix 2

The dramatisation of Fanny's story and revisions to nomenclature

Name changes occur frequently throughout the holograph manuscript of *Far from the Madding Crowd*. This tallies with much of what we have already seen of Hardy's creative activity – his constant experimentation with morphologies, modalities and dialectal formations, and his constant juggling with his text which he elects to preserve in a state of mutability or indeterminacy for as long as possible before the day of publication. I am not assured, with Robert Schweik, that Hardy's name changes, cancelled numeration, refoliation and redrafting in general necessarily indicate an earlier (different) version of the book, or that Hardy had not originally intended to dramatise Fanny's story.[1] What is immensely valuable in Schweik's approach is his detailing of Hardy's self-borrowings from earlier drafts and notes. This is particularly illuminating in his essay, 'A first draft chapter of Hardy's *Far from the Madding Crowd*'.[2] Here, Schweik's perceptive analysis shows how adept Hardy was in his self-borrowings, in so far as portions of a swamp description from a redundant draft focusing on Troy's malfeasance are transferred and reshaped for use in Chapter XLIV, where the focus is now upon Bathsheba's Slough of Despond – so to speak. This provides a marvellous example of Hardy's imaginative ability to craft and reshape his text from the most unlikely material.

Hardy, in creating the manuscript of *Far from the Madding Crowd*, changes his mind repeatedly, and as Schweik shows, his skilful incorporation of early drafts reveals a fascinating and distinct progression from rough-note starts to literary finish. Reworking character and incident from preliminary drafts is characteristic of Hardy's approach to the literary creation of text, which is, for him, in some degree an extempore arrangement between himself and his narrators and characters. Much depends on how things shape up as they first appear on the page, then how they appear in improved (or otherwise) form in interlinear revision and proof changes. And when Hardy seizes the words and knocks them into shape, he is not always certain what they will make, and when they are made, whether or not he will keep them. But nothing, up until the denouement, alters his original vision, his overall conceptual framework. Just as Oak remains in Hardy's first conception of things and throughout the manuscript, patient, sturdy, uncomplicated and enduring,[3] and Bathsheba remains compelling, headstrong, passionate and sensitive, so Fanny too, remains tender, brave, gullible and stoic. She is vivid for Hardy from his very first glance at her in the redundant draft of the shearing-supper to his very last gaze upon her in her coffin 'framed in by that yellow hair of hers'.[4]

In the first instance, Hardy's cancelled numeration, throughout his manuscript, provides no evidence of late additions made to his manuscript (as both Schweik and Gatrell claim). The only evidence it provides is that of augmentation. There is nothing to suggest that this augmentation is not simply the recopying of earlier leaves in either an abbreviated or amplified form. Working on the assumption that Hardy, in the process of composing the manuscript, incorporated as much draft and notebook material as he possibly could, thus making numerous recopyings as he went along (which his foliation bears out), my own view of Hardy's early work on Fanny's role and his changes to Chapters VII and X (in which she features) is as follows. Leslie Stephen commends Hardy, in a letter dated 17 February 1874, for having 'judiciously reduced' the 'paying scene'. This – and not Hardy's 'decision to dramatise Fanny's story' – is, I believe, the cause of foliation changes to Chapter X (the paying scene) which was once considerably longer than it is now. For example, whereas Fanny is briefly mentioned (in the MS renumbered section) in Bathsheba's enquiry, to which one of the responses is that 'the new shepherd have been to Buck's Head . . . but nobody had seed her', the focus is not upon her, as yet, but almost entirely upon the paying scene ('judiciously reduced'). Since in the first foliation (FF = before cancellation) the story continues in its reduced form from the last passage in Chapter IX, where Bathsheba asks Maryann to show the workfolk into the hall (FF 106, MS), and picks up in Chapter X where Bathsheba enquires of Laban's wife, 'What woman is that?' (FF 107, MS), it appears that Hardy had certainly 'reduced' the 'paying scene' and now simply needs to condense and rewrite earlier parts of it (from the draft version) in order to bridge the gap from showing the men into the hall to actually dealing with the payroll.[5] Hence the rewritten leaves and the cancelled numeration: Chapter X now runs in the manuscript from page number 111 onwards.

Gatrell (following Schweik's idea) favours Chapter XI (barracks scene) as the turning point in Hardy's decision about Fanny's story. While disagreeing with Schweik's suggestion that Hardy's decision to dramatise Fanny's story came as a new idea this far into his composition, Gatrell does feel that 'the close sympathy felt by Gabriel for Fanny was a late thought on Hardy's part'. His reasons are, in part, that Chapter XI is clearly a 'patchwork from perhaps three periods of conception'. It has to be said, however, that this 'patchwork' quality is a characteristic of the entire manuscript. Moreover the most obvious 'patch' in Chapter XI consists of a 'set piece' on Melchester Moor which runs to a couple of pages. Again, there is nothing to indicate that Hardy's reworking of this chapter turns upon Fanny – rather it turns upon his lovingly painted portrait of the Melchester landscape (which he had either overwritten and now needed to condense, or had composed with hindsight – as with parts of the storm episode – and now wanted to insert). Gatrell also bases his claim for the 'new' closeness of the Fanny–Oak relationship upon the fact that in Chapter X it is mentioned that Oak has gone to look for Fanny at the Buck's Head; this, he says, makes it 'certain that some encounter must have taken place between Gabriel and Fanny on the original two leaves which Chapter VII now replaces. . . . the inn must have figured in some original meeting'. The inn certainly does figure in some original meeting, but not in one necessarily pre-existing the manuscript version. In Chapter VII, Fanny asks Oak: 'Do you know how late they keep open the Buck's Head Inn?' Where else, then, would he go in search for her?

Gatrell also finds Hardy's elaboration, in Chapter XLI, upon Fanny's hair, to be an indication of his 'new view of the event'. The manuscript shows a cancelled passage:

> You won't burn that curl of hair, and you said 'ties' just now, and Frank, that woman we met.
> O that's nothing, he said hastily. You like the woman . . .

Hardy revises this dialogue in interlinear revision and we now have:

> You won't burn that curl. You like the woman who owns that pretty hair –

and 'ties' is brought in a little later. Contrary to Gatrell's claim that the colour of Fanny's hair is 'newly stressed in the manuscript', there is, in fact, no further 'addition' to the original and, rather than seeing this dialogical interlinear revision as an altered view on Hardy's part, it seems to me to be quite simply a clarification of an important issue.[6] Bathsheba has to have some means of instantly identifying Fanny's corpse if Hardy is not to incur some delay in the action at this highly tense and dramatic moment in the coffin scene. Thus the issue of the 'curl' of hair in Chapter XLI must be drawn out a little more (it is too compacted in the manuscript version), and must also be made vivid and significant to allow the attentive reader a glimmer of *déjà vu*. For, of course, this moment for Bathsheba has been foreshadowed when it was *her* curl of hair that Troy kept in his pocket! Hence her intense emotional pain now as he springs open his watchcase revealing 'snugly stowed within it, a small coil of [golden] hair'. This is patently not the jet-black 'winding lock which he had severed from her manifold tresses' and had put carefully in his pocket in the seductive ferns scene!

Ultimately, Hardy's haphazard foliation[7] provides no clear guide to his purposes, except to indicate rewritten sections which cannot be determined as late entries, or as an 'altered' view on Hardy's part, since so many of them are clearly reworked from earlier set pieces or, as in the section we have looked at in Chapter X, the paying scene, from cancelled portions of an earlier draft.[8] Their main importance to our understanding of Hardy's creative mind at work is, as Schweik demonstrates, that they show a most complex patchwork arrangement of narrative composition.

As it happens, the major problem with Fanny is that Hardy is obliged to keep her on the periphery of the novel because of her 'fallen woman' status. Leslie Stephen was watching out, hawk-eyed, for each and every sign of impropriety from the outset (he had, early on, read the 'shearing-supper' draft), and, as is evident from his pencil markings in the manuscript, he pounced on anything remotely connected with Fanny at every opportunity.[9] With that kind of surveillance, Hardy would not have been inclined to feature Fanny more centrally, but it is evident from her appearance throughout the book – in her churchyard meeting with Oak, in her (rather fine – for a maidservant) letter to him, in the Melchester barracks scene, in the abortive wedding episode, in the memorable 'Casterbridge Highway' chapter, and so on, not to mention that she regularly crops up in conversations – that she remained fairly central in Hardy's imagination, from first to last. It is worth mentioning, in support of this view, that whereas Boldwood enters the scene with hindsight, and does not feature in Hardy's original description of his novel to Stephen (as depicting a young woman-farmer, a shepherd and a sergeant of cavalry), he, unlike Fanny Robin, does not at any point inhabit Hardy's local colorist's world. Boldwood lives in a farmhouse of indeterminate name and location (in the manuscript), and the extent of his movements in Wessex, as descriptively evoked by Hardy, goes no further than Casterbridge market-place. But – and this is one of the reasons why we feel her dramatic presence to be at the very centre of the story – Fanny is omnipresent in Hardy's Wessex. As Ian Gregor so aptly puts it: 'We are made to *walk* with Fanny.'[10] She inhabits the distant towns and nearby churchyards, and the highways and bridges and byways and thickets in between.[11] And even in her pauper's grave, she rests in ground poetically and iconoclastically hallowed by Hardy (an aspect of his iconoclasm that is to return for fuller treatment in *Tess* – with the joint outrage of both author and heroine at the church's attitude towards the burial of unbaptised infants). Fanny 'belongs' at the very epicentre of *Far from the Madding Crowd*: her story is a perennial for Hardy, and one he would have found it hard not to dramatise – we have only to think of her affinity with certain characters in his poems, such as Melia in 'The Ruined Maid' (in her fallen-woman role in the first draft of the shearing-supper),[12] or, in her death, with Fanny Hurd in 'Voices from Things Growing in a Churchyard',[13] or even, in her 'triumph' in death, with 'Friends Beyond' – one of Hardy's levelling poems which, in Fanny's case, shows an interesting affinity of theme.[14]

However, if Hardy's conceptual framework from first draft to holograph manuscript remains self-consistent, this does not by any means obviate evolutionary development within the mutable text. And a small part of this development arises from Hardy's poetic love of playing with words. Most of his changes to characters' names are, I think, purely playful. And he does not, as some scholars have claimed, confine these changes, in any manner of high-seriousness, to Oak, who was first named Strong. Nor to his occasionally ghosted counterpart, Poorgrass, who was first named Poorheed (I bow here to others, although this very often looks to me like Poorhead – which, of course, rather befits this man with the 'multiplying eye'). We also have Frank Troy who was, at one stage, Alfred; Temperance Miller who was originally Temperance Winkler; and Fanny Robin who was once Fanny Robbin. Then, in the customary way of Hardy's shufflings and jugglings, we have the following interlinear changes in the manuscript. Jacob Smallbury becomes Billy Smallbury (MS 1–59), Poorgrass's father becomes his 'granfer' (MS 1–75), Henery becomes Coggan (MS 1–85), Jacob Smallbury becomes Henery (MS 1–87), Laban Tall becomes Susan Small's husband (MS 1–95), and, as late as the April issue, Poorgrass becomes Fray and Fray becomes Moon (MS 1–198). By the time Hardy has reached Part 2 (the May issue) and the vexed shearing-supper chapter, he has more or less settled his nomenclature. But not absolutely: we find in his revisions for the Wessex edition that Mr Granthead, the surgeon (an appropriate name!), has now, for reasons that remain obscure, become Mr Aldritch.

Appendix 3

Revisions to topography

The following section outlines some of the topographical changes made by Hardy either in proof for the *Cornhill* or in revisions for the Osgood, McIlvaine complete collected edition (1895), hereafter called the Wessex version. These revisions were part of Hardy's scheme of bringing each text into line with the Wessex landscape he latterly developed into a coherent and self-consistent partly real, partly dream country.

Chapter I

Manuscript version:

> The field he was in sloped steeply to a ridge called Norcombe Hill, through an adjunct of which ran the highway from Norcombe to Casterbridge, sunk in a deep cutting.

Cornhill version:

> . . . Hill. Through a spur of this hill ran the highway from Norcombe to Casterbridge, sunk in a deep cutting.

Wessex version:

> . . . Hill. Through a spur of this hill ran the highway between Emminster and Chalk Newton.

Chapter II

Manuscript version:

> Norcombe Hill – forming part of Norcombe Ewelease, was one of the spots which suggest to a passer-by that he is in the presence of a shape approaching the indestructible as nearly as any to be found on earth.

Cornhill version: no change.

Wessex version:

> Norcombe Hill – not far from lonely Toller-Down – was one of the spots . . .

Chapter V

Manuscript version:

> she had gone to a place called Weatherbury, more than twenty miles off,

Cornhill version: no change.

Wessex version:

> . . . Weatherbury, nearly twenty miles off,

Chapter VI

Manuscript version:

> Where do you come from?
> Norcombe.
> That's a long way.
> Twenty miles.

Cornhill version: no change.

Wessex version:

> 'That's a long way.'
> 'Fifteen miles.'

Manuscript version:

> Where is Shottsford?
> Eight miles t'other side of Weatherbury.

Cornhill version: no change.

Wessex version:

> 'How far is Shottsford?'
> 'Ten miles t'other side of Weatherbury.'

Manuscript version:

> The path wended through water-meadows traversed by little brooks . . . the stream was marked with spots of white froth. . . . On the high road . . . leaves tapped the ground as they went along. . . . He passed through a wood . . .
> By the time he had walked half-a-dozen miles. . . . He ascended a hill and could just discern ahead of him a wagon . . .

Cornhill version: no change except for the substitution of 'pied' for 'marked'.

Wessex version:

> The road stretched through water-meadows . . . the stream was pied with spots of white froth. . . . On the higher levels . . . leaves tapped the ground as they bowled along. . . . He passed by Yalbury wood . . .
>
> By the time he had walked three or four miles. . . . He descended Yalbury Hill and could just discern . . .

Chapter VII

Manuscript version:

> The young girl remained motionless by the tree, and Gabriel descended into the village.

Cornhill version: no change.

Wessex version:

> . . . and Gabriel descended into the village of Weatherbury, or Lower Longpuddle as it was sometimes called.

Chapter X

Manuscript version:

> And the new shepherd have been to Buck's Head, thinking she had gone there,

Cornhill version: no change.

Wessex version:

> . . . Buck's Head, by Yalbury, thinking . . .

Chapter XI

Manuscript version:

> For dreariness nothing could surpass a prospect in the outskirts of the city of Melchester, at a later hour on this same snowy evening –

Cornhill version: no change.

Wessex version:

> . . . in the outskirts of a certain town and military station, many miles north of Weatherbury, at a later hour on this same snowy evening –

Manuscript version:

This climax . . . had been reached on Melchester Moor

Cornhill version: no change.

Wessex version:

. . . on the aforesaid moor

Manuscript version:

We are all of us as good as in Melchester gaol

Cornhill version: no change.

Wessex version:

. . . in the county gaol

Chapter XII

Manuscript version:

Farmer Everdene's niece; took on Weatherbury Lower Farm;

Cornhill version:

. . . took on Weatherbury Upper Farm;

Wessex edition: no change.

Chapter XVIII

Manuscript version:

Boldwood was tenant of what was called Weatherbury Lower Farm,

Cornhill version: no change.

Wessex version:

. . . of what was called Little Weatherbury Farm.

Chapter XXXI

Manuscript version:

She had walked nearly two miles . . . when she beheld advancing over the hill the very man she sought so anxiously to elude.

Cornhill version: no change.

Cancelled Words

Wessex version:

> . . . she beheld advancing over Yalbury Hill the very man . . .

Chapter XXXII

Manuscript version:

> Again they hastened on. Coggan's watch struck two.

Cornhill version: no change.

Wessex version:

> Again they hastened on, and entered Blackmore Vale. Coggan's watch struck two.

Chapter XXXIII

Manuscript version:

> Cainy's grandfather. . . . Invented a' apple tree. . . . A Quarrington grafted on a Tom Putt

Cornhill version: no change.
Wessex version:

> . . . A Quarrenden grafted on to a Tom Putt

Note: Apple varieties are sometimes named after the people who 'invented' them, as also after their place of origin.

Chapter XXXIV

Manuscript version:

> Just arrived from Melchester, I think?

Cornhill version: no change.

Wessex version:

> 'Just arrived from up the country, I think?'

Chapter XXXIX

Manuscript version:

> On the turnpike road, between Casterbridge and Weatherbury, and a mile from the latter place, is one of those steep long ascents which pervade the highways of this undulating district.

Cornhill version: no change.

Wessex version:

> . . . between Casterbridge and Weatherbury, and about three miles from the former place, is Yalbury Hill, one of those steep long ascents which pervade the highways of this undulating part of South Wessex.

Manuscript version:

> Never did I see such a day as 'twas! 'Tis a wild open place, not far from the sands, and a drab sea

Cornhill version: no change.

Wessex version (post-Osgood, 1895):

> . . . a wild open place, just out of Budmouth, and a drab sea

Chapter XL

Manuscript version:

> Thus she progressed till the beginning of a long rail fence came into view. She staggered across to the first post, clung to it, and looked around. Another milestone was on the opposite side of the way.

Cornhill version:

> . . . beginning of a long railed fence. . . . milestone was on the opposite side of the road.

Wessex version:

> Thus she progressed till descending Mellstock Hill another milestone appeared, and soon the beginning of an iron-railed fence came into view. She staggered across to the first post, clung to it, and looked around.

Manuscript version:

> The half-mile stood now before the sick and weary woman like a stolid Juggernaut. . . . The road here ran across a level plateau with only a bank on either side. She surveyed the wide space . . . and lay down on the bank.

Cornhill version: no change.

Wessex version:

> . . . The road here ran across Durnover Moor, open to the road on either side. She surveyed the wide space . . . and lay down against a guard-stone of the bridge.

Chapter XLII

Manuscript version:

As the clock from the tower of St George's church pointed to five minutes to three

Cornhill version: no change.

Wessex version:

As the clock over the South-street Alms-house pointed . . .

Manuscript version:

Situated by the roadside in the midst of this wood was the old inn Buck's Head.

Cornhill version: no change.

Wessex version:

At the roadside hamlet called Roy-Town, just beyond this wood, was the old inn Buck's Head.

Chapter XLVIII

Manuscript version:

Her husband was drowned . . . in Carrow Cove.

Note: 'Carrow' is inscribed in the manuscript in a carefully marked hand on the outer margin of the leaf. It looks as though Hardy was undecided at the time of writing and left a small space for a later inclusion of the name.

Cornhill version: no change.

Wessex version:

. . . in Lulstead Cove [shortly after changed to Lulwind].

Manuscript version:

and bore her along the pavement to the Three Choughs Inn.

Cornhill version: no change.

Wessex version:

. . . to the Kings Arms.

Chapter L

Manuscript version:

> Greenhill was the Nijni Novgorod of Wessex

Cornhill version: no change.

Wessex version:

> Greenhill was the Nijni Novgorod of South Wessex

Manuscript version:

> Gabriel . . . accompanied them along the way – Old George the dog of course behind them.

Cornhill version: no change.

Wessex version:

> . . . along the way, through the decayed old town of Kingsbere, and upward to the plateau, – old George the dog . . .

Chapter LI

Manuscript version:

> They soon passed the merry stragglers in the immediate vicinity of the hill, and got upon the high road.

Cornhill version: no change.

Wessex version:

> . . . vicinity of the hill, traversed Kingsbere, and got upon the high road.

Chapter LIV

Manuscript version:

> Boldwood passed into the high road. . . . walked at an even steady pace by Buck's Head, along the dead level beyond, mounted Casterbridge Hill, and between eleven and twelve o'clock descended into the town.

Cornhill version: no change.

Wessex version:

> . . . high road . . . walked at an even steady pace over Yalbury Hill,

along the dead level beyond, mounted Mellstock Hill, and between eleven and twelve o'clock crossed the Moor into the town.

Chapter LV

Manuscript version:

After waiting half-an-hour a faint dust was seen in the expected quarter, and shortly after a travelling-carriage, bringing one of the two judges on that circuit came up the hill and halted on the top.

Cornhill version:

At the end of half-an-hour . . .

Wessex version:

At the end of half-an-hour . . . one of the two judges on the Western Circuit, came up the hill . . .

There are several altered chapter headings made in proof revisions for the *Cornhill*, but only one significant topographical change for the Wessex version. This occurs in Chapter XI, which Hardy originally entitles, 'Melchester Moor: snow: a meeting'. This remains intact for the *Cornhill* but is later altered for the Wessex version to 'Outside the Barracks – Snow – A Meeting'. This alteration conforms to Hardy's practice in his post-*Cornhill* revisions of eliminating most references to Melchester (Salisbury), where originally he had stressed this as the location for the barracks of the Dragoon Guards and Fanny's destination in her long walk from South to Mid-Wessex.

Notes

1 Preamble

1 See F.E. Hardy, *The Life of Thomas Hardy, 1840–1928* (London: Macmillan, 1962), p. 99. Although written under his second wife's name, *The Life of Thomas Hardy*, hereafter referred to as the *Life*, was largely drafted by Hardy himself.
2 *Life*, op. cit., p. 100.
3 See details in my Foreword. Hardy's letter (now attached to the front endpage of the holograph manuscript), referring to the discovery of his manuscript in 1918, is printed in full in Volume 5 of *The Collected Letters of Thomas Hardy, 1914–1919*, edited by Richard Little Purdy and Michael Millgate (Oxford: The Clarendon Press, 1978–90), pp. 243–4.

   Given Hardy's modest appraisal of the worth of his manuscript (see the excerpt from his letter in the Foreword), it may be of interest to note that first editions of his novels were, by 1918, fetching a high price at Sothebys. First editions of *Far from the Madding Crowd*, in particular, had a scarcity value that placed them second only to *Desperate Remedies* in the estimation of prospective buyers. Hardy might have enjoyed the irony implicit in the fact that whereas he had had to finance *Desperate Remedies* for publication himself, and whereas this first published novel had been remaindered rather shortly afterwards, by 1916 it was fetching the highest price, in the salerooms, of all his first editions! See Henry Danielson, *The First Editions of the Writings of Thomas Hardy and their Values* (London: George Allen & Unwin Ltd, 1916). A copy of this book is held in the Beinecke library at Yale University.

   For Hardy's personal account of the rediscovery of his manuscript, see the *Life*, p. 385.
4 Hardy began his literary career with *The Poor Man and the Lady* (1868), which was rejected by his publisher who, nevertheless, recommended that he try his hand at a Wilkie Collins-type novel. The melodramatic sensation-novel *Desperate Remedies* was the outcome (1871), and despite feeling almost suicidal about the savagery of one critical attack, Hardy went on to write his first rural novel, *Under the Greenwood Tree* (1872), which was received favourably. This led to an invitation to write a serialised novel, *A Pair of Blue Eyes* (1873), which brought acclaim from Coventry Patmore and a success which surpassed Hardy's expectations. It was, however, his achievement in writing a best-selling novel for *The Cornhill Magazine*, a leading literary periodical commanding, at this time, a wide and sophisticated readership and considerable high esteem, that brought Hardy into the limelight. *Far from the Madding Crowd* was published seven times in 1874 alone, twice in London, and five times in America,

171

and Hardy was now launched upon a career as a novelist, which he was to
pursue with huge success for another two decades.

5 See, for example, Stephen's own account of his ethical concerns in his remi-
niscences entitled, *Some Early Impressions*, 1903, reissued by Burt Franklin, New
York, 1924. See also Frederick William Maitland, *The Life and Letters of Leslie
Stephen* (London: Duckworth & Co., 1906), pp. 266, 276.

6 Of the verso augmentations made in the manuscript, all of which take the form
of reflective commentary – frequently ironic in tone – eight are given over to
Bathsheba, three to Troy, three to scenic/artistic observations, two to the rustics
and two to Oak.

7 It is customary for Stephen to recommend changes in proof. As, for example,
in his letter to Hardy of 17 February 1874, where he says in reference to the
proposed cuts to the sheep-shearing scene.

> Very likely, it will be best for you to see the whole in print before acting;
> if so, let it go to the press as it stands.

Or, alternatively, in a letter of 12 March 1974, where he explains that he himself
has 'ventured to leave out a line or two in the last batch of proofs'; or, yet
again, in a letter of 13 April, where he tells Hardy that,

> these changes can be easily made when the story is in type and I shall
> send it to the printers now; and ask you to do what is necessary to the
> proofs.

(For these letters in full, see Richard Little Purdy, *Thomas Hardy: A Bibliographical
Study* (Oxford: The Clarendon Press, 1968), pp. 337–9.)

8 Trevor Johnson tells me that when Edward Thomas (c. 1916), submitted his
poem 'Lob' with the line, 'That Mother Dunch's buttocks should not lack/Their
name was his [Lob's] care . . .', this was objected to and subsequently changed
to 'That Happer Snapper Hanger should not lack'. It seems (even in poetry)
that 'buttocks' was still unacceptable some forty years on!

9 With Troy's departure in Chapter XLVII, serialised in the October issue, this
temporal correspondence abruptly ceases. The November instalment shoots
ahead to the following spring in Chapter XLIX, then to the autumn in Chapter
L. The December instalment moves forward to Christmas Eve in Chapter LII,
to the following spring in Chapter LVI, and concludes the novel vaguely, 'some
time after', with Bathsheba's marriage to Oak. This last, in terms of time and
space, is the 'foggiest' episode in the entire book.

10 *Life*, op. cit., p. 100.

11 See Maitland, op. cit., pp. 266–7. Maitland does not name the recipient of this
letter. He writes: 'the following words from a letter, written in 1867, will show
us that the editor of the *Cornhill* was not likely to sympathise with any revolts
against English traditions.

> You say you have been reading some French novels lately. . . . On which I
> could be voluminous.

Though this is criticism in undress, it sufficiently indicates an opinion that
Stephen maintained to the end of his life' (Maitland pp. 266–7).

12 Stephen to Hardy, 30 November 1872. Published in Richard Little Purdy, op.
cit., pp. 336–7.

13 See Maitland, op. cit., p. 270. See also Hardy's account in the *Life*, pp. 95–6.

14 For a fuller discussion of symbolic action in the sheep-shearing scene see
Rosemarie Morgan, *Women and Sexuality in the Novels of Thomas Hardy* (London
and New York: Routledge & Kegan Paul, 1988), pp. 54–6. See also, Robert C.

Schweik's discussion of symbolic action in the fir plantation episode in, 'The narrative structure of *Far from the Madding Crowd*', in *Budmouth Essays on Thomas Hardy*, ed.: F. B. Pinion (Dorchester Thomas Hardy Society, 1976), p. 34.

15 As indicated in the title which refers (subversively) to the line in Gray's 'Elegy': 'Far from the madding crowd's ignoble strife'.

16 There is a definite tendency towards genre-breaking in certain Victorian literary forms of melodrama; a kind of dissolution of the traditional boundaries of the genre which, according to its established conventions, may be broadly defined as a heavily stylised form of sensational/romantic stagework relying on extravagance for its artistic effects (Martin Meisel, in *Realizations: Narrative, Pictorial, and Theatrical Arts in Nineteenth-Century England* (Princeton, NJ: Princeton University Press, 1983) points to a similar tendency towards genre-breaking in the Victorian narrative poem). Hardy's form and style dissolves fluently from the melodramatic staginess of, say, Troy's death, into the psychological realism of Bathsheba's shock as she methodically, but numbly, lays out his body for the coroner; there is no apparent attempt, on Hardy's part, to establish a bridging discourse, a tonal shift, or any narrative indicator of genre readjustment; similarly Dickens, in his treatment of Nancy's violent death in *Oliver Twist*, where he slips almost imperceptibly from the weird and grotesque hyperbole of melodrama to the blunt, brutal, and horribly factual blow-by-blow account of a woman's death by beating.

A fairly reliable measure of melodrama lies in its scenic potential for the 'musical' or melody-drama. As these events are narrated in the novel, it is hard to imagine either Nancy's murder or Bathsheba's laying-out of Troy's body as scenically (or tonally and dramatically) appropriate to melody-drama, whereas preceding and subsequent scenes in both Hardy and Dickens present no such conceptual problem, as the producers of the musical *Oliver* discovered. A modern parallel to this kind of genre-breaking in Hardy and Dickens might be the cinematic method of juxtaposing film animation and 'live' performance in the same scene.

2 'What sort of man is this?'

1 This is an allusion to the Cretan poet Epimenides, who uttered the paradox, 'All Cretans are liars'. This overweighty allusion thus undermines less than it ironises. Hardy clearly assumes an educated reader in his literary and classical borrowings and, although the *Saturday Review* (9 January 1875) rebuked him for his 'clumsy and inelegant metaphors', this did not deter him, throughout his career in fiction, from incorporating his extensive reading into the fabric of his novels. The pleasure this stylistic treatment gave him – 'the word', he said, 'is meant to express something more than literary finish' – no doubt evoked a similar pleasure in the more learned among his audience who were thus invited to share with the author the ambiguity, wit or irony of an allusion which also offered the pleasurable satisfaction of recognition. This quote by Hardy is taken from his article 'The profitable reading of fiction' which first appeared in *Forum* (New York), in March 1888, pp. 57–70. It is reprinted in *Thomas Hardy's Personal Writings*, ed. Harold Orel (New York: St Martin's Press, 1990), pp. 110–25.

2 Nevertheless we may glean, from Stephen's letters to Hardy, something of the continuous and subtle pressure he puts on his susceptible author to submit to his own critical views. There is, for example, the cumulative effect and, no doubt to Hardy, the palpable effect, of 'objections' raised (however mildly expressed) in each and every editorial letter sent during the months of Hardy's most creative writing period in 1874. Stephen clearly intends giving Hardy the

impression that the author has the final say; this is what I would call his 'overt message'; but on closer examination a more complex and even contradictory set of meta-messages begins to emerge. For instance, Stephen begins, in January, by congratulating Hardy on the reception of his first 'number'; then goes on to advise alterations to Chapters XV and XVI; then concludes by saying:

> The story comes out very well, I think, and I have no criticisms to make. In Chap X the paying scene is judiciously reduced and I think is now satisfactory.

So, clearly, 'criticisms' have already been made (of Chapter X); and whether they have been made in letters that are no longer extant or have not yet been found the meta-message is, as Stephen's tone subtly conveys with the repetition of 'I think', that while he is offering congratulations on the one hand, with the other he is offering a kind of half-withheld approval that makes one feel he expects to be pleased a little better. Given that Chapter X still contains abbreviated references to both Baily Pennyways and Fanny Robin in precisely that section now 'judiciously reduced' (see Appendix B for more details), and given that Pennyways is evidently meant to be well informed about Fanny's exploits (as in the cancelled section of the shearing-supper, where he speaks of her as 'too well-off to be anything but a ruined woman'), it may well be that the 'judicious' cuts requested of Hardy to Chapter X involved excising 'objectionable' references of a similar kind. Nothing else explains the cuts to this chapter, which otherwise stands as a humorous and highly entertaining episode dramatically setting off the dismal event which follows – namely Fanny's long and futile trek through the winter snow in the hope of nuptials with Troy at Melchester. The point is that Hardy has evidently dealt, in Chapter X, with one set of objections and is now faced, in Chapters XV and XVI with more – not an altogether encouraging prospect. However, it is in Stephen's February letter, in which he deals directly with the shearing-supper chapter, due to appear in the May issue of the *Cornhill*, where we find him at his most subtly coercive. On the basis that the preceding chapter dealing with the sheep-shearing is 'rather long', he recommends that Hardy should:

> simply omit the chapter headed the 'shearing supper' and to add a few paragraphs to the succeeding or preceding, just explaining that there has been a supper. . . . I don't know whether anything turns on the bailiff's story; but I don't think it necessary. . . . I shall take the MS to Smith and Elder's today and will tell them that they will hear from you. Please write to them (to S.E. & Co 15 Waterloo Place S.W.) and say whether the whole is to be printed as it stands; or whether the chapter I mention is to be omitted; or whether you would like to have the MS again to alter previously to printing. Do whichever your judgement commends.

So evidently the 'bailiff's story' is still causing difficulties! It is at this point that one doubts whether Stephen intended to leave Hardy with any judgement whatsoever to commend, for he now goes on to say:

> I have heard of the story from many people and have only heard one opinion of its merits, wh. coincides with my own. As it goes on and gets more into the action, I am sure that the opinion will be higher still.

(See Purdy, *Thomas Hardy: A Bibliographical Study* (Oxford: The Clarendon Press, 1968), pp. 337–8, for the complete version of these letters.) 'Only . . . one opinion of its merits': Stephen here adopts the not uncommon way of inflicting hurt without seeming to do so by repeating criticism from other sources. Certainly Hardy (painfully sensitive to criticism) would have endowed Stephen's words with the darkest possible meaning; and, certainly, he rushes, the very same day, to report back his good intentions to Stephen and to express his willingness – no, indeed his anxiety – to 'give up any points which may be desirable in a story when read as a whole' (*Life*, p. 100). And although he does resist Stephen in keeping the shearing-supper, he writes immediately – again the very same day – to Smith, Elder & Co., to ask for the return of his manuscript for reconsideration, and instantly rewrites the entire chapter.

3 It is not possible to determine from all of this quite how much a part of Hardy's response to Stephen, at this early stage of their acquaintance, had to do with his sense of intimidation. How bitterly reactive, angry, self-mutilating and defensive he might have felt can only be gauged by his 'willingness' to concede to his editor's authority over his own authorised text. This mirrors his response – throughout his entire novel-writing career – to negative criticism which follows a similar pattern of self-annihilating tendencies. From his first suicidal wish to be 'dead', following an unfavourable review of *Desperate Remedies* (*Life*, p. 84), to his last despairing cry, following the furore over *Jude*, that 'if he wished to retain any shadow of self-respect' he should simply give up writing novels altogether (*Life*, p. 291), Hardy encounters his critics at a level of such highly suppressed aggression and rage that, in becoming introverted and morbid, this becomes in turn self-destructive: he would either annihilate himself or his self's fictional creation.

As to the aspect of literary reputation and Stephen's more immediate, self-regarding concerns, I should mention that at this time (1874) Stephen was not only deeply committed to the press as a powerful shaper of public opinion, but he also had the literary repute and renown that Hardy, at this stage of his career, did not have. Hardy was merely the anonymous author of *Far from the Madding Crowd*.

4 These allusions linking Troy with the world of Greek culture are either deliberately mock-heroic ('sacrifices to Venus'), playfully ironic ('Cretan Liars'), or even deliberately incongruous – the citizens of Corinth were renowned for a life of dissipation and love of luxury the likes of which an enlisted soldier at Melchester barracks will never encounter! At the same time they serve to isolate Troy from the rustic community for whom Hardy customarily reserves biblical allusions. If, in his use of Greek allusions here, Hardy seems more intent upon impressing his reader than buttressing his own characterisation by reinforcing his air of benevolence concerning Troy, or endowing his microcosmic Wessex world with the universality of the macrocosm, he himself would justify his technique on two counts. The first is that in his view the most elusive of tropes is not the less auspicious for its obscurity:

> the appreciative, perspicacious reader . . . will see what his author is aiming at, and by affording full scope to his own insight, catch the vision which the writer has in his eye, and is endeavouring to project upon the paper, even while it half eludes him.
>
> (T. Hardy, 'The profitable reading of fiction' in H. Orel (ed.), *Thomas Hardy's Personal Writings* (New York: St Martin's Press, p. 117))

And the second, with a keen eye to the *craft* of fiction:

> The whole secret of fiction and the drama – in the constructional part – lies in the adjustment of things unusual to things external and universal. The writer who knows exactly how exceptional, and how non-exceptional, his events should be made, possesses the key to the art.
>
> (*Life*, p. 252)

Clearly, the *Saturday Review* did not accord to Hardy that 'key': 'eccentricities of style are not characteristic of genius, nor of original thinking' (9 January 1875). And, indubitably, Hardy's experimental play with allusive words and phrases allows for considerable extratextual interruption and obtrusion in his prose. If this stylistic 'eccentricity' does not conform to genre specifications, no doubt he would be the first to smile.

5 The original (cancelled) word looks like 'modestly'.

6 This chapter was originally entitled, 'A morning meeting: the letter: a question', but is changed in proof for the *Cornhill* to read, 'A Morning Meeting: the Letter Again'. The omission of the 'question' may well indicate that originally the discussion about Troy ('What sort of man is this?') featured more centrally, and (knowing Hardy) possibly contained rather more injudicious material than Stephen would allow – notably the mention of the unmentionable 'infant'.

7 Stephen to Hardy, 12 March 1874. Purdy, op. cit. pp. 338–9.

8 As later with 'honest girls' (see note 8 to Chapter 8), Liddy's use of 'virtue' implies a silent nod and a wink at an expression intended to convey the opposite of its conventional meaning. 'Virtue', meaning 'chastity' in Victorian parlance, makes mischief as Liddy uses the word (tongue-in-cheek) to suggest not its presence but its absence.

9 In Chapter XXIV, the fir plantation scene, Troy makes a witty play on words (Bathsheba's gimp being 'knotted' in his spur) with the line 'I wish it had been the knot of knots, which there's no untying'. This echoes Thomas Campbell's line from his song 'How Delicious is the Winning'.

In Chapter XXVI, the 'hay-mead' scene, Troy refers to himself as 'a plain blunt man', which is an allusion to Mark Antony's 'I am no orator, as Brutus is:/ But, as you know me all, a plain blunt man/ That love my friend' (*Julius Caesar*, III. ii. 222). Troy, like Antony, is aware of the ironic ambiguity of his words.

Shortly afterwards, he quotes a French proverb:

– and there's a proverb they have, *Qui aime bien châtie bien* – 'He chastens who loves well'.

And later, in the same scene, he begs Bathsheba not to 'take away the one little ewe-lamb of pleasure that I have in this dull life of mine'. This alludes to 2 Samuel 12:3, where a poor man has 'nothing but one little ewe lamb'.

Following hard upon these words, the motto on Troy's watch, *Cedit amor rebus*, is translated from Latin by this sergeant of cavalry! The motto comes from Ovid's *Remedia Amoris* I, 144.

In Chapter XXXV, on taking occupation of Bathsheba's farmstead, Troy says he feels 'like new wine in an old bottle', which are Jesus's words in Mark 2:22, 'And no man putteth new wine into old bottles'. And in Chapter XLVII, as he struggles with the treacherous currents at Lulwind Cove, he recalls the comic prayer for death from *The Tempest* (I.i. 71) where Gonzalo 'would fain die a dry death'.

More aptly in line with Hardy's own pagan allusions made in reference to himself, Troy speaks of Bathsheba as this 'Juno-wife of mine' – Juno was a Roman goddess who was both sister and wife of Jupiter (Chapter LII); and later in the same chapter, he alludes to a ballad by Monk Lewis (1775–1818), 'Alonzo the Brave and Fair Imogene', when he speaks of himself as a 'sort of Alonzo the Brave' who will enter Boldwood's party where all 'the guests will sit in silence and fear, and all burn blue'. These words echo Lewis's: 'All pleasure and laughter were hush'd at his sight/ The dogs as they eyed him drew back in affright/ The lights in the chamber burnt blue!' But unlike the disdained suitor in Lewis's poem, Troy is not the deserted lover here. He is presumably using these words self-mockingly.

10 This literariness may of course be attributed to Troy's schooling. But I am persuaded here by Peter Coxon's comment that Hardy, in the *Life*, stresses his own mother's literariness, that 'she appears to have mollified her troubles by reading every book she could lay hands on' (p. 12). Given that Hardy was still under his mother's wing while writing *Far from the Madding Crowd* at his childhood home in Bockhampton, and that he, self-confessedly, incorporated into his fiction the real world around him at the time, it seems reasonable to suppose that a 'literary mother' not only became extended into his wish-fulfilment dreams, but also vividly filled his creative imagination.

11 More customarily one thinks, in this context, of Hardy's lost 'prizes' – the Lizbies, Tryphenas, Elizas, Florences and maybe even Emma, who lived on in his imagination and poems in seeming proportion to the poet's own unresolved conflicts of attachment, rejection and loss. Tess, though, about whom Hardy could say that no one would ever know how much she meant to him, is perhaps the most notable of his literary creations to haunt his poetic imagination. For the following, see *The Complete Poems of Thomas Hardy*, ed. James Gibson (London: Macmillan, 1976).

    For Lizbie: 'To Lizbie Browne' (ibid., p. 130).
    For Tryphena: 'Thoughts of Phena' (ibid., p. 62).
    For Eliza: 'She, to Him, I, II, III, IV' (ibid., pp. 14–16).
    For Florence (Henniker): 'A Broken Appointment' (ibid., p. 136).
    For Emma: 'When I Set Out for Lyonesse' (ibid., p. 312).
    For Tess: 'Tess's Lament' (ibid., p. 175).

12 Robert Schweik's analysis of the shore section in 'The narrative structure of *Far from the Madding Crowd*' (op. cit., p. 36), discusses Hardy's revisions here as heightening reader suspense as the story builds up to its melodramatic climax.

13 Phillip Mallett adds here that Troy's return sets up one of the rules of Wessex as a fictional world, that those who leave always return! (Clym, Angel, Newson, Arabella, etc.).

14 Dick Turpin was a highwayman of historical renown who featured as a character in Harrison Ainsworth's melodramatic Gothic novel, *Rookwood* (1834). It has also been suggested that Hardy drew inspiration from Ainsworth's novel for his storm scene. See Penelope Vigar, *The Novels of Thomas Hardy: Illusion and Reality* (London: The Athlone Press, 1974), pp. 101–23. See also, Carl Weber, *Hardy of Wessex: His Life and Literary Career* (New York, 1965), pp. 9–10, and F. B. Pinion, *A Hardy Companion* (London: Macmillan, 1968), p. 154.

    'Noachian' comes from the Hebrew 'Noach' which refers to Noah (descendent of Adam) and, in common parlance, to objects that are antique or ancient.

3 'The proper artistic balance'

1 F. E. Hardy, *The Life of Thomas Hardy, 1841–1928* (London: Macmillan, 1962), p. 100. (Shortened ref.: *Life*.)

2 This occurs in the October issue. Hardy hurriedly wrote and corrected the last few chapters in late July and early August. If we can go by the evidence of Stephen's letters, these chapters were destined for the November/December issues and cover the sequence from Troy's disappearance to his return at

Greenhill Fair through to the finish. These chapters not only break with Hardy's time scheme of matching the internal seasons of his Weatherbury world to those beyond the novel, they also compress one-and-a-half years of action into nine chapters, including one betrothal, one murder and one marriage.

3 I share with Roy Morrell the view that the end of *Far from the Madding Crowd* 'is emphatically not a romantic happy-ever-after affair'. See Morrell, *Thomas Hardy: The Will and the Way* (Kuala Lumpur: University of Malaya Press, 1965), pp. 59–64.

4 *Life*, op. cit., p. 100.

5 ibid., p. 101.

6 The 'peculiar attractiveness' of the mentor is one thing. But as Hardy's lifelong friend, Mrs Anne Benson Proctor, put it in her characteristically forthright manner when she discovered 'the divine Hardy' in the pages of *Belgravia* (and not in the *Cornhill*), for the publication of *The Return of the Native*:

> I suppose Hardy could not stand Leslie Stephen; I could not.

Mrs Proctor, a prominent 'salon' member of the London literati who once told Hardy she was his 'truest friend' and was most certainly one of his greatest admirers, spent countless lively hours with him at her flat in Queen Anne's Mansions. There, they gossiped and debated and enjoyed the company of writers, artists, critics and poets from all walks of life. This feisty old lady had a particular fascination for Hardy. He relished her wit, her outspoken opinions, her intuitive perception of people and relationships, and there was no doubt that she knew something sufficiently substantial about his relationship with Stephen that not only allowed her to be perfectly blunt about it but also led others to quote her on it – including Hardy himself! (See sections on Mrs Proctor in the *Life*.)

7 Hardy later repeated this disclaimer to Blackwood over the publication of *The Return of the Native*. He wishes to insist that:

> should there accidentally occur any word or reflection not in harmony with the general tone of the magazine, you would be quite at liberty to strike it out if you chose. I always mention this to my editors, as it simplifies matters.
>
> (Michael Millgate, *Thomas Hardy: A Biography* (Oxford and Melbourne: Oxford University Press, 1982), p. 188)

However, we should bear in mind that Leslie Stephen, to whom Hardy had earlier offered *The Return of the Native*, was already demurring, and that Hardy, now anxious about publication, was no doubt willing to supplicate at all costs. Blackwood declined, in turn, and the serial version was finally published by *Belgravia*, at a figure (£20 for each instalment) substantially less than Hardy had received for *The Hand of Ethelberta*. Evidently, neither Stephen nor Blackwood felt sufficiently reassured by Hardy's words to assuage their fears that the relationships in *The Return of the Native* might not (in Stephen's words), 'develop into something too "dangerous" for a family magazine'. Hardy's claim that 'it simplifies matters' was apparently taken by his editors as a statement of form not of intent.

8 For further elaboration see Millgate, op. cit., p. 171.

9 Millgate observes of *Ethelberta*, that 'instead of building upon the success of *Far from the Madding Crowd* . . . Hardy set off, with what seems in retrospect an almost perverse determination, upon an entirely different tack' (ibid., p. 173); and shortly after the publication of this social comedy, Stephen himself

Notes

tried to persuade Hardy to follow his true bent (as Stephen saw it) – his own 'perfectly fresh and original vein' as in *Far from the Madding Crowd*, and to follow, above all others, the novelist George Sand, 'whose country stories seem to me perfect and have a certain affinity to yours' (Stephen to Hardy, 16 May 1876. See Maitland, *The Life and Letters of Leslie Stephen* (London: Duckworth & Co., 1906), pp. 291–1).

Of Hardy's progress with *The Return of the Native*, Millgate comments, first that,

> Because he expected only a relatively small financial reward . . . Hardy was prepared to pursue other forms of literary remuneration

and second that,

> He had striven more deliberately than ever before to make the book an unmistakeable work of art, not just another run-of-the-mill serial, and hence to prove himself not merely a good serial hand but . . . 'a great stickler for the proper artistic balance of the completed work'.

And third:

> But while the critical reception of the work . . . was indeed characterised by general respect for Hardy as an artist, it displayed a disappointment . . . as a manifestation of that art.

(Millgate, op. cit., pp. 195–8)

10 See also the *Life*, pp. 98–9.
11 I would agree, in general, with Rosemary Sumner's observation that Hardy's tendency,

> to tell editors that he is writing a story suitable for their magazines, a story which will, he thinks, be entirely 'proper', and then to find that it is going in quite a different direction and proving itself quite unsuitable for serial production, demonstrates his intuitive understanding of human beings, and his honesty in portraying them; in spite of bowdlerisation for magazines, he refused, in most of his final versions, to force events and characters into a preconceived direction.

(Rosemary Sumner, *Thomas Hardy: Psychological Novelist* (London and Basingstoke: Macmillan, 1981), p. 4)

But given the tendency, in his later novels, to 'pay homage to the human scale', as Gillian Beer puts it, 'by ceasing as the hero or heroine dies', there is every sense that Hardy's closure of *Far from the Madding Crowd* forces events and characters, if not into a 'preconceived direction', at any rate into serial form requirements. See Gillian Beer, *Darwin's Plots* (London, Boston, Melbourne, Henley: Routledge & Kegan Paul, 1983), p. 239.
12 Peter Coxon brings to my attention the 'sun on red' image which remained vivid in Hardy's memory from recollections of the sunset beams on the Venetian red of the staircase at Bockhampton. This memory is recorded in the *Life*, where Hardy recalls that the sunset glow added 'great intensity' to the colour red. Sun-on-red also pairs Bathsheba imagistically, with Troy, her soldier-lover, who later enters the scene also cutting a handsome figure in his crimson jacket. Bathsheba is also paired with Troy in being aligned with Venus and other pagan deities to which Hardy alludes (as with Troy) with light irony – notably where she sweeps out of the hall on payday, in her new role as bailiff, and is described as a 'small thesmothete' (the name given to high judges in ancient Athens); or where, in the Cornmarket, she is seen as 'a queen among these

179

gods of the fallow, like a little sister of a little Jove' (Chapter XII). 'Jove' is derived from Jovis, the genitive of the Latin name for Jupiter, the chief of the Roman gods. Earlier (Chapter X) Hardy had observed, on Gabriel's behalf:

> But perhaps her air was the inevitable result of the social rise which had advanced her from a cottage to a large house and fields. The case is not unexampled in high places. When, in the writings of the later poets, Jove and his family are found to have moved from their cramped quarters on the peak of Olympus into the wide sky above it, their words show a proportionate increase of arrogance and reserve.

This weighty allusion invites the reader to share a smile with the author at the mock-elevation of Bathsheba's status, at her own high-seriousness in her own role, and at poor Gabriel's perplexity who sees nothing to smile about at all!

13 Hardy names Milton (in this allusion) for the first time between the serial and first edition. In Milton's *Paradise Lost*, book 4, Satan looks down on Paradise while sitting 'like a Cormorant' in the Tree of Life.

14 'Innocent' is changed in proof for the *Cornhill* to 'nesh young' – possibly Stephen, unlike Hardy, found the original adjective inappropriate to an unmarried mother.

'Nesh young' does not, however, fulfil Liddy's meaning here. In traditional Christian ghostlore, youth alone does not disallow for the unrested spirit's night-walking, whereas 'innocence' does. The belief is that the unrested spirit (or ghost) is condemned to walk the earth until released from earthly burdens of sin or lack of spiritual grace, both of which may be purged by a mediating act on the part of the living. Prayer, acts of penitence, martydom and so forth, are deemed acts of mediation, as also (in pre-Lutheran tradition) the vindicating act of revenge – as demanded of Hamlet. Therefore, in keeping with ghostloric tradition, no innocent soul passes into this realm – as in Liddy's (iconoclastic) conviction that Fanny 'was such a childlike innocent that her spirit couldn't appear to anybody if it tried'. Stephen's bowdlerised version makes nonsense of Liddy's meaning.

4 'A rich mine of quaintnesses and oddities'

1 See Stephen's letter to Hardy, 17 February 1874, in which he approves the 'Great Barn' and 'merry mist' sections as 'excellent and I would not omit them or shorten them'. They are, indeed 'excellent' – Hardy at his poetic best – and one wonders why he needed Stephen's approval at all! Perhaps, in feeling the discomforts of his subservient role, he simply wanted to bring these particularly fine sections to his editor's attention in the hope of receiving (for once) some unqualified praise for his efforts. For Stephen's letter in full, see Purdy *Thomas Hardy: A Bibliographical Study* (Oxford: The Clarendon Press, 1968), pp. 337–8.

In referring to the 'merry mist' section, Stephen was probably speaking of the descriptive passage in Chapter XXIII beginning 'It was still the beaming time of evening', and including the paragraph beginning, 'The sun went down in an ochreous mist'. My reasons for making this claim are threefold. First, there is the obvious thematic connection: a misty sundown is now enveloping the shearers as they feast at Bathsheba's supper table, and as they gradually sink under their own alcoholic 'merry mist'. Second, this section features descriptively in the shearing-supper chapter which follows immediately upon the sheep-shearing chapter itself (Chapter XXII), which contains Hardy's other descriptive 'set piece' on the Great Barn (Hardy evidently sent 'pieces' to Stephen for approval – actual chapter structures were fairly fluid). It would be reasonable to suppose that while Stephen was checking through the May instalment in which both these chapters occur, he would mention both passages held up for approval, including the sundown section. Third, Hardy's manuscript title for the shearing-supper chapter stands as 'A merry time: a second declaration'. This may have stood (at the draft or set-piece-fragment stage) as 'A merry mist'. Hardy then revises this title, in interlinear revision, to 'A pleasant time: a second declaration', and finally, in proof, to 'Eventide – A Second Declaration'. With all this revisionary work, it is evident that Hardy was concerned about this segment up to the very last moment. If he had felt a certain pride in his set pieces (the poetry diffused through the prose) and was simply looking for a little praise from Stephen in these instances, this does not fully explain his continuing concern with this episode. Could it have been that Stephen at some point (prior to his letter of approval) passed comment on Hardy's uncensorious treatment of his inebriates? Does this explain the evolution of the title (and no doubt the chapter contents) from 'merry mist' (?) to 'merry time', to 'A pleasant time: a second declaration' to 'Eventide: A Second Declaration'? I think this may explain the obvious shift in focus, suggested by the changed titles, from 'Merry' celebrations (including Hardy's celebratory tone) to Boldwood's second declaration. This is also an atmospheric shift from misty alcoholic hazes to the falling shades of night – the latter more suitable to Stephen's country parsonage.

2 Debates on marriage, women, and property, continued to be vigorous throughout the late century. John Stuart and Harriet Taylor Mill (and their ilk) picked up the anti-marriage question in mid-century, where the Foxites had left off, and the legislature, with (most notably) the Matrimonial Causes Act and the Married Woman's Property Act (which packed the Commons Listeners' Gallery with militant women for months on end), extended debates into the political arena. At the time of the publication of *Far from the Madding Crowd*, stories and satirical sketches abounded on the women-and-property question, one of them being a tale told by the militant feminist, Millicent Garrett Fawcett, who went in search of her pocket-book at a local Lost Property office only to discover that it was not her property. As a married woman it was owned by her husband and had been filed as his lost property.

3 Robert Schweik provides an interesting commentary on Hardy's cuts and expansions of this chapter (VI) in which he takes foliation changes as an indication of an altered plot arrangement: that Hardy revised from a different earlier version of the novel; that the altered segment beginning 'He resolved to walk' is part of a reorganisation of material which serves to strengthen the 'new ending' to Chapter VI: that Chapter VI did not originally conclude with Oak's words ('Do you want a shepherd ma'am?') but in the Malthouse scene (Chapter VIII); that the new arrangement opened up the way for an additional chapter (VII) in which Hardy introduces another new element, namely Fanny's story. (See Robert Schweik, 'The early development of Hardy's *Far from the Madding Crowd*', *Texas Studies in Literature and Language*, vol. IX, no. 3, 1967, pp. 415–28.)

If we trace Hardy's foliation changes, in which Chapter VI ends on f. 63, and Chapter VIII begins with f. 70 and numbers its second leaf f. 71 with f. 66 (marked in ink) cancelled, the resulting gap, in which Chapter VII is inserted, was originally one of two pages – the missing f. 64, and f. 65. Hardy's augmentation of this segment to what is now Chapter VII (ff. 64–9) adds four leaves to the original missing two, two of which (ff. 65, 69) look like possible recopyings – the others bearing interlinear revisions. So what was the original content of the missing pages? I find no clear indications of an earlier, different tale, nor any evidence that Fanny's story did not exist in the original f. 64 and f. 65. How could we possibly know this? Schweik takes signs of erased foliation of ff. 65–6 to show that only the sections of Chapter VII treating with Oak's acceptance as the new shepherd and his setting out for the Malthouse existed in the original version. But I do not take signs of erased foliation as a reliable guide: why would Hardy use pencil in this instance when customarily he marks leaf numbers with pen, as evidenced by ink coloration of text and foliation? There is plentiful evidence throughout the text of reused papers showing signs of false starts, etc. Why would ff. 65, 66, be an exception to this? More to the point, though, is the fact that of the two possible recopyings (clean script, no interlinear revisions), the first (f. 65) deals with Oak's conversation with the bailiff while the second (f. 69) completes the meeting between Fanny and Oak by the churchyard. So whereas I see Chapter VII as Schweik sees it, as augmented text, I do not see it as necessarily departing in any substantial way from Hardy's original story in which Fanny features dramatically (for further details see Appendix 2). The augmentation, in so far as it provides dramatic interest at a point in the story where we have dwelt at some considerable length (and will continue to dwell in Chapter VIII – the Malthouse scene) with the rustics, fulfils, I think, Hardy's interest (and no doubt Stephen's) in intensifying the action and varying the dramatic focus. This is the work of the artist, simply. And by now we know we can expect this of Hardy – especially when there is a lull in the story.

As to which leaves provide augmentary detail in Chapter VII, we may take our pick. Assuming that f. 65 and f. 69 are recopyings from the original in which the bailiff and Fanny both feature, which details did Hardy add? Bathsheba's thoughts on Oak's declaration of love at Norcombe and that she had 'nearly forgotten it', or the villagers' fervent recommendations to Bathsheba that Oak is 'the man truly' – that she should take him on (f. 64)? Oak's thoughts on the rencounter with Bathsheba – the 'supervising, cool woman', or his passage to the churchyard (f. 66)? The description of Fanny and her opening conversation with Oak concerning the whereabouts of the Malthouse and Buck's Head (f. 67)? Or the continuance of this conversation which is, in fact, partly cancelled by Hardy at the foot of the page (f. 68)? – at the point where Fanny accepts Oak's shilling: '"Yes, I will take it", said the stranger gratefully.' Here the manuscript continues with what looks like:

> Stretching out his hand [then something illegible] before the money could be put into her palm, Gabriel's [*sic*.] recognized . . .

This is cancelled by Hardy. Instead he starts again on f. 69 with the segment we have today which opens with:

> She extended her hand; Gabriel his. In feeling for each other . . .

So, there were cuts as well as additions in Chapter VII! This opens up the way for yet another interpretation: not Fanny's absence in the original but her larger presence.

Schweik is surely right to stress 'Hardy's addition of a carefully dramatized account of the meeting' between Fanny and Oak, but 'carefully' is, I think, the operative word.

4 See Simon Gatrell for a contrary view: 'Hardy the creator: *Far from the Madding Crowd'*, in Dale Kramer (ed.), *Critical Approaches to the Fiction of Thomas Hardy* (New York: Barnes & Noble, 1979), pp. 74–98. This essay is reprinted in the

W.W. Norton edition of *Far from the Madding Crowd*, ed. Robert C. Schweik, pp. 347–61. On the basis of Hardy's altered numeration (see Appendices), Gatrell takes the verso passage as an indication 'that in the original version no proposal of marriage had taken place'. What then did Hardy intend as subject matter in the earlier chapter (IV) entitled (originally), 'Short account of Gabriel's love affair till a crisis came'? (the 'crisis' at this stage being separate from the 'farming incident' in the ensuing Chapter V). And what, too, of Oak's obsessive spying on Bathsheba, from the turnpike incident in Chapter I, to the 'Milton's Satan' incident in Chapter II, to the outlandish riding incident in Chapter III? These all, in one way or another, dramatise Oak's increasing desire to 'possess' Bathsheba by spying, and this appears to come to a 'crisis' in Chapter IV with the marriage proposal. For, thereafter, as a shepherd and manager in her employ, Oak's power threshold changes. He is now less the Peeping Tom of the opening chapters who seems to feel that he has the right to peer through crevices at her body in various performances of intimacy. Following her rejection of him, Oak takes on the role of the disdained lover who alternately defends her interests to the last moment in jeopardy or attacks her sexual behaviour to the last insinuation of irresponsibility. Chapter IV provides the dramatic pivot on which all of this swings, but how would it 'pivot' without the proposal scene, without Bathsheba's rejection, and without some action on her part to drive Oak from encroaching on her private space thence to take on a more circumspect, socially responsible role in her life?

5 In so far as Hardy reflects contemporary issues in the real world, in this instance, the issue of emigration – currently the Government of Brazil was offering assisted passages to 500,000 working men (possibly an incentive to Angel Clare some years on) – he evidently gives some thought to Oak's best destination since he alters the original in interlinear revision in the manuscript from 'British Columbia' to 'California'. Was it easier to imagine Oak a gold-prospector in California in continued pursuit of wealth and property than a hunter-trapper in British Columbia in line with his career as a husbander of meat?

6 Gatrell claims a greater change in Oak than is, in fact, apparent in Hardy's manuscript revisions. In support of this claim he cites, for example, a revision 'related to his growth . . . where Oak is added to Coggan in making a respectful nod to [farmer Boldwood] – primarily to emphasise his sense of inferiority in status at that stage of the novel' (Gatrell, op. cit.).

   The first thing to mention is that this revision directly refers to Coggan's recommendation to Oak (a few minutes before) that he pay a little more respect to his superiors – notably to Troy – 'to keep the man civil'. So evidently Oak is not sensing his 'inferiority' enough!

   The next point is that the respectful nod to Boldwood has now to be entered in revision because Hardy has interpolated (in proof) Troy's question about Boldwood's insanity, which includes Oak's query:

   There's Mr Boldwood. . . . I wonder what Troy meant by his question.

With this accentuated focus now on Boldwood (as he appears at their side), and now upon Oak (with his query), and now also upon the need for a more respectful attitude on his part, Hardy now could not possibly overlook Oak (after all this refocusing and added emphases) and have Coggan the only one to nod respectfully to Boldwood. This is yet another example of Hardy's attempt to keep Oak in focus, but that the revision is meant to emphasise Oak's sense of inferiority simply does not follow. The actual situation is that Oak is overcome by the ghastly shock of losing Bathsheba to Troy and has (like Giles after him) become, in his pain, boorish and socially clumsy. Coggan picks him up on this (or Hardy does) and Oak responds accordingly.

7 See the 'Buck's Head' discussion in Appendix 2.

8 *Life*, p. 99.

9 In the Norton Critical Edition of *Far from the Madding Crowd*, 1986, Robert Schweik (ed.) observes in 'Textual Notes' the following:

> Finally, in one case, Hardy made a revision for the Wessex edition which created a marked inconsistency that, nevertheless, has been allowed to stand. From the manuscript onward, all texts of *Far from the Madding Crowd* contain a speech by Troy in chapter 35 . . . which makes emphatically clear that he suspects Boldwood's sanity. . . . And, up to the Wessex edition, a subsequent passage in chapter 55 . . . read as follows:
>
>> nobody imagined that there had shown in him unequivocal symptoms of the mental derangement which Bathsheba and Troy, alone of all others and at different times, had momentarily suspected.

For the Wessex edition, Schweik goes on to say,

> Hardy changed the name *Troy* in this passage to *Oak*, even though later in the same chapter he has Oak say he does *not* think Boldwood was insane. The change certainly created an inconsistency; but many of Hardy's other late revisions made clear that he was intent on strengthening Oak's character, and this revision does attribute to Oak a somewhat greater insight and keenness of perception that Hardy no doubt thought important.

I should repeat here that Troy's speech in Chapter XXXV, in which he questions Boldwood's sanity, does not, in fact, appear in the holograph manuscript at all. Hardy added this in proof and it makes its very first appearance in the *Cornhill*. As to the inconsistency of the late revision for the Wessex edition and the strengthening of Oak's character, the problem arises (in the latter instance) that if, as Schweik says, this was a matter of importance to Hardy, why then is his method so horribly slipshod? I am not convinced of 'importance'. On the contrary, for Hardy to create such an inconsistency in characterisation it seems more likely, especially at this late stage of definition, that the problem was Oak's *unimportance*: his lack of presence, force of character, fascination, allure, in Hardy's own eyes. This, I would think, might well undermine the 'import' of such revisions as may have suggested themselves to him (as perhaps by such disparaging criticisms as Henry James's).

10 Schweik covers part of this ground when he calls attention to changes made to the manuscript passage in which Oak speaks of Boldwood's mind being 'quite a wreck'. (See R. Schweik, 'The narrative structure of *Far from the Madding Crowd*', in *Budmouth Essays on Thomas Hardy*, ed. F.B. Pinion (Dorchester: The Thomas Hardy Society Ltd, 1976), p. 37.)

11 See Stephen to Hardy, 25 August 1874, Purdy, op. cit., p. 339.

12 Robert C. Schweik infers from Stephen's letter to Hardy of 25 August 1874, that Hardy 'revised the final chapters of his manuscript to put more dialect in Oak's speech'. See *Far from the Madding Crowd*, ed. Robert C. Schweik (New York and London: W.W. Norton & Co., 1986), p. 344, note 4. See also Simon Gatrell, op. cit. Gatrell takes this further and claims that adjustment to the role of Gabriel Oak exercised Hardy 'more than any other topic'. A close study of Hardy's manuscript does not bear out this last claim, although his revisions to dialect certainly apply as much to Oak as to the rustics in general. Dialectal revisions to all of his characters did not stop at the manuscript and proof stage

of revision. Some brief examples of changes made to Chapter XXXIII for the Osgood, McIlvaine edition (1895) are: 'unfortunate', to 'onfortunate' (Cainy Ball); 'we are born' to 'we be born' (Poorgrass); 'nature' to 'nater' (Poorgrass); 'with you' to 'with 'ee' (Coggan); 'soldier' to 'sojer' (Cainy); 'almost' to 'a'most' (Cainy); 'without' to ''ithout' (Cainy); 'have' to 'hae' (Cainy); 'before' to 'afore' (Oak); 'you are no longer' to 'you be no longer' (Poorgrass).

13 See Gatrell, op. cit.

14 *Life*, p. 97. The artist, Helen Paterson, to whom Hardy later referred as the best illustrator he had ever had, does not feature these 'out-of-the-way things' in her woodcut illustrations to the *Cornhill* text (see the 'Foreword' of this book for more details). Bathsheba does carry a small wooden pail in the insert vignette to the January number, but mainly Paterson keeps such details to a minimum. However, her illustration of the Casterbridge Union (insert vignette to the September number), follows Hardy's description down to the last picturesque detail – the stone edifice with two wings smothered with masses of ivy – but bears little resemblance to the same building which still stands today in Dorchester behind the open-air market.

15 Part of the problematic in Hardy's struggle to strike the right balance might well arise from his own torn loyalties – now writing for a metropolitan audience, now also enjoying life in the metropolis himself, yet rooted heart and soul in Wessex – perhaps he needed a way of mediating his divided loyalties? It is interesting to note, as Phillip Mallett reminds me, that Andrew Lang seems to have found patronising tones in *Far from the Madding Crowd*, in so far as he accuses Hardy of 'telling clever people about unlettered people'.

16 See 'The Wessex Labourer', *Examiner*, 15 July 1876, pp. 793–4. Michael Millgate attributes this anonymous article to Charles Kegan Paul, and goes on to say that,

> Hardy put this article . . . in his scrapbook, and obviously had it in front of him many years later when writing the preface to the 1895 edition of *Far from the Madding Crowd*. He mentions it specifically as the first occasion when the term Wessex was 'taken up elsewhere' (viii), and adopts some of its phraseology in speaking of his appropriation of the old Saxon name for 'a modern Wessex of railways, the penny post, mowing and reaping machines, union workhouses, lucifer matches, labourers who could read and write, and National schoolchildren' (vii). Hardy must have found, in 1876, great reassurance in the article's informed and unhesitating endorsement both of the method and of the authenticity of his work; he may also have been grateful for the defence of his fiction against those (among them R.H. Hutton in the *Spectator*) who had found his rural characters extravagantly philosophical and articulate.
>
> (Michael Millgate, *Thomas Hardy: His Career as a Novelist*
> (New York: Random House, 1971) pp. 95–104)

17 *Spectator*, 19 December 1874, pp. 1597–9.

5 'Close intersocial relations, and eccentric individualities'

1 See, for example, *The Times*, 25 January 1875, p. 4. The reviewer praises *Far from the Madding Crowd* for its,

> delicate perspective faculty, which transforms, with skilful touch, the matter-of-fact prosaic details of every-day life into an idyl or a pastoral poem.

See also one of Hardy's own favourites:

> Perhaps the greatest beauty of the new novel escapes readers who only see in it a diverting history with the kind of dramatic situations one might find elsewhere. Mr Hardy, in effect, has intended to go beyond that. He has determined to revive the old-fashioned and often tedious form of the pastoral, and has put into it such a fidelity of observation, a feeling so profound, a poetry so fresh, a style so powerful, so much of the ideal and the real at one and the same time, that this transformation is able to almost pass for an original creation.
>
> (Léon Boucher, 'Le roman pastoral en Angleterre', *Revue des Deux Mondes*,
> *45e année*, 15 December 1875, p. 843 (Robert Schweik's translation))

2 J. Hillis Miller observes that the events of the story,

> are placed in a particular moment in the past. This seems to be no more than another way to hold the story at arm's length and see it in the perspective of the centuries which preceded it.
>
> The conventional past tense of the narration is a way of expressing the separation of the narrator from the culture he describes. . . . This distancing undercuts the assumptions and values which the characters share.
>
> (J. Hillis Miller, *Thomas Hardy: Distance and Desire*,
> (Cambridge, Mass.: Harvard University Press, 1970), pp. 57–70)

This manner of presentation, as Hillis Miller says, throws the 'immediate experience of each moment' back into the past, and no doubt this temporality of experience assists Hardy in reaching his contemporary Victorian reader with a comfortable degree of distance (given his treatment of seduction and illegitimacy). The question of separation is arguable, however. As the temporal correspondence between the two worlds (within and without the novel) becomes manifest – if we can read the novel with this in mind, in line with Hardy's contemporaries – the distance between reader and character as between reader and narrator is almost non-existent. The confrontation between Hardy's Weatherbury world and Stephen's country parsonage is extraordinarily direct. Virtually every new instalment includes a vivid evocation of the month or season – snowflake for snowflake, flossy catkin for flossy catkin, diaphanous fern for diaphanous fern, just as it was taking place beyond the reader's very own window.

See also Howard Babb, 'Setting and theme in *Far from the Madding Crowd*, *A Journal of English Literary History* 30 (1963), pp. 147–61. Babb discusses setting in this novel as establishing the moral values of the central characters, or as an oblique commentary on the character in view. While this is a truism of Hardy's novels in general, setting also functions in this early novel as a critical statement upon working and living conditions. It is not only that the long highway treks trodden by Fanny bespeak her deprivation and poverty (each time we meet her she is looking either for care or for shelter), or that the storm rages while Oak battles to forestall its damage to the corn stacks, or that Bathsheba's house clearance banishes the outmoded and defunct (including the thieving bailiff) and introduces a new form of female government, it is also Hardy's treatment of the tiniest of mundane details. It is, for example, the scene of the Malthouse, where hungry men do not 'chaw' too close because the bread might not be too 'clane'; it is Buck's Head Inn where jaded workfolk drink too long and too hard and a burial has to be postponed; it is the unheated cottages where the breath of the sleepers freezes to the sheets; or it is a lambing-hut so icy that ventilators are not opened and a shepherd is almost suffocated to death.

Practically every chapter in the novel provides some kind of documentation of rural labour conditions, and they are not 'idyllic'.

For an exemplary setting devised by Hardy partly as a socio-political statement on a particular working environment, as opposed to the 'church' and the 'castle' of the ruling classes, see his description of the Great Barn in Chapter XXII.

3 See 'The progress and spirit of physical science,' *Edinburgh Review,* 108 (1858) p. 71. The writer of this article, purported to be Sir Henry Holland, identified mid-Victorian Britain as the 'age of transition' and this became the predominant epithet of the age for countless Victorians – from Matthew Arnold to Disraeli to Tennyson, Harriet Martineau, Prince Albert, John Stuart Mill, William Morris, Carlyle and many many more.

4 See Walter Houghton:

> The feeling of isolation and loneliness, so characteristic of modern man, first appeared in the nineteenth century. With the break-up of a long-established order and the resulting fragmentation of both society and thought, the old ties were snapped, and men became acutely conscious of separation. They felt isolated by dividing barriers; lonely for a lost companionship, human and divine; nostalgic for an earlier world of country peace and unifying belief.

And for those adapting to life in the modern city,

> the romantic love of nature passed into a new phase. It became the nostalgia for a lost world of peace and companionship, of healthy bodies and quiet minds. The image had its basis in memory, for every Victorian in the city had either grown up in the country or in a town small enough for ready contact with the rural environment. 'When I was a child [in the 1830s],' Frederick Harrison remembered, 'in every city in the kingdom, and even in most parts of London, an easy walk would take a man into quiet fields and pure air'
>
> (Houghton, *The Victorian Frame of Mind, 1831–1870* (New Haven and London: Yale University Press, 1957), pp. 77, 79)

We might, in this instance, look to the great poets of the age, all of whom dealt with this topic in one way or another. If we move from mid-century with Matthew Arnold's 'The Scholar Gypsy':

> And wish the long unhappy dream would end,
> And waive all claim to bliss, and try to bear;
> With close-lipp'd patience for our only friend,
> Sad patience, too near neighbour to despair

to Hardy's *fin de siècle* poem, 'In Tenebris II', and the poet's cry that 'if a way to the Better there be, it exacts a full look at the Worst', we find the mood of melancholia and despair still governs, but where Arnold has lost a world, Hardy has buried it.

5 See Charles Kingsley's essay on the National Gallery, *His Letters and Memories of His Life,* ed. Fanny Kingsley, 2 vols (London, 1877), vol. 1, pp. 138–9. Kingsley writes in praise of picture galleries:

> There, in the space of a single room, the townsman may take his country walk – a walk beneath mountain peaks, blushing sunsets, with broad woodlands spreading out below it; a walk through green meadows, under cool mellow shades, and overhanging rocks, by rushing brooks, where he watches and watches till he seems to *hear* the foam whisper, and to *see* the

fishes leap; and his hard-worn heart wanders out free, beyond the grim city-world . . . into the world of beautiful things.

6 Mill writes that

mankind have outgrown old institutions and old doctrines, and have not yet acquired new ones

See John Stuart Mill, *The Spirit of the Age*, ed. F.A. von Hayek (Chicago: Chicago University Press, 1942), p. 6. Mill is referring to the England of antiquity – medieval or feudal – which saw its end during and after the period of the Enlightenment, the nineteenth-century rise of democracy and agnosticism, the emancipation of the Catholics and the crumbling of the old religious and civil orders.

Carlyle, Ruskin and Arnold saw the period as one of 'decaying or dying feudalism' (see Houghton, op. cit., pp. 2–8); Bulwer Lytton saw it as the age of destruction in preparation for reconstruction; Leslie Stephen followed suit with 'the old ideas have become obsolete, and the new are not yet constructed' (Hardy records this in the *Life*, p. 308) – but often liked to speak, rather more illuminatingly, of the 'macadamisation' of Victorian society.

7 The *Telegraph* reviewer, following his visit to Dorset, writes that 'Piddletown' (Hardy's Weatherbury),

rejoices in most of the essentials of Arcadian felicity. The squire takes a direct and fatherly interest in his villagers. He has built them from time to time numbers of good cottages, and he has furnished them with ground for garden allotments. . . . [Workers receive] full standard wages of the county. . . . Small kindnesses are also practised by the farmers, which go a long way in promoting friendly feeling amongst the labourers. . . . [the Labourer] stands a chance, provided he be faultless as a labourer, and properly deferential as an inferior, of having a hundredweight or two of firewood delivered at his door in the cold weather.

('The Arcadians of Dorset', *Daily Telegraph*, 30 April 1872, p. 5)

See also, Francis George Heath, *The English Peasantry* (London, 1874), pp. 27–40, in which this article is printed in full.

The Dorset agricultural labourer comes off rather well in the *Telegraph*'s account, which sounds, in tone and focus, rather as if the local squire may have entertained the reporter to some good hospitality as well as to some good news! By way of contrast, Michael Millgate notes that:

The 1867 Royal Commission on the Employment of Children, Young Persons, and Women in Agriculture, to which submissions were made by such Dorset figures as William Barnes and Henry Moule, gave ample coverage to Dorset as, by common consent, one of the areas where wages were lowest, cottages the least sanitary, landlords the most unenlightened, and the plight of the labouring class nearest to desperation.

(Michael Millgate, *Thomas Hardy: His Career as a Novelist* (New York: Random House, 1971), pp. 97–9)

Barnes and Moule were both personally known to Hardy and no doubt shared their views on social conditions with him. In *Far from the Madding Crowd* Hardy seems to steer somewhere between the 'Arcadia' of the first report and the feudalism of the second – the latter considerably muted by his technique of infusing touches of comic-absurdity into his portrayal. Hardy was, no doubt, wary of treading too closely upon neighbourly toes in his choice of a local

Notes

Dorset setting:

> I have decided to finish it here [Bockhampton], which is within a walk of the district in which the incidents are supposed to occur. I find it a great advantage to be actually among the people described at the time of describing them.
>
> (*Life*, p. 99)

But clearly this close proximity would not be a 'great advantage' to any popular novelist wishing to write in criticism of the harsher realities of life in the neighbourhood.

8 Lang continues:

> The old and the new must meet here and there, with curious surprises, and our world may find itself face to face with the quaint conceited rustics of Shakespeare's plays.
>
> (*The Academy*, 2 Jan. 1875, p. 9)

Lang criticised *Far from the Madding Crowd* for its lack of contingency,

> the country folk in the story have not heard of strikes, or of Mr Arch; they have, to all appearances, plenty to eat, and warm clothes to wear

and, moreover, 'Mr Hardy', Lang complains, is 'somewhat patronising' (ibid.).

Hardy's relationship with Lang did not improve over the years. Lang appears, in this instance, to be asking for a rural version of something akin to the industrial novel of the mid-century (such as Gaskell's *Mary Barton*, 1848, or *North and South*, 1855; Dickens's *Hard Times*, 1854; Disraeli's *Sybil*, 1845; Kingsley's *Alton Locke*, 1850; or Eliot's *Felix Holt*, 1866).

Millgate notes that:

> if Hardy does not draw attention to the miseries of the farm labourer's lot he does not seek specifically to conceal them.
>
> (Millgate, op. cit., p. 104)

9 This is Millgate's (op. cit., p. 96) view:

> It is not until the early 1880s that the first clear indication of agricultural distress and discontent appears, somewhat unexpectedly, in *Two on a Tower*, where the labourers refer to themselves as 'folks with ten or a dozen shillings a week and their gristing, and a load o' thorn faggots when we can get 'em'.

Millgate concludes that in *Far from the Madding Crowd*, 'Hardy seems to have chosen his setting with a deliberate eye to its remoteness from the current unrest.'

As to that 'deliberate eye', 'remoteness' is emphatically arguable. I notice, for example, that in Chapter X, 'Mistress and Men', when Bathsheba asks Poorgrass what she owes him for carting, shooting rooks and sparrows and helping at pig-killing, he replies in the manuscript with, 'seven and ninepence'. This is increased, in proof revision, to 'nine and ninepence', which would approximate the average weekly wage for labourers of the 1870s.

10 K.D.M. Snell argues against rural realism in Hardy, but he does so from the point of view of the social critic and statistician, not the local colorist nor the native returning with a deep sense of nostos. Hardy's Wessex is not only a partly real, partly dream country but it is also *his* country. He is on the inside; the rural world is familiar, safe and very much taken for granted. When facing the urban outside, Hardy becomes the harsh social critic, but in confronting

189

conditions in Wessex he, quite naturally, experiences an ambience no outsider possesses. He, apparently, feels no need to hold forth about squalor, he simply gives us the eating habits of the Malthouse: grimy cider mugs, potatoes in the ashes, and a bacon sandwich passed from hand to hand, grit and all. Nor poverty – the breath of sleepers simply freezes on the sheets. Nor contemptuous class attitudes which Hardy, who reserves polemics for thematics, delivers with his customary irony by allowing us to know that if a field worker is addressed contemptuously by a farmer and takes it all with 'no more resentment than the blow of the wind and rain', this is not because the contempt is acceptable. Snell fails to pick up on the irony – which here lies in the unpalatable fact that inured field workers find class abuse as inevitable as foul weather. Snell also fails to locate Hardy's centre of consciousness which comes close, in terms of artistic representation and mimesis, to Ruskin's (in *Modern Painters*), who develops the idea of art being 'of' rather than 'from' nature. Not exactitude but essence, not copying but rather a 'faithful statement' of the 'mind and senses'. This artistic affinity between Hardy and Ruskin is nowhere more imaginatively wedded than in their mutual admiration for Turner!

See Snell's *Annals of the Labouring Poor* (Cambridge University Press, 1985), in particular his section on Hardy, pp. 374–411.

11 On the question of 'real-life' representations and freedom of expression, Stephen was, throughout his life, ethically concerned to preserve 'Freethinking and Plainspeaking' (see his essays under this title). But, in truth, this ethical principle only really took form in the practice of religious freethinking. He observes in the freespeech context that 'Whatever reticence may be desirable, we ought not to tell lies, or to countenance the telling of lies.' But in this he is aiming quite specifically at 'one of the superstitions against which we have specially to contend in England' which 'is the excessive idolatry of the Bible'. Stephen was a fervent disbeliever in the divinity of Christ and the authenticity of the Old and New Testaments. This, of course, makes him very much a freethinker, but also very much a freethinker of his time – that is, a radical critic of Christian doctrines. Yet even then he had misgivings about shocking the morality 'and lofty sentiments' of others: 'Is not silence in such a case better than a rash proclamation of a bare truth?' He would not, under any circumstances of freethinking and plainspeaking, have 'ignorant' people 'suppose that I mean to strike at the very foundation of morals'. See Janet E. Courtney, *Freethinkers of the Nineteenth Century* (New York: E.R. Dutton & Co., 1920), pp. 171–97.

In this respect, although we hear a good deal about freethinking with regard to Stephen, this does not encompass free-expression or freethinking on such issues as class oppression, sexual relationships or, indeed, any kind of heterodoxy beyond religious politics.

12 Likewise, in some of his most sympathetic poems as in some of his most anarchic moods, Hardy tempers much of his social criticism with a wry humour, a mischievous play on the absurd, and a wicked eye upon life's little ironies.

13 *Life*, p. 98.

14 See, for example, Raymond Williams, *Culture and Society 1780–1950*, (Harmondsworth: Penguin, 1968). Williams explains (ibid., pp. 14–15) that the word 'class', before about 1740, referred to

> a division or group in schools and colleges. . . . It is only at the end of the eighteenth century that the modern structure of *class*, in its social sense, begins to be built up. First comes *lower classes*, to join *lower orders*, which appears earlier in the eighteenth century. Then, in the 1790s, we get *higher*

classes; middle classes and *middling classes* follow at once; *working classes* in about 1815; *upper classes* in the 1820s. *Class prejudice, class legislation, class consciousness, class conflict,* and *class war* follow in the course of the nineteenth century. The *upper middle classes* are first heard of in the 1890s; the *lower middle classes* in our own century.

It is obvious, of course, that this spectacular history of the new use of *class* does not indicate the *beginning* of social divisions in England. But it indicates, quite clearly, a change in attitudes towards them. . . . at a crucial phase in the development of political democracy.

In amendment to Williams, Phillip Mallett points out that, whereas this may not reflect a prevailing or common parlance. Ruskin uses the term 'lower middle class' in the 1870s. And taking the cue from Mallett, I would add that (in the 1890s) Hollingshead also uses the term to describe his own early Victorian background.

15 Stephen to Hardy, 8 January 1874, in R.L. Purdy, *Thomas Hardy: A Bibliographical Study* (Oxford: Clarendon Press, 1968), p. 337.

16 See Leslie Stephen, *History of English Thought in the Eighteenth Century* (1876), pp. 290–325.

17 See Jeffrey Paul von Arx, *Progress and Pessimism: Religion, Politics and History in Late Nineteenth Century Britain* (Harvard University Press, 1985), pp. 32, 45.

18 See Mrs Sara Ellis, *Daughters of England, Wives of England* and *Women of England,* published and continuously reprinted as standard manuals from the 1830s onwards.

See also John Ruskin:

> The very removal of the massy bars which once separated one class of society from another, has rendered it tenfold more shameful in foolish people's, i.e., in most people's eyes, to remain in the lower grades of it, than ever it was before. . . . Now that a man may make money, and rise in the world, and associate himself, unreproached, with people once far above him . . . it becomes a veritable shame to him to remain in the state he was born in, and everybody thinks it is his *duty* to try to be a 'gentleman'.

John Ruskin, 'Pre-Raphaelitism' (1851), *Works*, ed. E.T. Cook and A.D.O. Wedderburn, (London, 1902–12), vol. 12, p. 342. Ruskin recurs to this topic in 'Of King's Treasuries' (1864). See also 'The bourgeois dream' and 'success' (Houghton, op. cit., pp. 189–95).

I should also mention that a respectable gentleman would have been identified by his top hat, frock coat and possession of a gig. It is no wonder, therefore, that Susan Tall (Chapter XLIX) mocks Oak for his 'tall hat a-Sundays, and 'a hardly knows the name of smockfrock'. This is not so much the dress of a master-farmer, as Schweik notes, as the dress of a gentleman! (See T. Hardy, *Far from the Madding Crowd*, ed. R.C. Schweik, (New York and London: W.W. Norton Co., 1986), p. 254.)

19 Hardy (like Stephen), as a follower of John Stuart Mill and Herbert Spencer – whose influence within the society pervaded mid- to late-century thought, disseminated in magazine articles and reviews – would no doubt have been familiar with their views on wealth and respectability as being two sides of the same coin. See, for example, Herbert Spencer, 'The morals of trade', *Essays: Scientific, Political and Speculative*, vol. 2, no. 141, pp. 139–48 and John Stuart Mill, *Letters*, ed. H.S.R. Elliot, 2 vols (London and New York, 1910), vol. 1, p. 74.

20 In Chapter IX in the manuscript, which opens with an account of housekeeping

with Bathsheba, Liddy, Maryann and Mrs Coggan all coming in for a considerable amount of closely depicted detail (another instance here of truncated script, where Hardy visibly curbs his interest in these details and pushes ahead with the action), I notice that Hardy has Bathsheba and Liddy originally 'lounging' together on the floor. This is altered in interlinear revision to the more ladylike and less informal 'sitting' on the floor.

6 'A man's Damn'

1 While Stephen insisted that his editorial principles did not express his feelings as a man, his views, according to Grosskurth, 'in fact accorded closely with the prevailing canons of Victorian taste'. See Phyllis Grosskurth, *Leslie Stephen*, (Harlow, Essex: Longmans, Green & Co. Ltd, 1968), p. 11. Grosskurth goes on to say that 'Stephen was extraordinarily conscious of the presence of Mrs Grundy at his shoulder.' I would go one step further, as regards those 'prevailing canons of Victorian taste', to emphasise that Stephen's editorial principles are actually more in line with an older tradition that considerably predates his own time and clime. In this sense he is very much the reactionary Grundyist. His influential predecessor, Hugh Murray, who published *The Morality of Fiction* as early as 1805, held that the novel should offer moral instruction and examples of excellence of conduct superior to those met with in ordinary life. Edward Mangin followed Murray in much the same vein with *An Essay on Light Reading As It May be Supposed to Influence Moral Conduct And Literary Taste* (1808), and Lord Brougham advanced the pedagogic cause in *Practical Observations on the Education of the People* (1825). Brougham, who also sponsored the Society for the Diffusion of Useful Knowledge, called specifically for the novel's moral edification of the sons and daughters of tradesmen. Likewise, Mrs Sara Ellis in 'An Apology for Fiction' in 1833; likewise the widely influential Harriet Martineau who advocated that 'man's natural imitative faculty' should be guided by examples (in the novel) of high conduct (Martineau's motto, attached to *Illustrations of Political Economy* was 'Example before Precept'). Finally, as perhaps one of the last of this line, one of the last of the Victorian Morality-of-Fiction advocates, there was Walter Besant whose 'The Value of Fiction' in the 1870s struggled to uphold the didactic role of fiction. For fuller discussion of this topic, see Robert A. Colby, '"Rational amusement" vs useful knowledge', *Victorian Literature and Society, Essays Presented to Richard D. Altick*, ed. James R. Kincaid and Albert J. Kuhn (Ohio State University Press, 1983), pp. 46–73.

   Stephen remains, in this sense, very much the old-fashioned pedagogue. In another sense, his partial attitude to the freedom of speech reflects his conflict over religious belief. Despite his abandonment of the pretence of faith, he shared Matthew Arnold's misgivings about unsettling the faith of the working classes. Arnold's intellectual agreement with Bishop Colenso's doubts about the historical validity of the Scriptures did not prevent him from doubting the wisdom of voicing these views to the masses. Likewise Stephen felt, and promoted in his 'Science of Ethics', that such revelation might have a devastating effect on the morality of the uneducated classes.

2 See his essay, 'Darwin and divinity', in *Essays on Freethinking and Plainspeaking* (New York: G.P. Putnam's Sons, 1877). Nor is Stephen very far in his thinking here from J.S. Mill in *On Liberty*.

3 Grosskurth observes that Pater's ideal of art – that 'art comes to you proposing frankly to give nothing but the highest quality to your moments as they pass' – would have appeared 'criminally irresponsible' to Stephen (Grosskurth, op.

cit. 18–27). However, Pater's view that one of the 'legitimate' functions of the novel is to 'trace the influence of religion upon human character', would probably have met with Stephen's approval (see Pater's review of Mrs Humphrey Ward's *Robert Elsemere*, published in *Essays from 'The Guardian'*, (London: 1901), pp. 56–7.

4 Stephen held the state of the nation to be disunited by sectarian strife and disrupted by party politics under Gladstone's timid administration. And this seems to have fuelled his conviction that men in his position of responsibility should set an example of moral firmness, especially in judging what was most beneficial for the masses.

5 In common with many of his contemporaries, Stephen felt ambivalent about the enfranchisement of the masses (as he viewed them) under the Reform Bill of 1867. He would not have gone as far as Carlyle in his anti-democratic beliefs, but he did believe that the working classes should only enter the electorate, 'not to govern but to support able and public-spirited University men'. See Von Arx, *Progress and Pessimism: Religion, Politics and History in Late Nineteenth Century Britain* (Harvard University Press, 1985), p. 18.

6 Noel Annan, *Leslie Stephen: The Godless Victorian* (New York: Random House, 1984), p. 67.

7 See Maitland, *The Life and Letters of Leslie Stephen* (London: Duckworth & Co., 1906), pp. 270–7. Interestingly, Hardy's account in the *Life*, copied almost verbatim from the account he submitted earlier to Maitland, differs in one or two minor details that in the aggregate actually lend the autobiographical account a greater degree of diffidence, or even indifference (to Stephen). For example, the following observation made by Hardy is absent in Maitland, where he says, in the *Life* (p. 97), that he 'feared the date at which he could write a story for the Cornhill would be too late for Mr Stephen's purpose' since he already had one on hand. Also at variance with the account given to Maitland is Hardy's anecdote about Stephen's letter (containing the invitation to write for the *Cornhill*) which according to the *Life*, only came to him at Bockhampton by accident. It had, he says, been found lying in the mud. However, in Maitland, the letter arrives safe and sound and is merely stained with 'rain-drops' (p. 270). And finally, there is some discrepancy over dates. Asserting with a longer hindsight a greater degree of indifference to Stephen's power and influence and a certain 'muddiness' attached to his correspondence in places, Hardy also records in the *Life* that he did not submit the first few chapters of *Far from the Madding Crowd* 'with some succeeding ones in outline' until the end of September 1873 (three months before publication). In Maitland, he says these chapters were submitted some months earlier in July (p. 272), which makes him sound more ready, willing and able to meet Stephen's demands than suits the proud Hardy's self-image in later years.

8 In his reminiscences, *Some Early Impressions* (New York: Burt Franklin, 1924), pp. 148–50, Stephen writes that,

> An editor, though authors sometimes forget the fact, is always in a state of eagerness for the discovery of the coming man (or woman). In spite of many disappointments, I would take up manuscript after manuscript with a vague flutter of hope that it might be a new *Jane Eyre* or *Scenes of Clerical Life*, destined to lift some obscure name to the heights of celebrity. That delight never presented itself; and yet I do not know that I ever rejected an angel unawares.

This is an attitude of Stephen's of which Hardy was surely aware. Who knows but that the copy of *Wessex Poems* he sent to Stephen in 1898 was not a way of demanding (but this time with the 'evidence') the unqualified praise of a man whose 'approval', Hardy says, 'is disapproval minimized' (*Life*, p. 171).

Stephen, at last, gave Hardy what he had been longing to hear for years:

> It gave me a real pleasure – I am glad to think you remember me as a friend . . . I am always pleased to remember that *Far from the Madding Crowd* came out under my command. I then admired the poetry which was diffused through the prose. . . . I will try not to criticise or distinguish, but will simply say that they have pleased me
>
> (*Life*, p. 298)

These are also the words of Coventry Patmore, who had earlier praised Hardy's novels for 'the poetry diffused through the prose'. But Patmore's praise had come instantly, as soon as the novels were published, and was not drawn from him with a book of verse some twenty years later.

9 Stephen does admit (in *Some Early Impressions*) to inheriting 'some admirable contributors'. He cites Matthew Arnold as one with whom he had to part company 'because he wished to discourse upon topics to which we had to give a wide berth'. John Addington Symonds was another – soon to become an invalid 'carrying on a precarious struggle' with his malady; R.L. Stevenson another – 'though I did not discover him'; Henry James another – whose *Daisy Miller* 'I hope I did something to establish'; and finally, 'Mr Hardy's *Far from the Madding Crowd* – a most delightful book of the kind in which he is unrivalled . . . and I hope I did the same kind of service for him.' But the only author lately under his wing who comes in for high praise as 'so versatile and ingenious an intellect, that one might have predicted for him a great success', is Grant Allen (ibid., pp. 148–50). However, those who fall short of 'the pure and lofty moral sentiment', who do not 'breathe in a wholesome social atmosphere', do not qualify for success in Stephen's book. Best is 'the admirable Trollope, content to provide his fellow with harmless and healthy amusement . . . increas[ing] the stock of innocent pleasure for the moment' (ibid., p. 192). We might infer from all of this that the iconoclastic Hardy and the circumspect Stephen spent considerably more time in bitter disagreement than either of these proud men would ever admit in public; although Hardy cannot resist putting into autobiographical form a rather oblique but not inoffensive last word on the subject. Approached by the Rationalist Press Association, in 1899, of which, he says pointedly in the *Life*, his 'friend Leslie Stephen was an honorary associate' he replies to the RPA to say:

> Though I am interested in the Society I feel it to be one which would naturally compose itself rather of writers on philosophy, science, and history, than of writers of imaginative works, whose effect depends largely on detachment.
>
> (ibid. p. 304)

This is Hardy at his most subversive and Stephen, whose writings stood at the centre of 'philosophy, science and history' (to wit, *The Science of Ethics*!), would surely have heard about it. In Stephen's 'rational' Darwinism, we see the beginnings of the present-day apotheosis or deification of science; whereas Hardy – also a Darwinist but inquiring rather than doctrinaire – nourished a deep distrust of 'facts', or of what he called 'empirical panaceas', and went so far as to claim for himself the title of 'Irrationalist'. This, in clear opposition to 'Rationalist', stands with 'Meliorist' as something of a ground-breaker for Hardy who generally had little time for the Victorian passion for 'ists' and 'isms'.

194

10 *Life*, p. 99.

11 The offending passage in question occurs in Chapter VIII, the Malthouse scene, where Coggan recounts the anecdote about Bathsheba's father, who cured his 'wandering heart' by making his wife take off her wedding ring so

> as he could thoroughly fancy he was doing wrong and committing the seventh . . . a perfect picture of mutel love.

12 To wit, the aforementioned episode of March 1875 where Stephen sends a 'mysterious note' to Hardy: 'he said he wanted me to witness his signature to . . . a deed renunciatory of holy-orders' (*Life*, pp. 105–6). In Maitland (op. cit., p. 277), Hardy also refers, rather cryptically, to a 'ten years chasm of silence' with Stephen, and likens him to the 'formidable peak of the "gaunt and difficult" Great Schreckhorn' (see his poem 'The Schreckhorn', 1897).

13 See Robert Schweik in 'The early development of Hardy's *Far From the Madding Crowd*', *Texas Studies in Literature and Language*, vol. IX (3), (1967) for a closely detailed discussion of Hardy's late introduction and development of Boldwood as a major character.

14 *The Athenaeum* (5 December 1874) found 'a sort of recklessness . . . [and] coarseness . . . [which] disfigures his work and repels the reader. . . . Such monstrous periphrases . . .' And the *Nation* (24 December 1874), criticised Hardy's 'ingeniously verbose and redundant style'.

15 It was R. H. Hutton who struck this blow. In his review of the first volume edition of *Far from the Madding Crowd* (1874), he cites the passage beginning 'The phases of Boldwood's life' (Chapter XVIII), as being a 'study almost in the nature of a careful caricature of George Eliot'. This snide remark, implying a cheap kind of plagiarism, was no doubt self-defensive, Hutton having been one of the first to mistake the author of the serial version of *Far from the Madding Crowd* for George Eliot.

16 Hardy's account of his reaction to the 'George Eliot' criticism reveals something of his bitterness. Moving on (in the *Life*) to describe his next novel, he writes:

> The *Comedy in Chapters* [*Hand of Ethelberta*], despite its departure from a path desired by his new-found readers . . . appeared in the *Cornhill* for May, when Hardy had the satisfaction of proving, amid the general disappointment at the lack of sheep and shepherds, that he did not mean to imitate anybody, whatever the satisfaction might have been worth.
>
> (*Life*, p. 103)

17 'Property' is certainly forcefully antagonistic here, especially at this time (1870s) when anti-marriage feeling is running high on the woman-as-property issue, and when countless numbers of women are flocking to London to support issues surrounding the 'Married Woman's Property Act'.

18 Hardy first gave this chapter the title of 'The sheep fair: Troy holds his wife's hand', but revised it in proof to 'The sheep fair: Troy touches his wife's hand'.

19 Here the manuscript has Dissenters where the *Cornhill* has chapel-members.

20 A 'gaffer' is an old overseer or foreman. The word is a metathesis of godfather.

7 'The form of its manifestation'

1 Hardy to Macquoid, 7 November 1874. Published in Purdy and Millgate, vol. 1, 1840–92, p. 33.

2 Henry James, *The Nation*, 24 December 1874. Robert Schweik offers an interesting footnote to James's letter in which he comments on James's reference to Poorgrass as a Dissenter:

Henry James's mistaken characterization of Joseph Poorgrass as a Dissenter was probably the result of his misreading or inaccurately remembering some of the dialogue in Chapter 42. 'Joseph and his Burden – Buck's Head,' where Mark Clark at one point taunts Poorgrass by saying, 'I believe ye to be a chapel-member, Joseph'.

(T. Hardy, *Far from the Madding Crowd*, ed. R. Schweik
(New York and London: W.W. Norton, 1986), p. 367)

Now the interesting point here is that 'Dissenter' does stand in the manuscript (see note to Chapter VI) but was revised for the *Cornhill* to 'chapel-member' – likewise 'Dissenter' is replaced by 'meetinger' shortly after the previous occurrence of the word in the same chapter. So James's 'misreading' or 'misremembering' comes (intuitively – or is he picking up on something else – 'chapel-member' as a euphemism perhaps?) closer, in fact, to Hardy's original conception of things than we might think!

3 J.R. Wise, *Westminster Review*, January 1875.
4 As Leslie Stephen himself advocated, women should *serve*, and Bathsheba does not; or at any rate she does not serve the right man. And by the time she marries Oak, however 'right' he may be in the reader's eyes, we know he will never be – body, heart and soul – 'right' for Bathsheba. It is interesting to note in this context that Stephen was later to complain to Hardy about the *The Trumpet Major* – that the heroine marries the wrong man. Hardy replied that they mostly did. 'Not in magazines', Stephen answered.
5 Fraser Harrison writes:

> The myth of marriage as a prize to be won only by those men who had demonstrated their material eligibility through spiritual self-denial depended on the readiness of women to play their part of complaisant victim.

Harrison, *The Dark Angel: Aspects of Victorian Sexuality*
(Glasgow: Fontana, 1979), p. 28

I think we may be fully assured that Oak fulfils his role of eligibility, in this context, but not so fully assured of Bathsheba's 'readiness' to play 'complaisant victim', despite the subduing of her spirit.
6 Of the codes of behaviour for women, Mill wrote in *The Subjection of Women* (1869) that,

> No other class of dependents have had their character so entirely distorted from its natural propensities by their relation with their masters.

He concluded that,

> men indolently believe that the tree grows of itself in the way they have made it grow.

Hardy later claimed that he could not remember reading this work when it first came out (Mill's views on this topic were widely broadcast), but he may well have encountered it in shorter anonymous form for it was fundamentally based on Harriet Taylor's work which had appeared even earlier in periodical publication.
7 Hardy had evidently conceived, in his early draft chapters and rough outline of *Far from the Madding Crowd* to Leslie Stephen, of making something more of Bathsheba's elopement, for Stephen responds at this time by hoping that Hardy would hurry on 'the elopement of the heroine' which had been 'foreshadowed' in the material Hardy had sent. Robert Schweik points out that there is no such

foreshadowing in Hardy's holograph manuscript:

> But if Stephen were looking at an earlier manuscript version of the novel
> which lacked the Fanny Robin and Boldwood episodes – a version con-
> fined to the affairs of a 'young woman farmer, a shepherd, and a sergeant
> of cavalry' – then its action could have proceeded much more rapidly to
> the point at which Troy seems likely to win Bathsheba than is presently the
> case. Stephen's response, in short, is consistent with what the manuscript
> evidence suggests – that the Boldwood episodes and the dramatisations
> of Fanny Robin's story were probably not part of Hardy's first version of
> the novel.
> (Schweik, 'The early development of Hardy's *Far from the Madding Crowd*',
> *Texas Studies in Literature and Language* IX (3), p. 426)

This provides an admirable solution to the puzzle of a foreshadowed elopement! There is only one difficulty. If Stephen were looking at an earlier manuscript version which lacked the Fanny and Boldwood episodes and was already
at (say) the 'hiving' or 'ferns' episodes he would have to wait no time at all for
'Horses tramping', in which Bathsheba elopes very shortly afterwards. So I
would like to suggest an alternative solution. Fanny Robin's story certainly
featured in Hardy's original conception of *Far from the Madding Crowd*, as
evidenced both by the discarded draft fragment treating with the shearing-
supper (see 'Foreword') and by Stephen's continuing concern, from January
1874 onwards, to have Hardy treat this subject judiciously. Boldwood, on the
other hand, may have featured, in Hardy's first conception of things, as a minor
character – much as he does in *The Mayor of Casterbridge* – who later took on a
larger life in Hardy's imagination as the story progressed month by month.
The full development within the serialised text of both Fanny and Boldwood
conforms to Hardy's artistic preference for a kind of natural growth, or evolution of his creations, as opposed to 'hot-housing' them into existence.

As to the foreshadowing, it is now evident that much of the original material
Stephen received from Hardy, especially the first few instalments, underwent
extensive cuts (as in the rustic scenes, see my Chapter 5; the shore scene, see
my Chapter 2; and the coffin scene, see my Chapter 8), as well as extensive
emendations and augmentations. My suggestion is then that in Chapter XIII,
'Sortes Sanctorum – The Valentine', Hardy may have originally created a more
substantial scene to fulfil the promise of his Latin title (translated as 'the oracles
of the holy writings'). As it stands, Bathsheba's Bible divination with Liddy
runs to not much more than half a page, and the remainder of this very short
chapter is given over to the Valentine. Does this brief focus justify Hardy's
title? Was the chapter originally longer? Could it have been, in the original
draft, that as Bathsheba lights upon the Book of Ruth that she divines there
her elopement?

> The special verse in the Book of Ruth was sought out by Bathsheba, and
> the sublime words met her eye. They slightly thrilled and abashed her. It
> was Wisdom in the abstract facing Folly in the concrete. Folly in the
> concrete blushed, persisted in her intention, and placed the key on the
> book. A rusty patch immediately upon the verse, caused by previous
> pressure of an iron substance thereon, told that this was not the first time
> the old volume had been used for the purpose.

We are told nothing more, other than that Bathsheba will not tell Liddy what
she has divined. Nor does she explain her blushes – or, more, to point, Hardy
doesn't! Could it have been that he had originally offered his reader a little

more than this? For instance, some clue to the divination which, as it now stands, signifies nothing? Could *this* have been the moment of the 'fore-shadowing'? If so – given that the elopement does not occur within the next twenty chapters – Stephen would naturally feel impatient to see this substantiated. Although he, at this time, would have only had Hardy's first few chapters and sketched outline for subsequent chapters, he might well have had 'Sortes Sanctorum' which features in the March issue, and fearing that it would still be some three or four more months before the elopement would occur, he would surely wish Hardy to hurry it on. The elopement eventually appears in Chapter XXXII, in the July issue. On Hardy's part – given the less-than-hurried momentum of the plot as the Boldwood episodes develop, and as he might have felt unwilling to 'hurry' on the elopement – it could have been that he decided to amend the Bible divination segment and any hint of foreshadowing simply because it had now lost its usefulness as dramatic pointing.

8 This is Peter Casagrande's view. See his essay, ill-titled: 'A new view of Bathsheba Everdene', in Dale Kramer (ed.), *Critical Approaches to the Fiction of Thomas Hardy* (New York: Barnes & Noble, 1979), pp. 50–73.

9 In the process of composition, Hardy takes more trouble with his allusions than might be apparent to the modern reader. A good example occurs in Chapter XII where he is describing Bathsheba's reaction to Boldwood's indifference to her in the cornmarket. Here, he has in the first writing (in the manuscript):

> If nobody had regarded her, she would have taken the matter indifferently – such cases had occurred. . . . just as it was the difference between the state of an insignificant fleece and the state of all around it, rather than any novelty in the states themselves, which arrested the attention of Gideon.

This rather lumpy allusion is later cancelled by Hardy in post-*Cornhill* revision, and now we have simply:

> But the smallness of the exception made the mystery.

10 Simon Gatrell feels that,

> It is probable. . . . that this long paragraph. . . . describing Bathsheba's instinctive allegiance to Diana was an afterthought, one in which [Hardy] was trying to offer some counterbalance to the impression given by the early chapters of the novel to many contemporary readers that she was a selfish and thoughtless flirt

S. Gatrell, 'Hardy the creator: *Far from the Madding Crowd*', in Dale Kramer (ed.), *Critical Approaches to the Fiction of Thomas Hardy* (New York: Barnes & Noble, 1979), pp. 74–98.

There is no evidence of 'afterthought' in the manuscript. This section is not even marked in verso on the preceding leaf, as is customary with Hardy's lengthier afterthoughts. The entire passage, in fact, flows evenly from Hardy's pen, and he was evidently sufficiently satisfied with it to have it published almost verbatim in the *Cornhill*. The only proof changes he made were as follows:

> *MS*: despairing perception of spoilation by marriage . . .
> *Cornhill*: despairing discoveries of her spoilation by marriage . . .
> *MS*: humbler half of an indifferent whole . . .
> *Cornhill*: humbler half of an indifferent matrimonial whole . . .

And the only significant interlinear revision within the manuscript is the deletion of 'like Fanny Robin', where Bathsheba 'had always nourished a secret contempt for girls [like Fanny Robin] who were the slaves of the first good-looking young fellow . . .' Clearly, Fanny Robin cannot feature in her thoughts at this stage, since this shows too much knowledge of events that have yet to be revealed.

11 See Gayle Greene and Coppélia Kahn (eds), *Making a Difference: Feminist Literary Criticism* (London and New York: Methuen, 1985), p. 22:

> Feminist critics find that the critical tradition reinforces – even when literature does not – images of character and behaviour that encourage women to accept their subordination, either by ignoring or degrading women, or by praising them for such virtues as obedience, meekness and humility. Moreover, literary history has canonised, designated as 'great', certain texts which are claimed to embody 'universal human truths': but such truths only appear so because of their congruence with the dominant ideology.

> In the gender ideology of the male critics I have cited, there is more recuperation and attempts at legitimisation of the dominant culture's preference for the 'obedient, meek and humble' woman than Hardy's conception of Bathsheba even begins to invite. In refusing the 'perfect woman of fiction', Hardy subverts the dominant ideology's preservation of the ideal of 'perfect womanhood', the 'angel', even the 'better half', which encourages women to accept themselves as aspirants to an impossible standard (of perfection) and who are thereby subordinated by being condemned to a perpetual sense of their own failure. In this early novel, however, on which his future reputation and popularity was to depend, Hardy finds a way of avoiding a collusion between literature and the dominant ideology with only limited success. Later in his career, when his literary reputation is assured (and his iconoclasm or avoidance of this collusion is more in evidence), he can better absorb the critical blast.

12 *Women's World*, May 1868, p. 26. Articles of, by and for the 'Strong-minded woman' abounded throughout the Victorian age. These included debates for and against female suffrage; short hair and 'bold' attire; mannishness; the Married Women's Property Bill; the 'shrieking sisterhood'; the 'Platform Woman'; the Anti-Marriage League; education for women; and sexual equality in general. See also 'Women with views' and 'The strong-minded woman', in Stella Mary Newton, *Health, Art and Reason: Dress Reformers of the 19th Century* (London: John Murray Ltd, 1974).

13 'The evolution of woman', Fraser Harrison writes,

> was, in effect, a process of continual rebellion, and the myriad struggles of which it was composed were undertaken as much by individuals on their own domestic battle-grounds as by groups and organisations in the public arenas.

By the mid- to late-nineteenth century, Harrison continues,

> the era of female submissiveness was on the decline and waning fast – the cumulative effect of this bewildering, and often humiliating revolution was to induce in men a profound sense of fear. This fearfulness involved an acute apprehension concerning their capacity to withstand the 'new woman's' aggression, as they saw it, and an intense dread [of women] . . . yearning for the chance to participate in sexual relations on equal emotional terms with their husbands.

(Harrison, op. cit., p. 122)

14 See pp. 52 and 60 of this volume for an example of Hardy's verso writing.
15 Hardy has 'had', not 'has' as printed in the Norton 'Authoritative Text'.
16 Female anger was unlovely and unlovable – an abhorrence to Victorians. Indecent, ugly and savage, it was at best rude and unladylike and, at worst, a pathological disorder of the mind and body.

A gentleman too, restrained his anger, just as he restrained every powerful emotion, even pleasure. Leslie Stephen has the story that once his father smoked a cigar and found it so delicious that he never smoked again. But intense emotion – laughter, rage, irritation – did not appear unattractive or unmanly in quite the same way that it appeared unattractive and unfeminine in respectable, middle-class women.

Even for Stephen's distinguished daughter, Virginia Woolf, if for reasons of art rather than decorum, anger was unlovely. It was the 'anger and rebellion' of Jane's soliloquy in *Jane Eyre* that, in Woolf's eyes, flawed Brontë genius 'whole and entire':

> Her books will be deformed and twisted. She will write in a rage where she should write calmly. . . . She is at war with her lot. How could she help but die young, cramped and thwarted?

See Cora Kaplan, 'Pandora's box: subjectivity, class and sexuality in socialist feminist criticism', in Gayle Greene and Coppélia Kahn (eds), op. cit., pp. 146–76.

Kaplan goes on to say that:

> Over and over again in her writing, Woolf tries to find ways of placing the question [subjectivity, class, sexuality, etc.] inside an aesthetic that disallows anger, unreason and passion as productive emotions.

(ibid., p. 173)

17 See John Paterson, *The Making of 'The Return of the Native'* (Berkeley: University of California Press, 1960). Paterson sees Hardy's original 'angry' Eustacia as a 'demonic', 'satanic' witch. For a rejoinder to Paterson's view, see Rosemarie Morgan, *Women and Sexuality in the Novels of Thomas Hardy* (London and New York: Routledge, 1988), p. 180, note 13.

Male dread of female anger had a socially recognised anxiety-base in the dread of hysteria. Caroll Smith Rosenberg looks to the socialisation of women as a major cause of hysteria:

> The tensions that existed between the two central roles the bourgeois matron was expected to assume – that of the True Woman [emotional, dependent, gentle – a born follower] and that of the Ideal Mother [strong, self-reliant, protective, efficient] – exemplify these disjointures which were simultaneously social and psychological.

Smith Rosenberg observes that one of the reasons for the medical profession's punitive treatment of the female hysteric can be attributed to male perceptions of deviance from the way women were expected to function – the hysteric was angry, hostile, violent, impatient and unconstrained. Thus her physician:

> felt threatened both as a professional and as a rejected male.

Afflicted with uncertainties and with a constant thwarting of their control, physicians resorted to suffocation, beating and ridicule in order to enforce their authority upon their unruly patients. See Caroll Smith Rosenberg, *Disorderly Conduct* (New York and Oxford: Oxford University Press, 1985), pp. 197–216.
18 In 'An appeal against female suffrage', *The Nineteenth Century*, 25 (1889), pp.

781–8, the women who signed the appeal – among them Mrs Leslie Stephen – were concerned that emancipation would reduce women's power and moral influence by infiltration of worldly preoccupations and that such pre-occupations – professional, political, commercial – would have a coarsening effect on the feminine sensibility. This leads one to consider that the very fact of Bathsheba's business-like approach to her farming enterprise – sacking the bailiff and taking on that role herself, dealing with men's paypackets, performing night surveillance 'with the coolness of a metropolitan policeman', and so on – might well have alarmed contemporary critics into thinking of her as already 'coarsened' by her unfeminine exploits.

Among the claims put forward by those antagonistic to the 'Strong-minded woman' as antithetical to ideal womanhood, there was the 'fact' that women moving into business and the professions developed a coarse look, a visible hardening of their 'gentle' feminine features. This was no new idea: the term 'strong-minded' as applied to women had become a familiar term of abuse from as far back as the 1840s, where it is used pejoratively by Dickens in *Martin Chuzzlewit*.

19 Elaine Showalter notes in her study of women and madness that great irregu-larities of temper, disobedience, and sexual assertiveness were regarded by clinicians in the mid-century as suitable reasons for controlling women's behav-iour by surgical means: hysterectomy, clitoridectomy, and other obstetrical practices. In the institutions in which such women were confined, their 'devi-ations from ladylike behaviour were severely punished': solitary confinement was enforced upon women 'on account of being violent, mischievous, dirty and using bad language'. See Elaine Showalter, *The Female Malady, Women, Madness, and Culture, 1831–1980* (New York: Penguin, 1985), p. 81.

In the novel, the rebellious woman, or the less-than-timid such as Maggie Tulliver or Tess, finds no comfortable space in the world where she is not subject to controls and prohibitions.

20 Marlene Springer makes out an excellent case for Hardy's deliberate efforts, by use of both negative and positive allusions, to stop short of presenting Bathsheba as 'a perfect woman nobly planned'. Although Springer finds a decidedly more stereotypical heroine – an arrogant and capricious Bathsheba whose 'gradual erosion' of hauteur is brought about 'by a series of tragedies' – she also argues for extraordinary complexity and depth of character in her astute analysis of Hardy's use of allusions. For example, 'where Bathsheba is threatened with financial ruin and even death':

> The hellishness of her predicament is made more acute when the narrator relates the blackness to a 'cave in Hinnom' . . . the valley near Jerusalem where human sacrifices and filth were burnt during the time of Josiah.

Specifically, *innocents* (children) were burnt as human sacrifices.

And if Hardy lightly mocks Bathsheba's efforts at dignity and high serious-ness by calling her one of the six inferior Archons in ancient Athens, and a 'queen among these gods of the fallow, like a little sister of a little Jove', he extends the deepest sympathy to her at Fanny's death:

> Before Bathsheba discovers the child, she is truly saddened by Fanny's fate, and she is allowed the narrator's sympathy: she does not feel vic-torious, though 'she was the Esther to this poor Vashti'.

Then, borrowing from Wordsworth the 'phantom of delight' image, Hardy alludes first to her charm in maturity, then, in a matter of a few pages, has Boldwood compare her to Rachel, 'asserting', as Springer says, 'his willingness to play Jacob', and almost in another breath, has Troy speak of her as his 'dashing piece of womanhood, Juno-wife of mine'. Springer sees this technique of juxtaposition and allusive diversity as a way of exploring 'new psychological levels' which 'reveal, enlarge, intensify, and solemnise' and even subtly undermine surface impressions. If Joseph Poorgrass were to leave us in any doubt about the marriage between Bathsheba and Oak – that 'why, it might have been worse' – Hardy apparently would not. Springer notes that in the final chapter of the novel, the wedding scene begins with, 'It was a damp disagreeable morning', and then:

> two allusions quickly follow: one to Keats's 'Eve of St Agnes', where Madeline is in a trance and has no idea of what is happening around her, and one to the bloody hands of Macbeth immediately after he has murdered Duncan (*Macbeth*, II, ii, 62).
>
> (M. Springer, *Hardy's Use of Allusion*, (London and
> Basingstoke: Macmillan, 1983), pp. 53–77)

21 Hardy is evidently keenly aware of the politics of language, of language as a structuring process. He cannot permit Bathsheba to take her strong-minded ideas too far, for fear of alienating Stephen's *Cornhill* reader, but that he has her introduce the notion that language is modulated and codified by prevailing patriarchal values, would, by itself, place her in the vanguard of contemporary feminism. Hélène Cixous writes (over a hundred years later):

> You'll understand why I think that no political reflection can dispense with reflection on language, with work on language. For as soon as we exist, we are born into language and language speaks [to] us, dictates its law, a law of death: it lays down its familial model, lays down its conjugal model, and even at the moment of uttering a sentence, admitting a notion of 'being', a question of being, an ontology, we are already seized by a certain kind of masculine desire, the desire that mobilizes philosophical discourse.
>
> (H. Cixous, 'Castration or decapitation?' trans.
> A. Kuhn, *Signs*, 7 (1) p. 45)

22 At this point, the poisonous swamp which exudes 'the essences of evil things', becomes just a little too graphically illustrated for Stephen, what with rotting fungi with 'clammy tops' and 'others with oozing gills. . . . marked with great splotches, red as arterial blood', and he draws the line (visibly in the manuscript) at 'others were scabbed . . .' Hardy had evidently gone too far – no 'scabs' for the *Cornhill*!

23 'Jineral' is a dialectal adjustment made in proof revision. It stands as 'general' in the manuscript.

8 'A curious frame of Nature's work'

1 Letter from Stephen to Hardy, 12 March, 1874. See Purdy, *Thomas Hardy: A Bibliographical Study* (Oxford: The Clarendon Press, 1968), pp. 338–9.
2 See Noel Annan, *Leslie Stephen: the Godless Victorian* (New York: Random, 1984) pp. 67–9. Annan notes that:

> A magazine which offended its readers went bankrupt. *Fraser's* lost readers from county families for publishing Kingsley's *Yeast* and for his verses denouncing the game laws; Trollope was sacked by *Good Words* under pressure from Evangelical fanatics; and Thackeray in the *Cornhill* had to

stop further publication of Ruskin's denunciations of orthodox political economy. Leslie Stephen was compelled in this atmosphere to safeguard the interests of his proprietor.

3 Among them, Henry James, Mrs Oliphant, Robert Louis Stevenson, Matthew Arnold, Symonds, and Eliza Lynn-Linton.

4 Annan, op. cit., p. 67.

5 Letter from Stephen to Hardy, 12 March 1874, in Purdy, op. cit., p. 338.

6 With the burgeoning of periodicals during this period, Stephen faced a challenge in competition that, ultimately, he could not meet. The *Cornhill* lost approximately 12,000 subscribers under his editorship, and by 1882 was running at a loss. James Payn, former editor of *Chambers' Journal*, was invited to take his place. Stephen, who seems to have erred on the side of conservatism and the 'country parson's daughters', while maintaining highbrow standards in scientific and literary articles, expressed his regrets to his publishers that his rule had been so 'prejudicial in the commercial sense': 'I do not fancy myself to be a good judge of public taste.' See Maitland, *The Life and Letters of Leslie Stephen* (London: Duckworth, 1906); Annan, *Leslie Stephen: the Godless Victorian* (New York: Random House, 1984).

7 Purdy, op. cit., pp. 338–9.

8 In Victorian parlance, 'honest' here is used ambiguously. In usage, a tone of light sarcasm would make it quite plain that the archaic meaning of 'honest' as 'chaste' was not intended literally. This usage combined with the more familiar meaning of 'honest' as 'frank and open' implied a nod and wink at any lack of sexual inhibition.

9 Letter from Stephen to Hardy, 13 April 1874 in Purdy, op. cit., p. 339.

10 Stephen was not only a parson's son and an apostate (agnostic), but he also regarded himself as a freethinking rationalist.

11 See Frederick William Maitland, *The Life and Letters of Leslie* Stephen (London: Duckworth & Co., 1906), p. 35.

Appendix 1 A survey of post-*Cornhill* substantive revisions

1 See also, Michael Millgate, *Thomas Hardy, A Biography*, (Oxford, Melbourne: Oxford University Press, 1982), pp. 162, 173, 181–2, 189, 200–1, 212, 224, 248–51, 268, 276, 278, 288, 292–3, 323, 324, 360–2, 394, 413–14, 421, 422–3, 442, 576. Millgate notes that by 1877 Hardy had begun 'his exploration of Hutchins's *History and Antiquities of the County of Dorset*, a resource of the first importance for Hardy's gradual evolution of Wessex as a total imaginative world with a solid, complex, comprehensively realised existence in space and time' (ibid., p. 189). Millgate goes on to say (p. 248) that it was in the writing of *The Mayor of Casterbridge*, in 1884, that,

> The solidity of the presentation of Casterbridge was intimately related to its role as the economic, and geographical centre of an entire Wessex world, hitherto evolved in somewhat piecemeal fashion, now for the first time perceived and projected as distinct, integrated, and autonomous.

But it was not until the 1890s that Hardy's textual revisions and prefaces were specifically

> designed to make the topographical references in the different works more consistent one with another and thus to enhance that sense of imaginative and regional coherence he had sought to emphasize in the title, 'Wessex Novels', chosen for the Osgood, McIlvaine edition as a whole. The prefaces, written over a period of more than a year and a

half, reflect Hardy's genial contemplation of the fictional world he had created over the previous quarter-century and was now about to leave permanently behind him.

(ibid., p. 360)

Emma, incidently, had kept for Hardy a listing of 'Wessex' names from the mid-1870s onwards.

2 It is characteristic of Hardy to view his texts as mutable and constantly evolving. A good example of this, noticed by James Gibson, occurs in the marginalia of Hardy's own copy of *Jude*. Here he has entered a phrase of Browning's against his own phrase referring to 'Arabella's inlated bosom'. The new phrase reads, 'Breasts' superb abundance.' Hardy was eighty years old at the time! See James Gibson, 'Hardy and his readers,' in *Thomas Hardy*, ed. Norman Page (London: Routledge & Kegan Paul, 1980), p. 207.

3 See Gatrell, 'Hardy the creator: *Far from the Madding Crowd*', in D. Kramer (ed.), *Critical Approaches to the Fiction of Thomas Hardy* (New York: Barnes & Noble, 1979), pp. 74–98.

4 I use the word 'reprieve' as Hardy uses it, to mean a 'remission of sentence' and not the postponement or delay of a death sentence. I understand from Phillip Smith (author of *Policing Victorian London: Political policing, public order and the London Metropolitan Police*, Westport, Conn.: Greenwood Press, 1984) that by the 1870s such 'reprieves' issued on the basis of insanity were becoming more common in practice, particularly in cases where the petitioner was deemed a member of the 'respectable' classes, as is Boldwood – a gentleman.

Appendix 2 The dramatisation of Fanny's story and revisions to nomenclature

1 See Robert C. Schweik, 'The early development of Hardy's *Far From the Madding Crowd*', *Texas Studies in Literature and Language* IX (3) pp. 415–28. Schweik makes a fascinating, closely detailed examination of Hardy's unusual foliation of his holograph manuscript and concludes from Hardy's renumbering of previously used leaves, internal shufflings of first drafts, revised drafts and rewritten pages, that a different version of the novel pre-existed the manuscript version. Schweik claims 'a profound change in Hardy's intentions', particularly his 'decision to dramatize Fanny's story rather than to develop it solely through the reports of others' (ibid., p. 420). I am not assured, with Schweik, that this is the case. I doubt any profound change; although it is true (as shown in the chapters of this book) that Hardy, possibly in an attempt to fulfil Leslie Stephen's hopes of a *Greenwood Tree*-type tale, originally drew more rural scenes and rustic dialogues in early drafts and (now-cancelled) portions of the holograph manuscript than finally transpired in the published version. But, with regard to 'a profound change', as indicated by foliation changes, it is worth repeating here that Hardy's unusual foliations are often at their most chaotic (see 'Foreword') well into the novel, where character and plot (and Fanny's story) are fully established and, moreover, where the damp imprint of the numbered leaf appearing in verso on the preceding leaf clearly indicates rapid, uninterrupted writing. These unusual foliations and interweaving of textual sources with new material, suggest not so much a change in intention as a continuing compositional practice – in particular, of using previously used and previously numbered leaves, many of which show sentences started and abandoned in verso. And with regard to Hardy's self-borrowings, we know that various segments from *The Poor Man and the Lady* (first unpublished novel, 1868), were incorporated into later novels; and we know that phrases from

hitherto unpublished poems also found their way into Hardy's prose. This practice, then, of kaleidoscoping his written material into new, evolving texts seems to be the hallmark of Hardy's compositional method, from which an 'unintentional' flow of thought could spring forth as readily as an 'intentional'.

2 *English Studies*, 53 (1–6), pp. 344–9.

3 In most instances, Hardy's incorporation of supplementary leaves into the holograph manuscript fulfils such a variety of literary functions that indications of 'an earlier version of the novel' (Schweik, 'Early development', pp. 416–18), are frequently undercut by contrary indications. A good example arises in the case of Oak in Chapters V ('Departure of Bathsheba – A Pastoral Tragedy'), and VI ('The Fair – The Journey – The Fire'). Schweik has already pointed out that the leaves numbered 45 and 45a 'suggest that a portion of the paragraph describing Oak's dogs' appears to be recopied and that 'the present 45 and 45a both take the place of an original f. 45'. But I would not necessarily conclude, as Schweik does, that this expansion of the text has 'been brought about by other more extensive alterations' (ibid., p. 416). There is nothing to indicate, for example, that the original f. 45 'contained a shorter account of Bathsheba's departure from Norcombe' or that Hardy had left Oak in ignorance of her whereabouts (ibid., p. 416). One could as easily argue that Hardy was just as interested here in introducing a few philosophical notes of his own. After all, the recopied leaves and supplementary material deal less with Oak's knowledge of Bathsheba's departure and whereabouts than with authorial musings. Oak is merely the cipher here. For example, on leaves 45 and 45a the manuscript has:

> The news which one day reached Gabriel, that Bathsheba Everdene had left the neighbourhood, had an influence upon him which might have surprised any who never had suspected that the more emphatic the renunciation the less absolute its character as a rule.
>
> It may be observed that there is no regular path for getting out of love as there is for getting in. Some people look upon marriage as a short cut that way, but it has been known to fail. Separation, which was the means that chance offered to Gabriel Oak by Bathsheba's disappearance, though effectual with people of certain humours, is apt to idealize the removed object with others – notably those whose affection, placid and regular as it may be, flows deep and long.

This passage featuring on the rewritten leaves f. 45 and f. 45a seems to me less indicative of an extensive alteration than a mild form of Hardyan peregrination.

4 Citing cancelled numeration in support of his view, Schweik suggests that the decision to dramatise Fanny's story was taken part of the way through the composition of Chapter X, entitled 'Mistress and Men'; that the cuts made to Chapter X were solely directed to that end; and that Chapter VII, in which we first encounter her in the churchyard meeting with Oak, was added later (Schweik, 'Early, development', pp. 418–22).

It is hard to accept the notion that the dramatisation of Fanny's story comes with hindsight to Hardy when she features in nearly all the Weatherbury sections leading up to Chapter X. For example, Bathsheba moves to Weatherbury, in Chapter V, Oak follows in Chapter VI, and Fanny is first encountered in Chapter VII. She has just left the farm and is on her way to find Troy; Hardy hints at the reasons for her fugitive situation and hasty departure in the very next chapter (VIII). Here Laban Tall hurries into the Malthouse in some excitement:

> Have you heard the news that's all over the parish? . . . Fanny Robin –

Miss Everdene's youngest servant – can't be found. They've been wanting to lock up the door these last two hours, but she isn't come in. And they don't know what to do about going to bed for fear of locking her out. They wouldn't be so concerned if she hadn't been noticed in such low spirits these last few days, and Maryann d'think the beginning of a crowner's inquest has happened to the poor girl.

The rustics now speculate on the various ways she might have committed suicide, but the unmentionable is not spelled out: that Fanny is pregnant. Possibly, given Laban's account, many readers would have hazarded a guess, and Hardy certainly offers them the chance. He already has Fanny's tragic story in view. Presently, Bathsheba calls the men in and after some detailed discussion she orders a search for Fanny. The extent of these dialogues in Chapter VIII run to several manuscript pages and include such personal details as Maryann's concern that Fanny left the house 'with only her indoor working gown on – not even a bonnet'. The next day (in Chapter IX) Boldwood calls on Bathsheba specifically to discuss Fanny's disappearance; later on that day (in Chapter X), the search parties make their reports, thus keeping the dynamic of Fanny's story in view as the story proper proceeds with Bathsheba's affairs. Had Hardy decided to dramatise Fanny's story as late as Chapter X, he would have had to make substantial revisions to all preceding (Weatherbury) chapters in order to include all of the above events!

Further, the 'judicious cuts' to the paying scene (Chapter X), referred to by Leslie Stephen, probably eliminated (in my view) Hardy's injudicious references to Fanny's lover and her pregnancy. This, to my mind, largely accounts for his refoliation of this section. My reasons for making this claim are supported by a related cancellation made earlier in the manuscript which is still visible – as opposed to being rendered entirely invisible through recopying on to a new leaf. This occurs on f. 97, in Chapter VIII, where dialogues concerning Fanny's lover turn upon the fact that he is a soldier and that Fanny was 'very close' about naming him: Bathsheba's concern intensifies:

> I feel more responsible than I should if she had had any friends or relations alive. I do hope she has come to no harm through a man of that kind

The manuscript evidently continued on at this point, but was subsequently cancelled; there is visible evidence of this; the lower quarter of the leaf is truncated, cutting off the remainder of this dialogue. We now have a rather abrupt transition in Bathsheba's speech:

> through a man of that kind. . . . And then there's this disgraceful affair of the bailiff – but I can't speak of him now.

In the light of this evidence, it seems probable that if Hardy's refoliations had anything to do with Fanny at all, it was due to Stephen's invocations of Mrs Grundy and his call for 'judicious cuts'. Hardy would then supplement the excised passages with short set pieces (as in Chapter XI with 'Melchester Moor'), or with philosophical musings (as in several of his verso afterthoughts), or with a little more detailed action and local colour as in the partly rewritten supplement to Chapter VII.

5 It is worth repeating here that it was Hardy's practice to send Stephen unchaptered passages and set-pieces for evaluation. The final shape and numbering of chapters sometimes took form as late as the proof stage of composition.

6 For all references to Gatrell, see 'Hardy the creator', op. cit.

7 The following presents a section of Hardy's manuscript foliation traced from

Chapter XL to XLIII, MS 2–181–224.

Note: The outer margin number is printed in bold, the inner margin number in standard, and the cancelled inner margin number is set in parentheses. Some of these last are omitted. They may be hidden in the gutter of the manuscript, but, at any rate, they are not visible.

Chapter XL
181, 1, -;
182, 2, -;
183, 3, -;
184, 4, -;
185, 5, -;
186, 6, -;
187, 7, -;
188, 7a,-;
189, 8, -;
190, 9, -;

Chapter XLI
191, -, -;
192, 12, -;
193, 13, -;
194, 14, -;
195, 15, -;
196, 16, -;
197, 16a,-;
198, 16b, (42);
199, 17, -;
200, 18, -;
201, 19, -;
202, 20, -;
203, 21, -;
204, 21a, -;
205, 22, -;

Chapter XLII
206, 22a, (17);
207, 23, (18);
208, 24, (19);
209, 25, (20);
210, 26, -;
211, 27, (22);
212, 28, -;
213, 29, -;
214, 30, (25);
215, 31, (26);
216, 32, (29);
217, 28, (33);
218, 29, -;
219, 30, -;
220, 31, -;
221, 32, -;
222, 32a, -;
223, 32b, -;

Chapter XLIII
224, 33, -;

8 There is nothing in the manuscript to indicate that Hardy's references to Fanny's baby were an afterthought (for a contrary view see Gatrell, op. cit,). The 'and child' part of the inscription of 'Fanny Robin and child' is not a late addition as Gatrell claims but forms an integral part of the text, in the last part of Chapter XLII where Oak erases it. This inscription was cancelled by Hardy in its earlier occurrence in the chapter (where Poorgrass picks up the coffin), presumably to delay this moment of recognition for the reader and also to keep Poorgrass in ignorance of the full facts. All references to Fanny's baby in the manuscript are inclusive and the only indication of emendation is where 'and babe' is inserted with a caret at, 'but to be vindictive towards a poor dead woman and babe recoils upon myself' (later cancelled by Stephen for the *Cornhill*).

9 We should not forget that it would be twenty-odd years before Hardy could present his readers with a fallen woman central character – Tess.

10 Ian Gregor, 'Reading a story: sequence, pace, and recollection', in Ian Gregor (ed.), *Reading the Victorian Novel: Detail into Form* (New York: Barnes & Noble, 1980), pp. 98–101. Gregor makes an interesting case for Fanny as the intensifier of feeling in *Far from the Madding Crowd*.

11 Hardy follows Fanny's journey in Chapter XL with painstaking care, and may well have originally overwritten parts of it. At the point where she whispers 'No further!', and closes her eyes, the manuscript leaf (2–186) is truncated and Hardy now introduces the dog. The augmented leaves (inner margin numeration 7 and 7a; outer margin, 2–187–188), which feature the assistance of the dog, constitute the only patchwork to this chapter which Hardy seems to have written at high speed. The inner margin numeration runs consecutively from 1 to 8, outer margin from 181 to 189, thus indicating, together with the damp imprint of inked numeration on the verso of the preceding leaf, that this was one of the chapters Hardy describes as having been written at a 'gallop' – the truncated leaf possibly indicating an abrupt if temporary halt of that 'gallop', in order to move ahead with the dog sequence.

12 See Gibson (ed.), *The Complete Poems of Thomas Hardy* (London: Macmillan, 1976), pp. 158–9.

13 ibid., pp. 623–4.

14 ibid., pp. 59–60. See stanza 3 in particular. I am indebted to Trevor Johnson for this reference.

References

Annan, Noel, *Leslie Stephen: the Godless Victorian* (New York: Random House, 1984).

Babb, Howard, 'Setting and theme in *Far from the Madding Crowd*', *E.L.H.* 30 (1963).

Beer, Gillian, *Darwin's Plots* (London, Boston, Melbourne, Henley: Routledge & Kegan Paul, 1983).

Casagrande, Peter, 'A new view of Bathsheba Everdene', in Dale Kramer (ed.), *Critical Approaches to the Fiction of Thomas Hardy* (New York: Barnes & Noble, 1979), pp. 50–73.

Cixous, Hélène, 'Castration or decapitation?' trans. Annette Kuhn, *Signs* 7 (1) (Autumn, 1981).

Courtney, Janet E., *Freethinkers of the Nineteenth Century* (New York: E.R. Dutton & Co., 1920).

Danielson, Henry, *First Editions of the Writings of Thomas Hardy and Their Values* (London: George Allen & Unwin, 1916).

Ellis, Sara, *Daughters of England; Wives of England; Women of England* (1830).

Gatrell, Simon, 'Hardy the creator: *Far from the Madding Crowd*', in Dale Kramer (ed.), *Critical Approaches to the Fiction of Thomas Hardy* (New York: Barnes & Noble, 1979), pp. 74–98.

Gibson, James (ed.), *The Complete Poems of Thomas Hardy* (London: Macmillan; 1976).

Gibson, James, 'Hardy and his readers', in *Thomas Hardy*, ed. Norman Page (London: Routledge & Kegan Paul, 1980).

Greene, Gayle and Kahn, Coppelia (eds), *Making a Difference: Feminist Literary Criticism* (London and New York: Methuen, 1985).

Gregor, Ian, 'Reading a story: sequence, pace, and recollection', *Detail Into Form* (New York: Barnes & Noble, 1980).

Grosskurth, Phyllis, *Leslie Stephen* (Harlow: Longmans, Green & Co., 1968).

Hardy, F.E., *The Life of Thomas Hardy, 1841–1928* (London: Macmillan, 1962).

Hardy, Thomas, *Far from the Madding Crowd*, ed. Robert C. Schweik (New York and London: W.W. Norton & Co., 1986).

Hardy, Thomas, 'The profitable reading of fiction', *Forum* (New York, 1888), pp. 57–70. Republished in *Thomas Hardy's Personal Writings*, ed. Harold Orel (New York: St Martin's Press, 1990), pp. 110–25.

Harrison, Fraser, *The Dark Angel: Aspects of Victorian Sexuality* (Glasgow: Fontana, 1979).

Heath, Francis George, *The English Peasantry* (London: 1874).

Holland, Henry, 'The progress and spirit of physical science', *Edinburgh Review* 108 (1858).

Houghton, Walter, *The Victorian Frame of Mind, 1831–1870* (New Haven and London: Yale University Press, 1957).

Kincaid, James R. and Kuhn, Albert J. (eds), *Victorian Literature and Society, Essays Presented to Richard D. Altick* (Columbus: Ohio State University Press, 1983).

Kingsley, Charles, *His Letters and Memories of His Life*, ed. Fanny Kingsley, 2 vols (London, 1877).

Kramer, Dale (ed.), *Critical Approaches to the Fiction of Thomas Hardy* (New York: Barnes & Noble, 1979).

Maitland, Frederick William, *The Life and Letters of Leslie Stephen* (London: Duckworth & Co., 1906; New York: G.P. Putnam's Sons.)

Mill, John Stuart, *Letters*, ed. H.S.R. Elliot, 2 vols (London and New York: Longmans, Green & Co., 1910).

Mill, John Stuart, *The Spirit of the Age*, ed. F.A. von Hayek (Chicago: University of Chicago Press 1942).

Mill, John Stuart, *The Subjection of Women* (D. Appleton & Co., 1869).

Miller, J. Hillis, *Thomas Hardy: Distance and Desire* (Cambridge, Mass.: Harvard University Press, 1970).

Millgate, Michael, *Thomas Hardy: A Biography* (Oxford and Melbourne: Oxford University Press, 1982).

Millgate, Michael, *Thomas Hardy: His Career as a Novelist* (New York: Random House, 1971).

Morgan, Rosemarie, *Women and Sexuality in the Novels of Thomas Hardy* (London and New York: Routledge, 1988).

Morrell, Roy, *Thomas Hardy: The Will and the Way* (Kuala Lumpur: University of Malaya Press, 1965).

Newton, Judith L., Ryan, Mary P. and Walkowitz, Judith R., *Sex and Class in Women's History* (London: Routledge, Chapman and Hall, 1983).

Newton, Stella Mary *Health, Art and Reason: Dress Reformers of the 19th Century* (London: John Murray, 1974).

Orel, H. (ed.), *Thomas Hardy's Personal Writings* (New York: St Martin's Press, 199).

Pinion, F.B., *A Hardy Companion* (London: Macmillan, 1968).

Purdy, Richard Little, *Thomas Hardy: A Bibliographical Study* (Oxford: The Clarendon Press, 1968).

Purdy, Richard Little and Millgate, Michael (eds), *The Collected Letters of Thomas Hardy*, 6 vols (Oxford: Clarendon Press, 1978–90).

Ruskin, John, *Works*, ed. E.T. Cook and A.D.O. Wedderburn, 39 vols (London, 1902–12).

Schweik, Robert C., 'A first draft chapter of Hardy's *Far from the Madding Crowd*', *English Studies* 53 (1–6).

Schweik, Robert C., 'The early development of Hardy's *Far from the Madding Crowd*', *Texas Studies in Literature and Language* IX (3) (Autumn 1967).

Schweik, Robert C., 'The narrative structure of *Far from the Madding Crowd*', in *Budmouth Essays on Thomas Hardy*, ed. F.B. Pinion (Dorchester: The Thomas Hardy Society Ltd, 1976).

Showalter, Elaine, *The Female Malady, Women, Madness, and Culture, 1831–1980* (New York: Penguin, 1985).

Smith Rosenberg, Caroll, *Disorderly Conduct* (New York and Oxford: Oxford University Press, 1985).

Snell, K.D.M., *Annals of the Labouring Poor: Social Change and Agrarian England 1601–1900* (Cambridge, England: Cambridge University Press, 1985).

Southerington, F.R., *Hardy's Vision of Man* (London: Chatto & Windus, 1971).

Spencer, Herbert, 'The morals of trade', in *Essays: Scientific, Political and Speculative*, 2, 141.

References

Springer, Marlene, *Hardy's Use of Allusion* (London and Basingstoke: Macmillan, 1983).

Stephen, Leslie, *History of English Thought in the Eighteenth Century* (1876).

Stephen, Leslie, *Some Early Impressions* (New York: Burt Franklin, 1924).

Sumner, Rosemary, *Thomas Hardy: Psychological Novelist* (London and Basingstoke: Macmillan, 1981).

Vigar, Penelope, *The Novels of Thomas Hardy: Illusion and Reality* (London: The Athlone Press, 1974).

Von Arx, Jeffrey, *Progress and Pessimism: Religion, Politics and History in Late Nineteenth Century Britain* (Cambridge, Mass.: Harvard University Press, 1985).

Weber, Carl J., *Hardy of Wessex: His Life and Literary Career* (New York: Columbia University Press, 1965).

Williams, Raymond, *Culture and Society, 1781–1950* (Harmondsworth: Penguin, 1968).

Index

Kingsley, Charles 187 n.5, 189 n.8, 202
  n.2
Kingsley, Fanny 187 n.5

ladylike 99–102, 114, 125–8, 191–2 n.20
Lang, Andrew 84, 185 n.15, 189 n.8
Lewis, 'Monk' 176–7 n.9
Lynn-Linton, Eliza 203 n.3
Lytton, Bulwer, 188 n.6

Macbeth-Raeburn H. 10
Macmillan 11
Macquoid, Kathleen 120, 122, 195 n.1
Maitland, F. W. 104, 150, 172 n.5, 172
  nn.11 and 13, 179 n.9, 193 nn.7 and
  12, 203 nn.6 and 11
Mallett, Phillip 177 n.13, 185 n.15, 191,
  n.14
Mangin, Edward 192 n.1
manliness 196 n.5, 200 n.16
mannishness 31, 199, n.12, 200–1 n.18
Mark, Book of (N.T.) 176 n.9
Married Woman's Property Act, The
  181 n.2, 195, n.17, 199 n.12
marriage 49, 67–71, 85, 122, 140, 181 n.2,
  195 n.17, 196 nn.4 and 5, 198 n.10,
  199 n.12, 202 n.20, 205 n.3
Martineau, Harriet 187 n.3, 192 n.1
Mayor of Casterbridge, The 197 n.7, 203
  n.1
Meisel, Martin 173 n.16
Mill, J. S. 121, 181 n.2, 187 n.3, 188 n.6,
  191 n.19, 192 n.2, 196 n.6
Mill, Harriet Taylor 181 n.2, 196 n.6
Miller, J. Hillis 186 n.2
Millgate, Michael 178 nn.7, 8 and 9, 185
  n.16, 188–9 nn.7, 8 and 9, 203–4 n.1
Milton, John 180 n.13
misprints 153–4, 200 n.15
Morgan, Rosemarie 172 n.14, 200 n.17
Morrell, Roy 178 n.3
Morris, William 187 n.3
mothers 177 n.10, 200 n.17
Moule, Henry 188 n.7
Murray, Hugh 192 n.1

Nation, The 195 nn.2 and 14
Newton, Edward A. 5, 6–7
Newton, Stella Mary 199 n.12
Nineteenth Century, The 200 n.18
Noah 177 n.14
nomenclature 161

Norton, W. W. & Co. 11
nostalgia 187 nn.4 and 5, 188 n.6

oaths 111–18
Oliphant, Mrs 203 n.3
Orel, H. 173 n.1, 175 n.4
Osgood, McIlvaine & Co. 10, 40, 111,
  152, 162, 203 n.1
Ovid 176 n.9

Pair of Blue Eyes, A 19, 171 n.4
Pater, Walter 192–3 n.3
Paterson, Helen 9–10, 136, 185 n.14
Paterson, John 200 n.17
Patmore, Coventry 171 n.4, 194 n.8
Payn, James 203 n.6
Pinion, F. B. 177 n.14
Poor Man and the Lady, The 49, 150, 171
  n.4, 204 n.1
pregnancy 61, 139, 206 n.4, 208 n.8
Proctor, Anne Benson 178 n.6
Purdy, Richard Little 172 nn.7 and 12,
  173 n.2, 176 n.7, 180 n.1, 184 n.11, 191
  n.15, 202 n.1, 203 nn.7 and 9
Purdy, Richard Little and Millgate,
  Michael (eds) *The Collected Letters of
  Thomas Hardy* (6 vols) 171 n.3, 195 n.1
Punch Magazine 125
Rationalist Press Association, The 194
  n.9
Red Cross 2
Reform Bill 193 n.5
Return of the Native, The 50, 85, 124, 150,
  152, 178 nn.6, 7 and 8, 200 n.17
Rosenberg, Caroll Smith 200 n.17
'Ruined Maid, The' 139, 141, 160
rural labour 2, 80, 85–96 186–90 nn.2, 7,
  8, 9 and 10
Ruskin, John 188 n.6, 190 n.10, 191
  nn.14 and 18, 203 n.2
Ruth, Book of (O.T.) 197, n.7

sacrilege 114–15
Samuel, Book of (O.T.) 176 n.9
Sand, George 18, 179 n.9
Saturday Review, The 173 n.1, 176 n.4
'Schreckhorn, The' 195 n.12
Schweik, Robert C. 11, 157–8, 172–3
  n.14, 177 n.12, 181 nn.3, 9, 10 and 12,
  184 nn.9, 10 and 12, 186 n.1, 191 n.18,
  195 n.13, 196 nn.2 and 7, 204 n.1, 205
  nn.3 and 4